GRIMM FAIRY TALES

CREATED AND STORY BY
JOE BRUSHA
RALPH TEDESCO

WRITTEN BY
JOE BRUSHA
TROY BROWNFIELD
PAT SHAND

TRADE DESIGN BY
CHRISTOPHER COTE
STEPHEN SCHAFFER

TRADE EDITED BY
RALPH TEDESCO
MATT ROGERS

THIS VOLUME REPRINTS THE
COMIC SERIES GRIMM FAIRY TALES
ISSUES #82-84 AND 86-88 PUBLISHED
BY ZENESCOPE ENTERTAINMENT

WWW.ZENESCOPE.COM

FIRST EDITION, SEPTEMBER 2013
ISBN: 978-1-939683-05-2

WWW.ZENESCOPE.COM
FACEBOOK.COM/ZENESCOPE

ZENESCOPE ENTERTAINMENT, INC.

Joe Brusha • President & Chief Creative Officer
Ralph Tedesco • Editor-in-Chief
Jennifer Bermel • Director of Licensing & Business Development
Raven Gregory • Executive Editor
Anthony Spay • Art Director
Christopher Cote • Senior Designer/Production Manager
Dave Franchini • Direct Market Sales & Customer Service
Stephen Haberman • Marketing Manager

Zenescope Entertainment presents:

Grimm Fairy Tales™

Volume 14

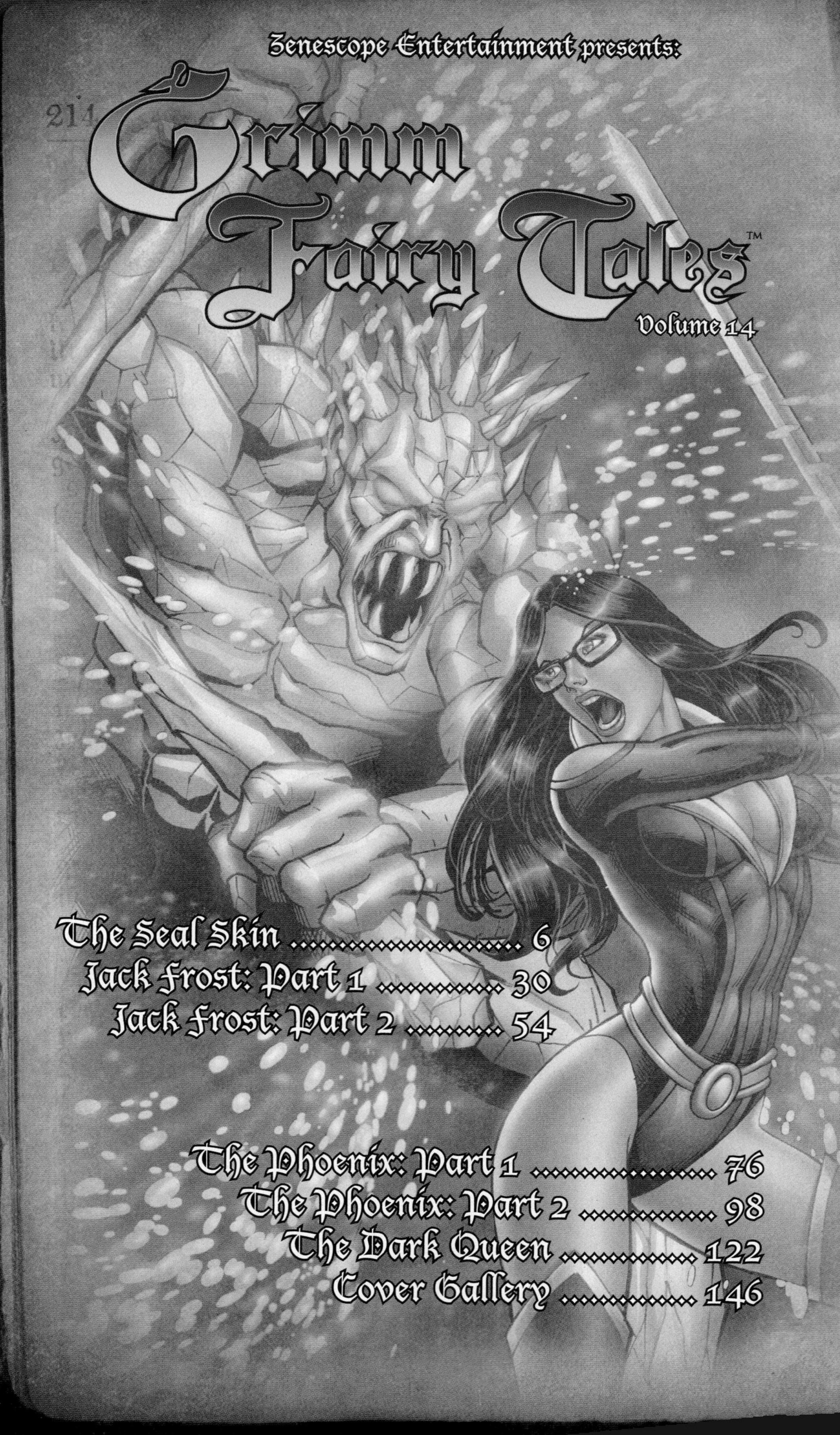

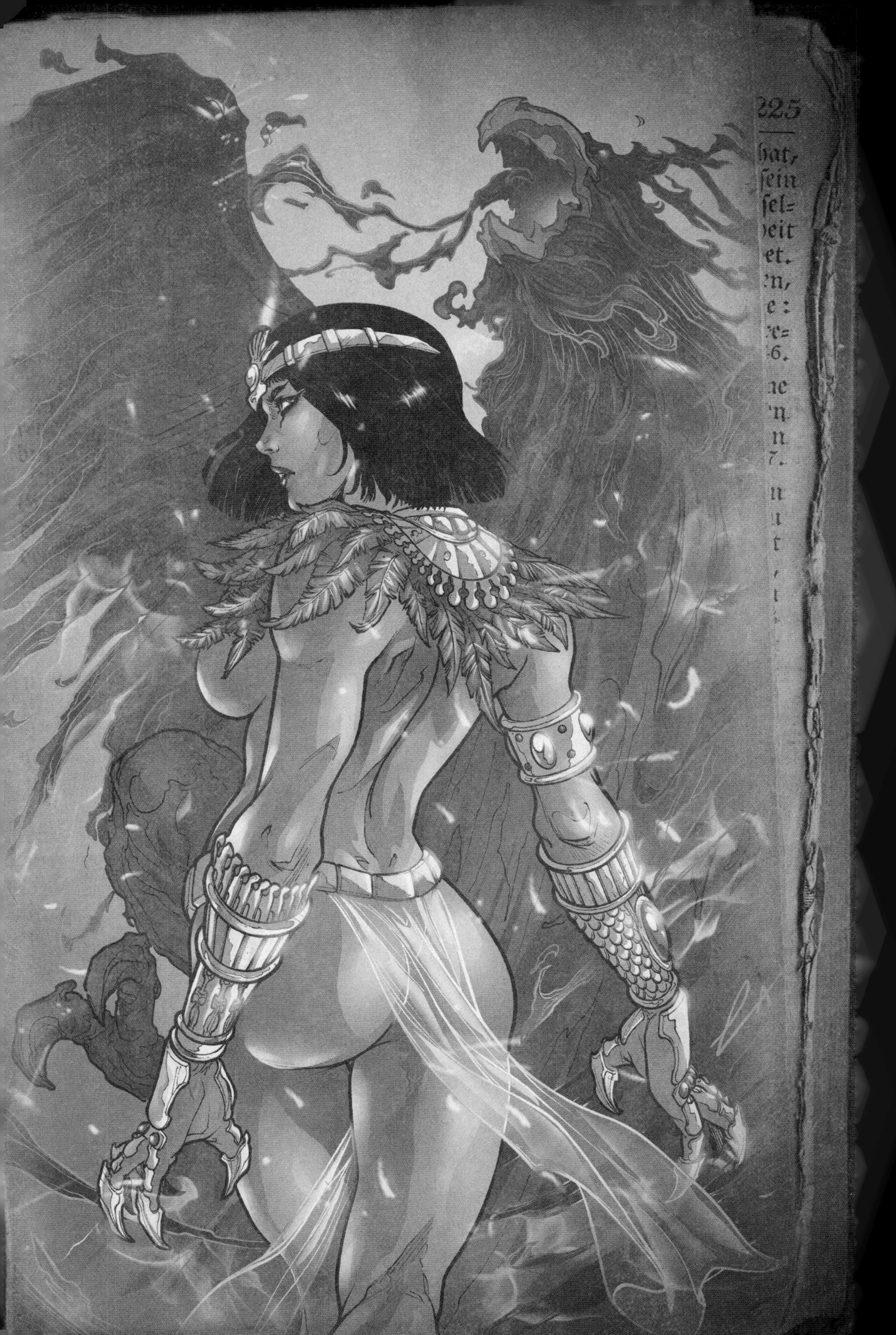

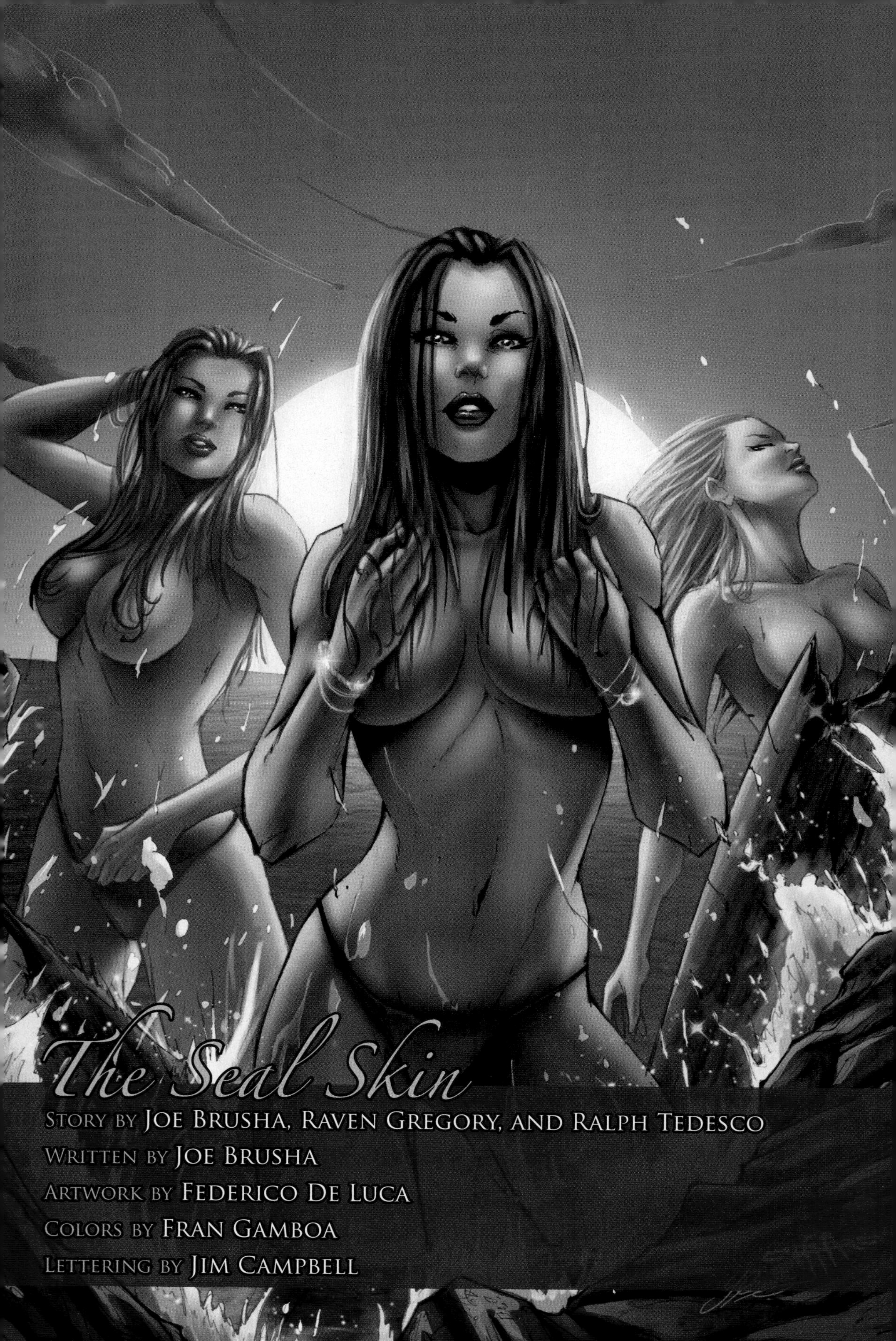
The Seal Skin
Story by Joe Brusha, Raven Gregory, and Ralph Tedesco
Written by Joe Brusha
Artwork by Federico De Luca
Colors by Fran Gamboa
Lettering by Jim Campbell

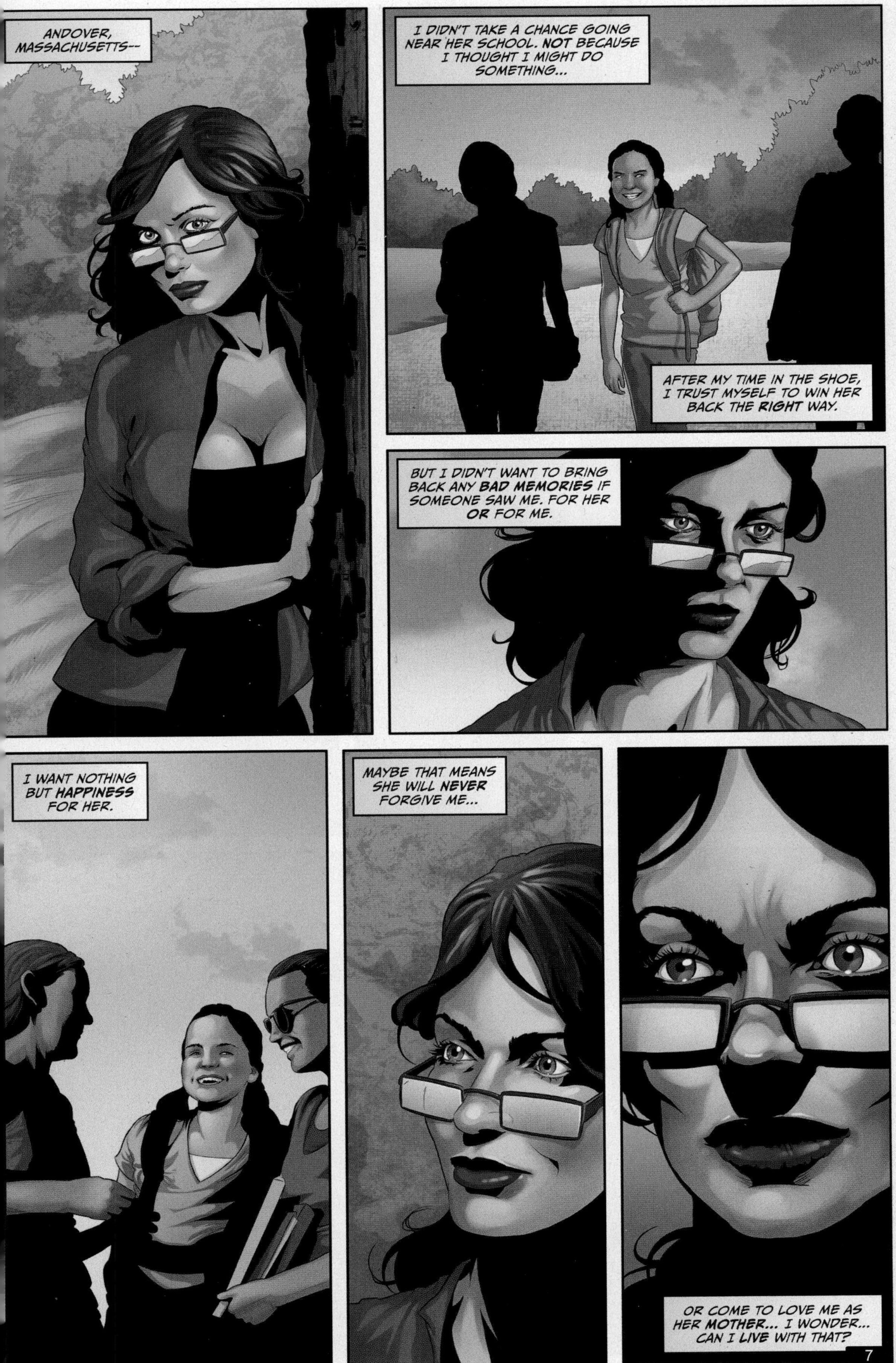

ANDOVER, MASSACHUSETTS--
I DIDN'T TAKE A CHANCE GOING NEAR HER SCHOOL. NOT BECAUSE I THOUGHT I MIGHT DO SOMETHING...
AFTER MY TIME IN THE SHOE, I TRUST MYSELF TO WIN HER BACK THE RIGHT WAY.
BUT I DIDN'T WANT TO BRING BACK ANY BAD MEMORIES IF SOMEONE SAW ME. FOR HER OR FOR ME.
I WANT NOTHING BUT HAPPINESS FOR HER.
MAYBE THAT MEANS SHE WILL NEVER FORGIVE ME...
OR COME TO LOVE ME AS HER MOTHER... I WONDER... CAN I LIVE WITH THAT?

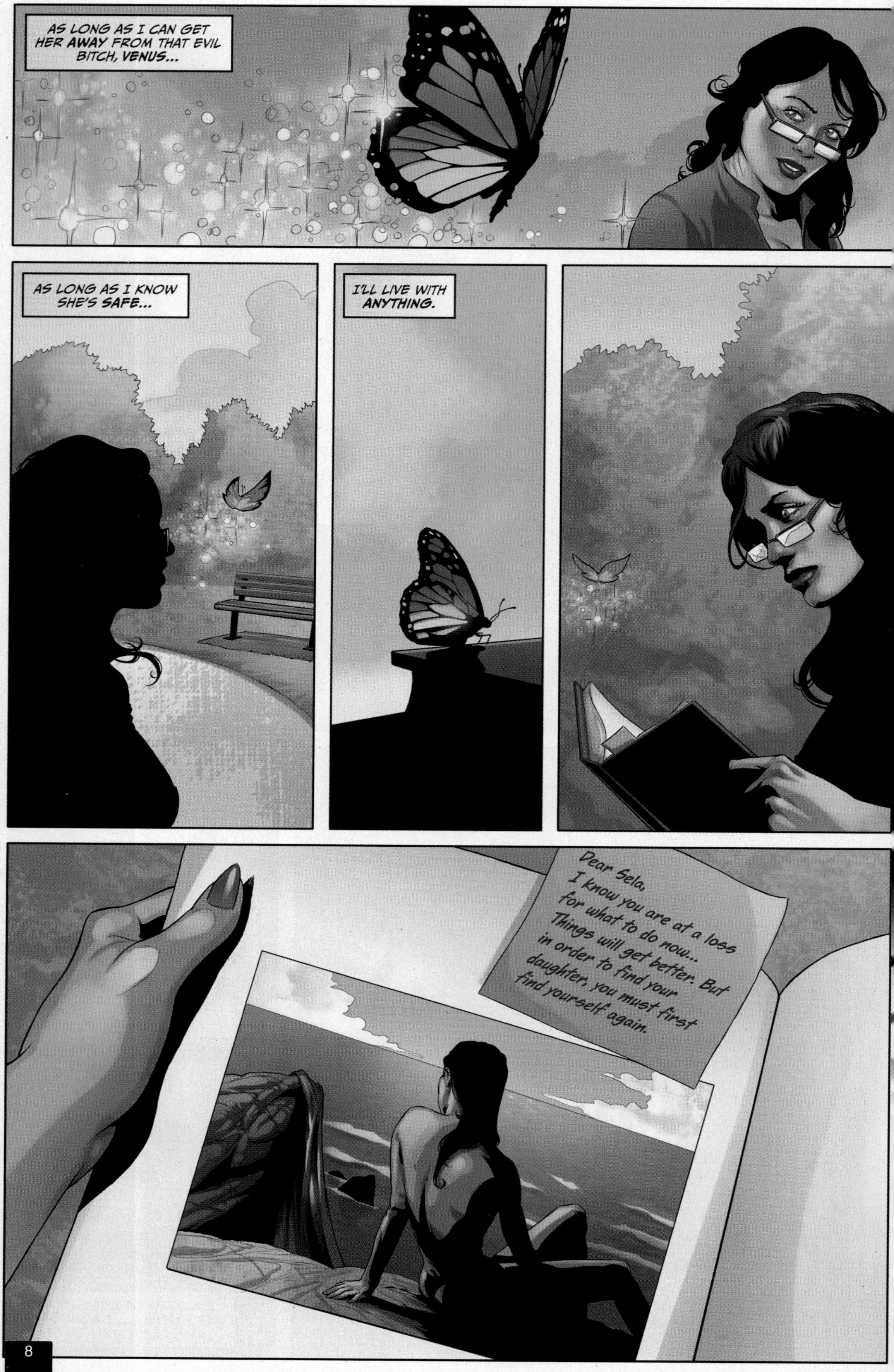
AS LONG AS I CAN GET HER AWAY FROM THAT EVIL BITCH, VENUS...
AS LONG AS I KNOW SHE'S SAFE...
I'LL LIVE WITH ANYTHING.
Dear Sela,
I know you are at a loss for what to do now...
Things will get better. But in order to find your daughter, you must first find yourself again.

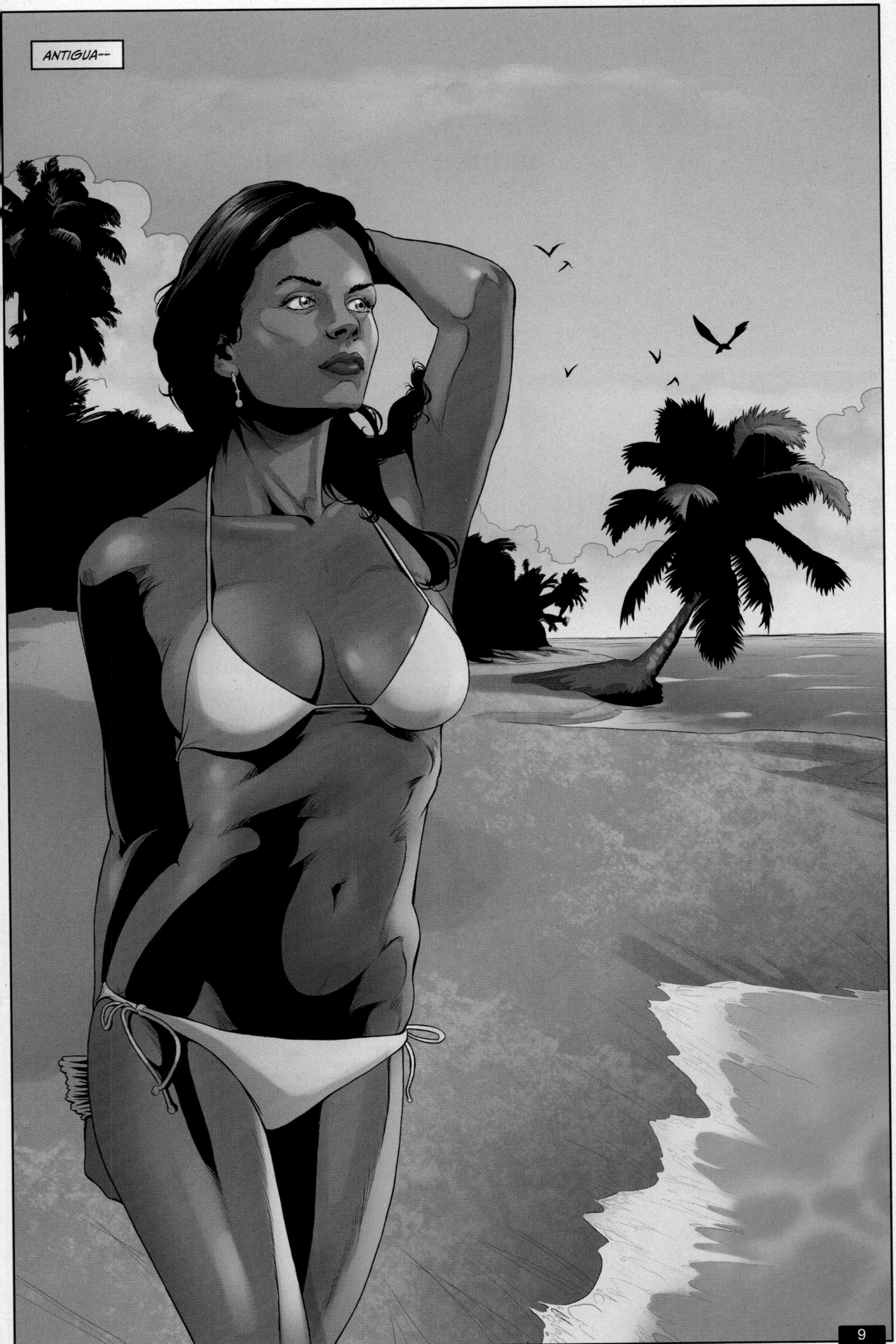
ANTIGUA--

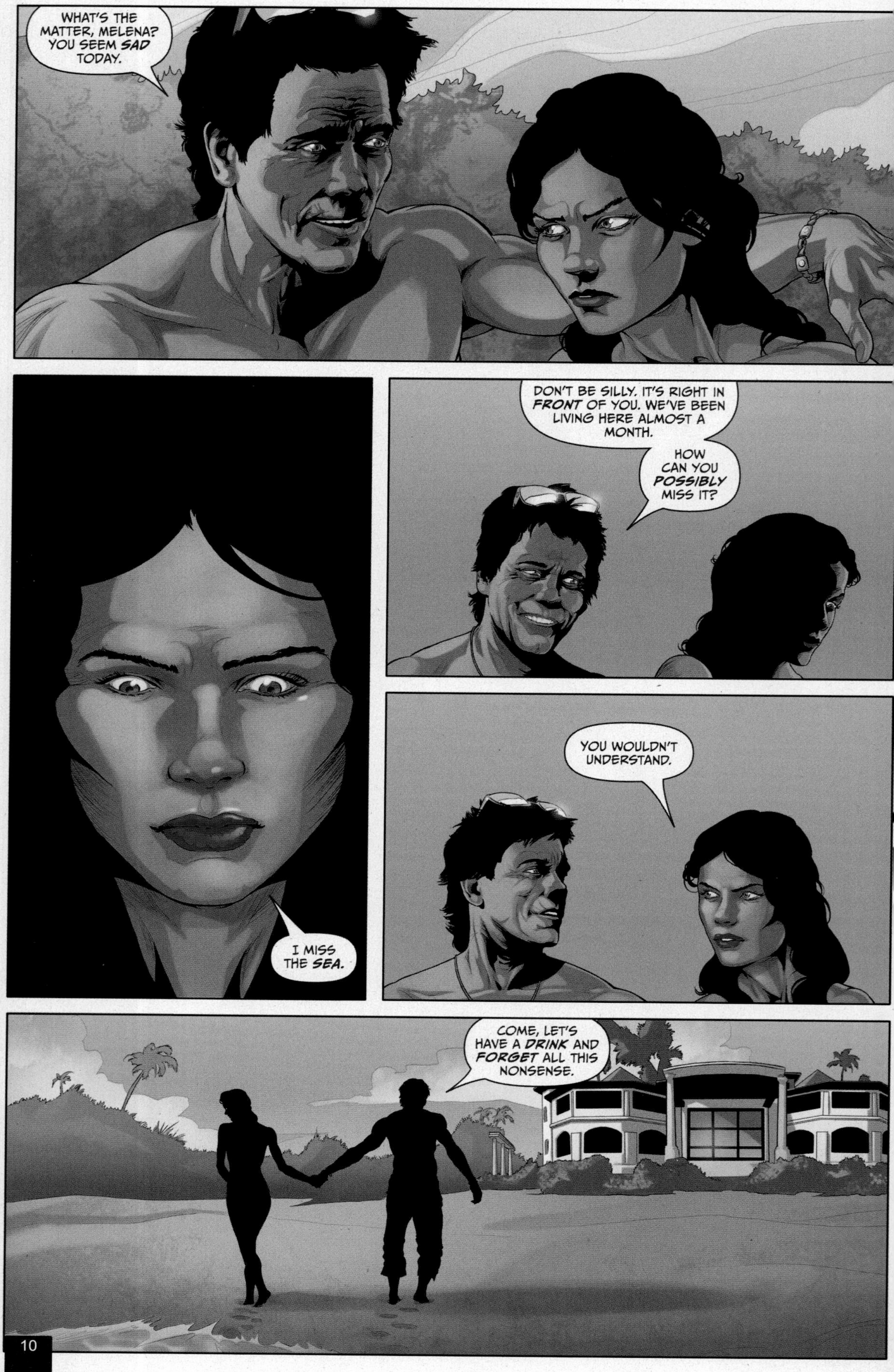
WHAT'S THE MATTER, MELENA? YOU SEEM SAD TODAY.
I MISS THE SEA.
DON'T BE SILLY. IT'S RIGHT IN FRONT OF YOU. WE'VE BEEN LIVING HERE ALMOST A MONTH.
HOW CAN YOU POSSIBLY MISS IT?
YOU WOULDN'T UNDERSTAND.
COME, LET'S HAVE A DRINK AND FORGET ALL THIS NONSENSE.

IT **CALLS** TO HER...

THEY CALL TO HER.

THE **LAND** HAS ITS PLEASURES...

BUT THE **SEA** IS FILLED WITH BEAUTY AND MYSTERY.

IT CALLS TO HER...

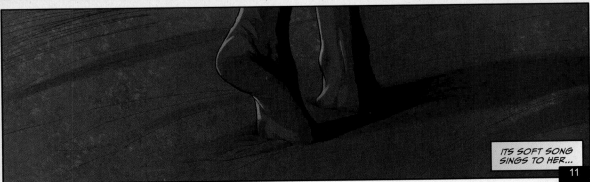

ITS SOFT SONG SINGS TO HER...

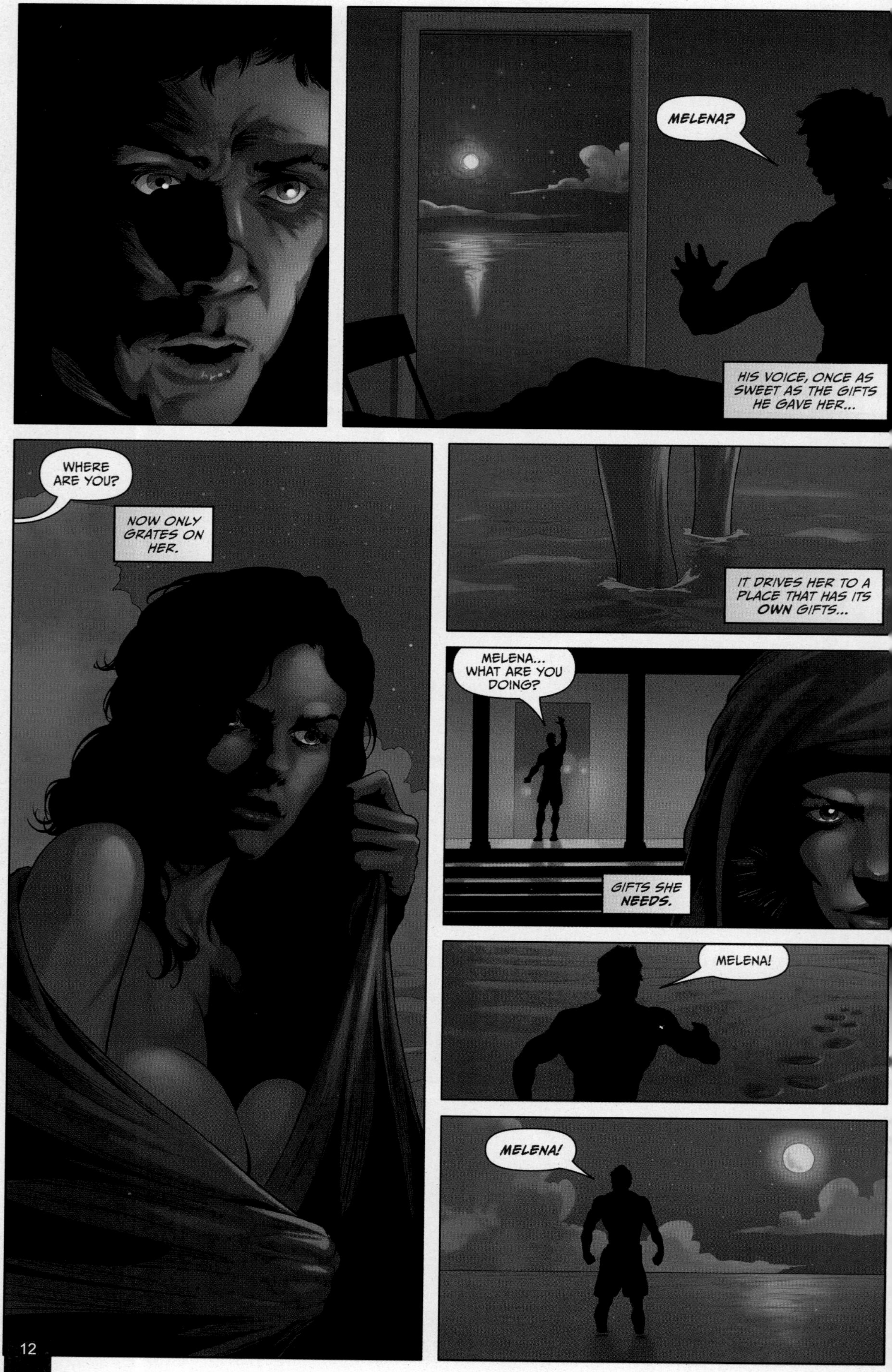
MELENA?
HIS VOICE, ONCE AS SWEET AS THE GIFTS HE GAVE HER...
WHERE ARE YOU?
NOW ONLY GRATES ON HER.
IT DRIVES HER TO A PLACE THAT HAS ITS OWN GIFTS...
MELENA... WHAT ARE YOU DOING?
GIFTS SHE NEEDS.
MELENA!
MELENA!

ONE MONTH LATER...
RIO DE JANEIRO--

DON'T YOU WANT TO COME IN THE WATER AND *PLAY,* SISTER?

YOU WERE THE ONE WHO WANTED TO TAKE A VACATION IN *RIO.*

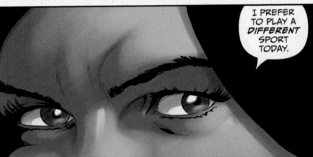

I PREFER TO PLAY A *DIFFERENT* SPORT TODAY.

EXCUSE ME...

YES...?

13

WHAT CAN I DO FOR YOU?

I WAS WONDERING IF YOU COULD HELP ME WITH A *PROBLEM?*

WHAT PROBLEM?

YOU SEE, I JUST ORDERED A BOTTLE OF *CHAMPAGNE* TO MY CABANA...

AND I HAVE NO ONE TO *SHARE* IT WITH.

DO YOU THINK YOU WOULD BE ABLE TO ASSIST ME?

I WOULD *LOVE* TO.

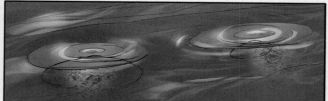

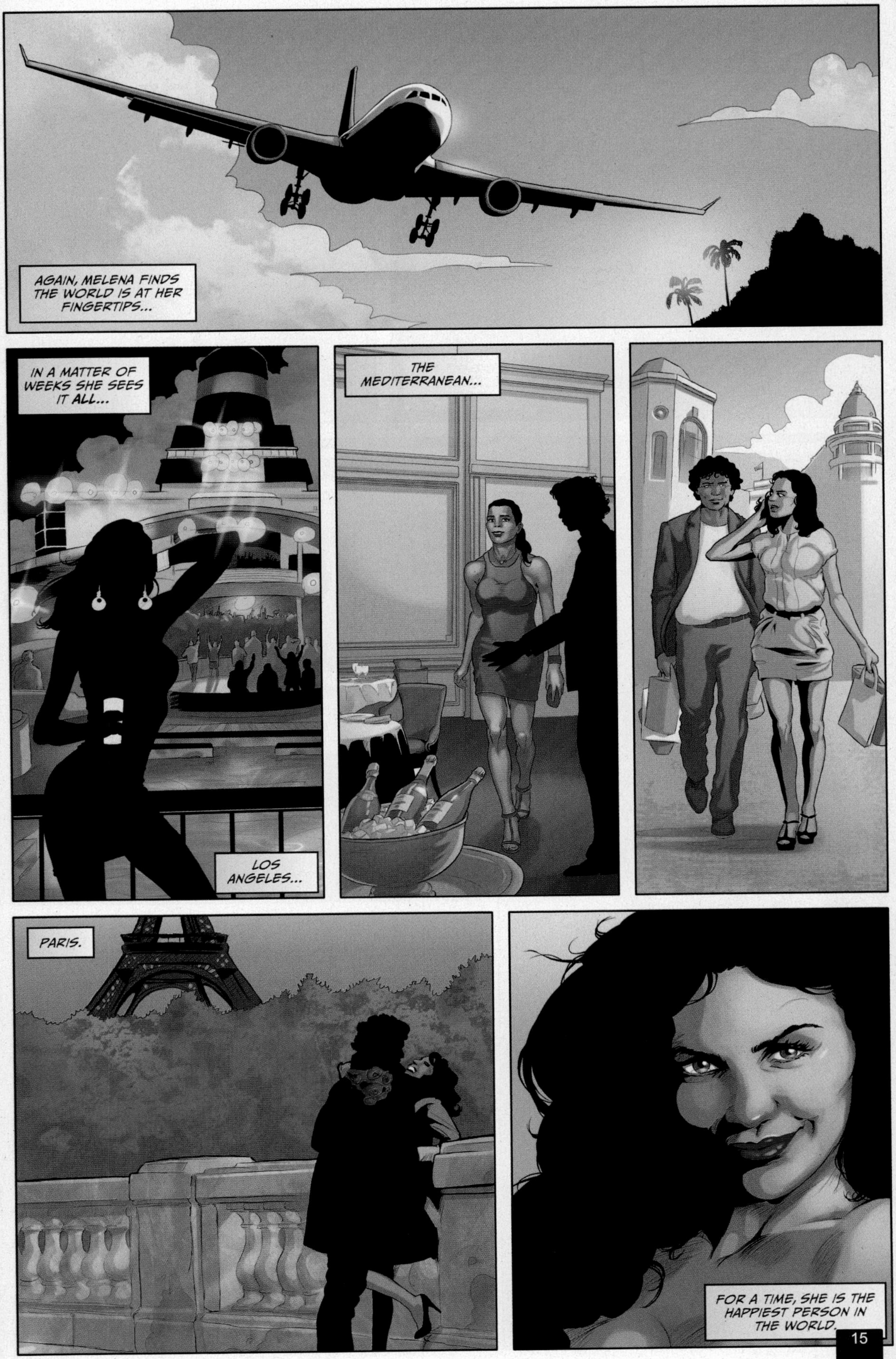
AGAIN, MELENA FINDS THE WORLD IS AT HER FINGERTIPS...
IN A MATTER OF WEEKS SHE SEES IT ALL...
LOS ANGELES...
THE MEDITERRANEAN...
PARIS.
FOR A TIME, SHE IS THE HAPPIEST PERSON IN THE WORLD.

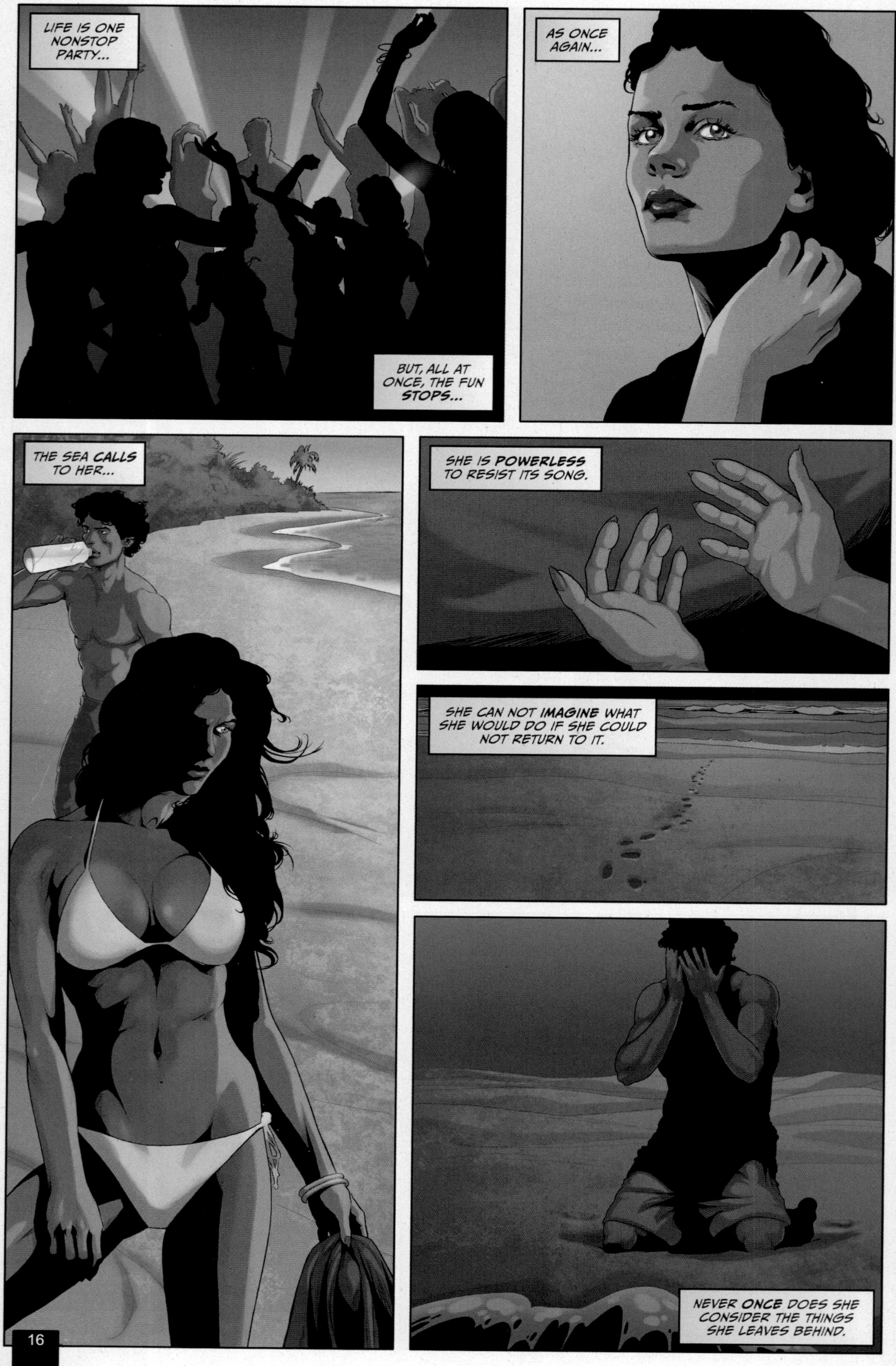
LIFE IS ONE NONSTOP PARTY...
BUT, ALL AT ONCE, THE FUN STOPS...
AS ONCE AGAIN...
THE SEA CALLS TO HER...
SHE IS POWERLESS TO RESIST ITS SONG.
SHE CAN NOT IMAGINE WHAT SHE WOULD DO IF SHE COULD NOT RETURN TO IT.
NEVER ONCE DOES SHE CONSIDER THE THINGS SHE LEAVES BEHIND.

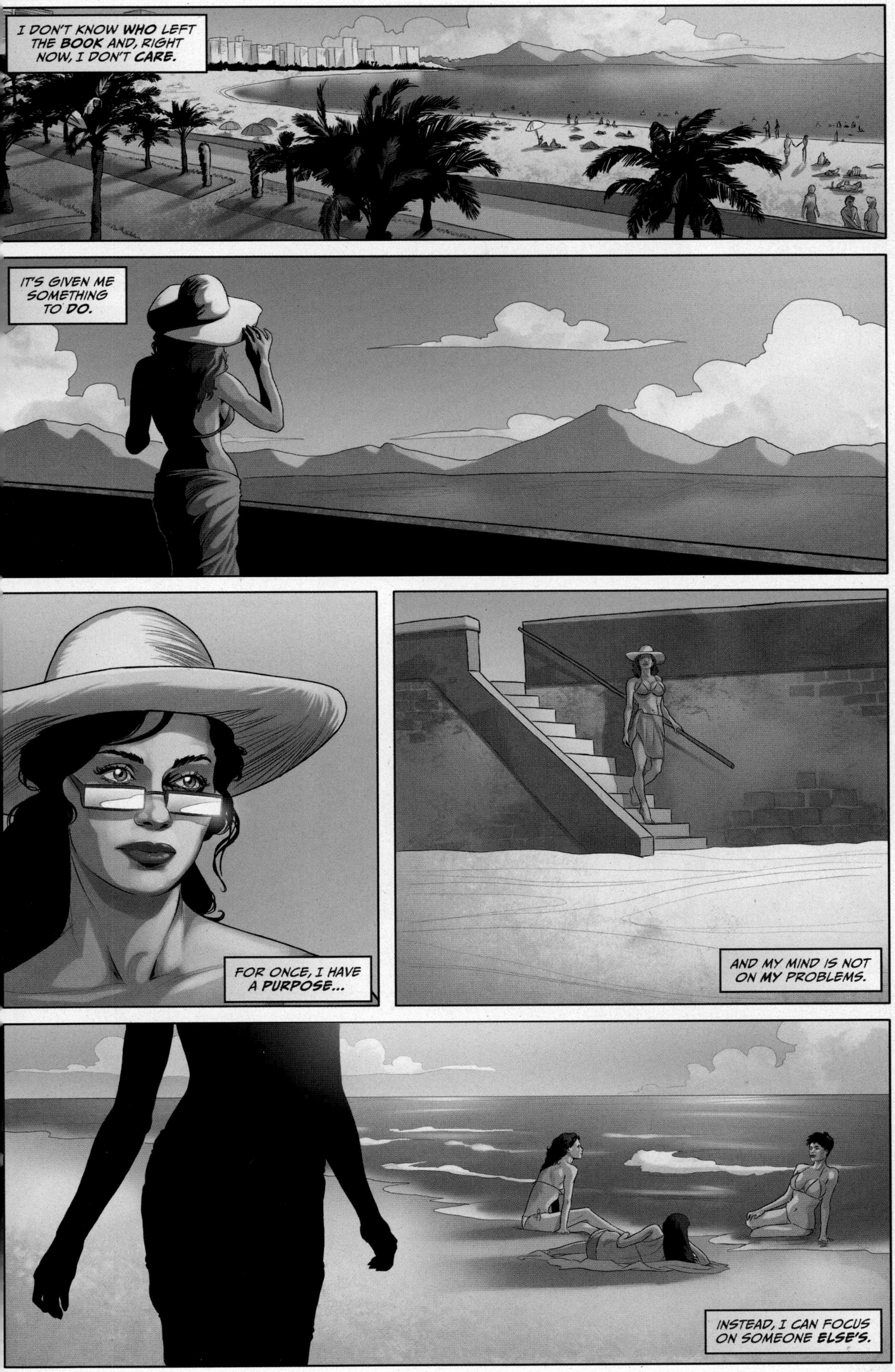
I DON'T KNOW WHO LEFT THE BOOK AND, RIGHT NOW, I DON'T CARE.
IT'S GIVEN ME SOMETHING TO DO.
FOR ONCE, I HAVE A PURPOSE...
AND MY MIND IS NOT ON MY PROBLEMS.
INSTEAD, I CAN FOCUS ON SOMEONE ELSE'S.

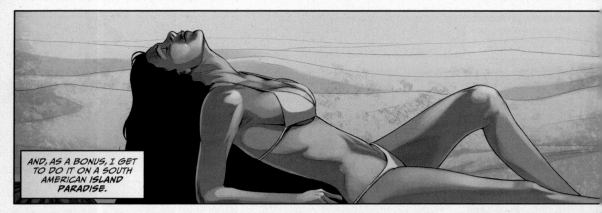

AND, AS A BONUS, I GET TO DO IT ON A SOUTH AMERICAN ISLAND PARADISE.

HELLO, MELENA?

DO I KNOW YOU?

WE'VE NEVER MET BEFORE, BUT YOU'VE PROBABLY HEARD OF ME.

MY NAME IS SELA MATHERS.

OF COURSE. YOU'RE ONLY THE MOST FAMOUS FALSE BLOOD OF ALL TIME.

BUT I HEARD YOU TOOK A ONE WAY TRIP TO MYST.

I DID. I'M BACK.

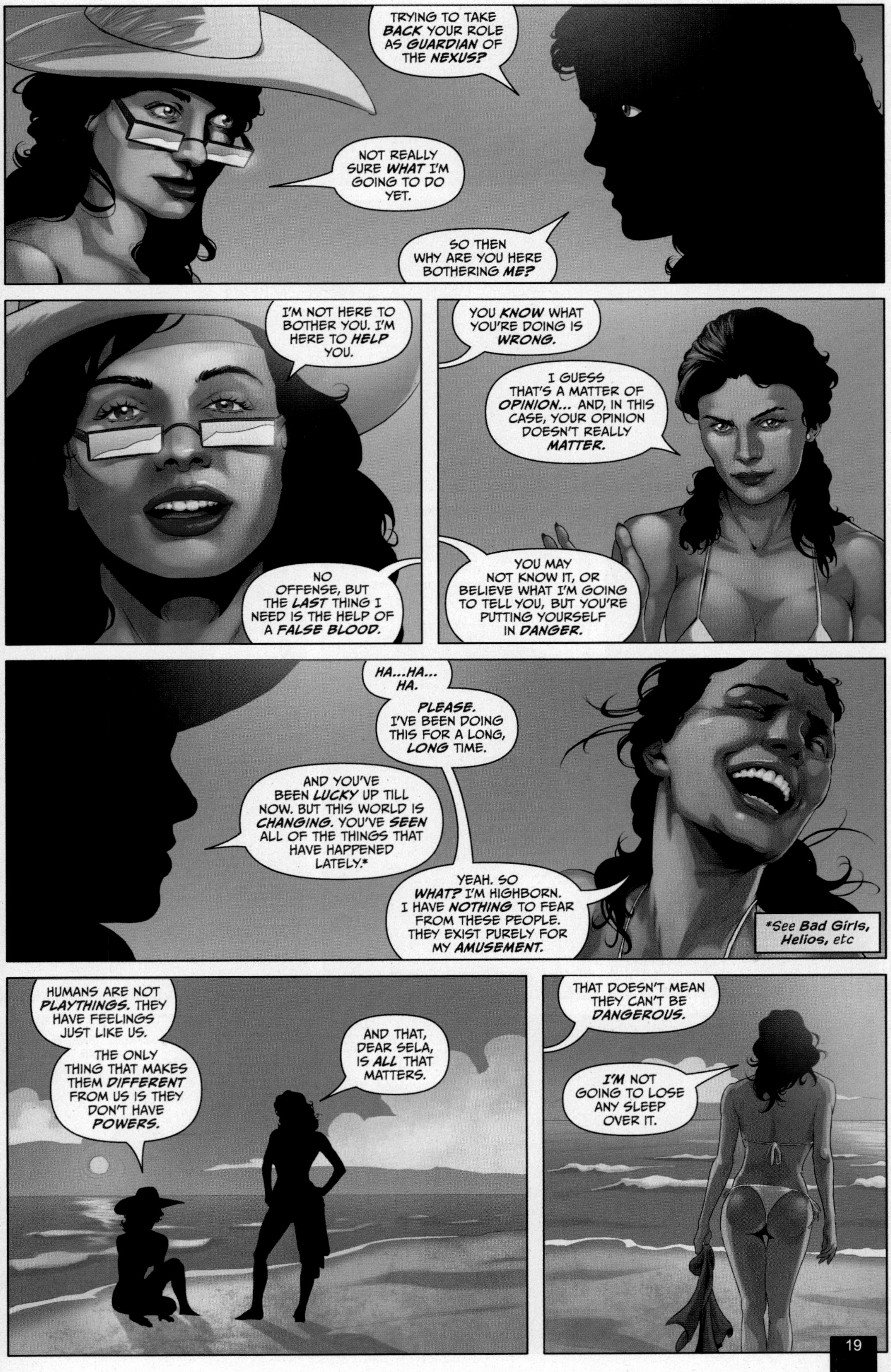

TRYING TO TAKE BACK YOUR ROLE AS GUARDIAN OF THE NEXUS?
NOT REALLY SURE WHAT I'M GOING TO DO YET.
SO THEN WHY ARE YOU HERE BOTHERING ME?
I'M NOT HERE TO BOTHER YOU. I'M HERE TO HELP YOU.
NO OFFENSE, BUT THE LAST THING I NEED IS THE HELP OF A FALSE BLOOD.
YOU KNOW WHAT YOU'RE DOING IS WRONG.
I GUESS THAT'S A MATTER OF OPINION... AND, IN THIS CASE, YOUR OPINION DOESN'T REALLY MATTER.
YOU MAY NOT KNOW IT, OR BELIEVE WHAT I'M GOING TO TELL YOU, BUT YOU'RE PUTTING YOURSELF IN DANGER.
HA...HA... HA.
PLEASE. I'VE BEEN DOING THIS FOR A LONG, LONG TIME.
AND YOU'VE BEEN LUCKY UP TILL NOW. BUT THIS WORLD IS CHANGING. YOU'VE SEEN ALL OF THE THINGS THAT HAVE HAPPENED LATELY.*
YEAH. SO WHAT? I'M HIGHBORN. I HAVE NOTHING TO FEAR FROM THESE PEOPLE. THEY EXIST PURELY FOR MY AMUSEMENT.
*See Bad Girls, Helios, etc
HUMANS ARE NOT PLAYTHINGS. THEY HAVE FEELINGS JUST LIKE US.
THE ONLY THING THAT MAKES THEM DIFFERENT FROM US IS THEY DON'T HAVE POWERS.
AND THAT, DEAR SELA, IS ALL THAT MATTERS.
THAT DOESN'T MEAN THEY CAN'T BE DANGEROUS.
I'M NOT GOING TO LOSE ANY SLEEP OVER IT.

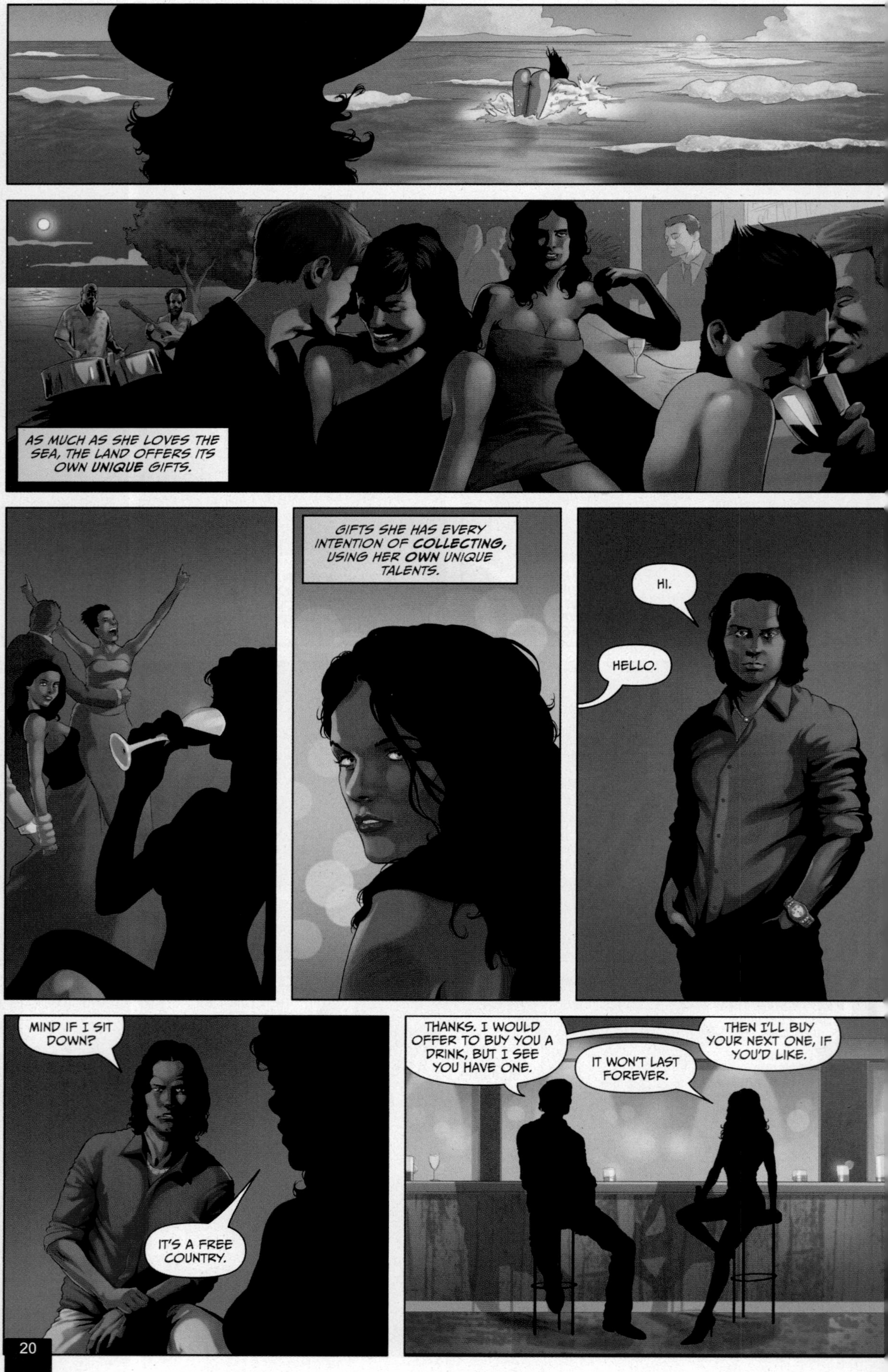
AS MUCH AS SHE LOVES THE SEA, THE LAND OFFERS ITS OWN UNIQUE GIFTS.
GIFTS SHE HAS EVERY INTENTION OF COLLECTING, USING HER OWN UNIQUE TALENTS.
HI.
HELLO.
MIND IF I SIT DOWN?
IT'S A FREE COUNTRY.
THANKS. I WOULD OFFER TO BUY YOU A DRINK, BUT I SEE YOU HAVE ONE.
IT WON'T LAST FOREVER.
THEN I'LL BUY YOUR NEXT ONE, IF YOU'D LIKE.

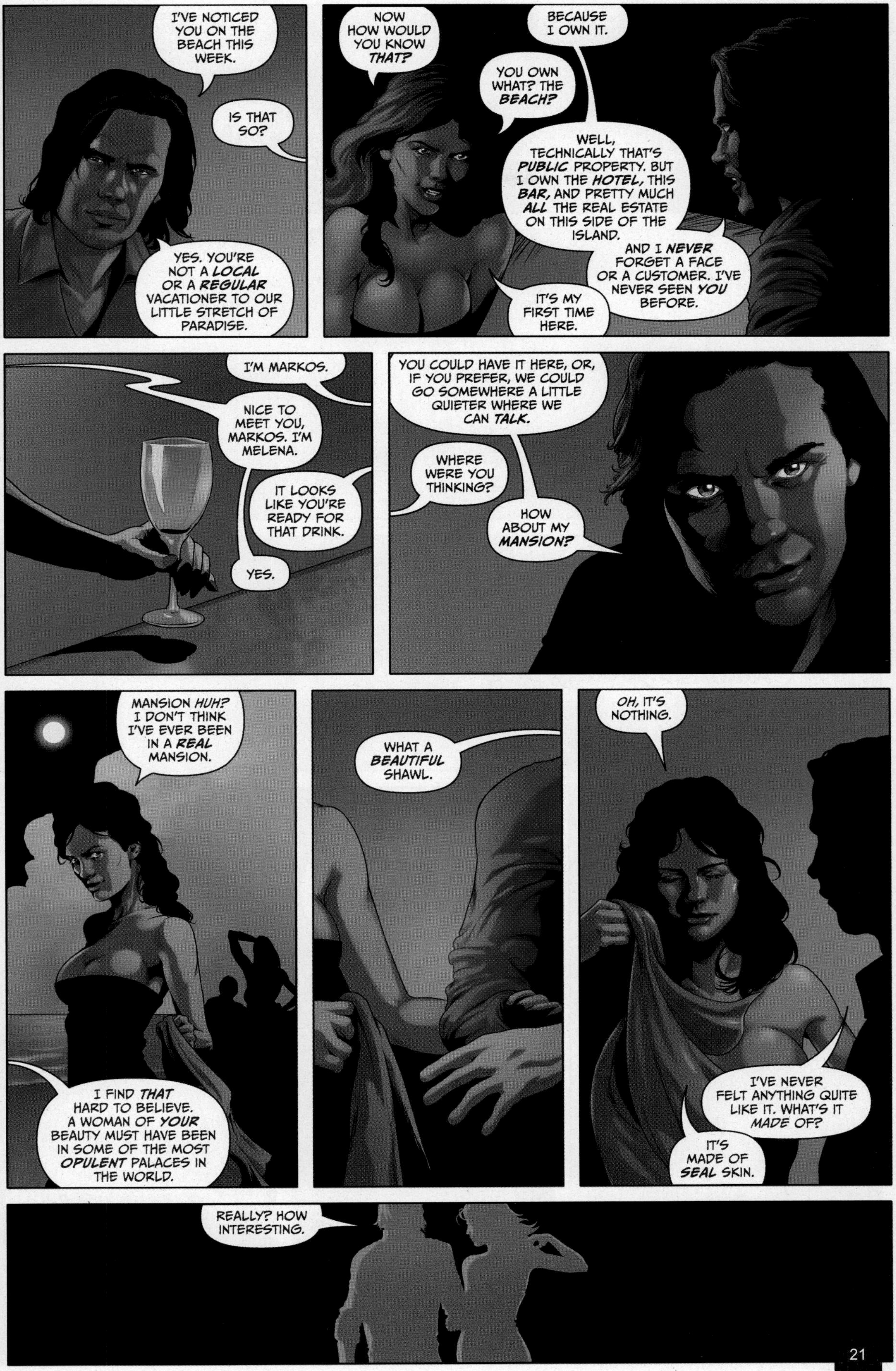
I'VE NOTICED YOU ON THE BEACH THIS WEEK.
IS THAT SO?
YES. YOU'RE NOT A LOCAL OR A REGULAR VACATIONER TO OUR LITTLE STRETCH OF PARADISE.
NOW HOW WOULD YOU KNOW THAT?
BECAUSE I OWN IT.
YOU OWN WHAT? THE BEACH?
WELL, TECHNICALLY THAT'S PUBLIC PROPERTY. BUT I OWN THE HOTEL, THIS BAR, AND PRETTY MUCH ALL THE REAL ESTATE ON THIS SIDE OF THE ISLAND.
AND I NEVER FORGET A FACE OR A CUSTOMER. I'VE NEVER SEEN YOU BEFORE.
IT'S MY FIRST TIME HERE.
I'M MARKOS.
NICE TO MEET YOU, MARKOS. I'M MELENA.
IT LOOKS LIKE YOU'RE READY FOR THAT DRINK.
YES.
YOU COULD HAVE IT HERE, OR, IF YOU PREFER, WE COULD GO SOMEWHERE A LITTLE QUIETER WHERE WE CAN TALK.
WHERE WERE YOU THINKING?
HOW ABOUT MY MANSION?
MANSION HUH? I DON'T THINK I'VE EVER BEEN IN A REAL MANSION.
I FIND THAT HARD TO BELIEVE. A WOMAN OF YOUR BEAUTY MUST HAVE BEEN IN SOME OF THE MOST OPULENT PALACES IN THE WORLD.
WHAT A BEAUTIFUL SHAWL.
OH, IT'S NOTHING.
I'VE NEVER FELT ANYTHING QUITE LIKE IT. WHAT'S IT MADE OF?
IT'S MADE OF SEAL SKIN.
REALLY? HOW INTERESTING.

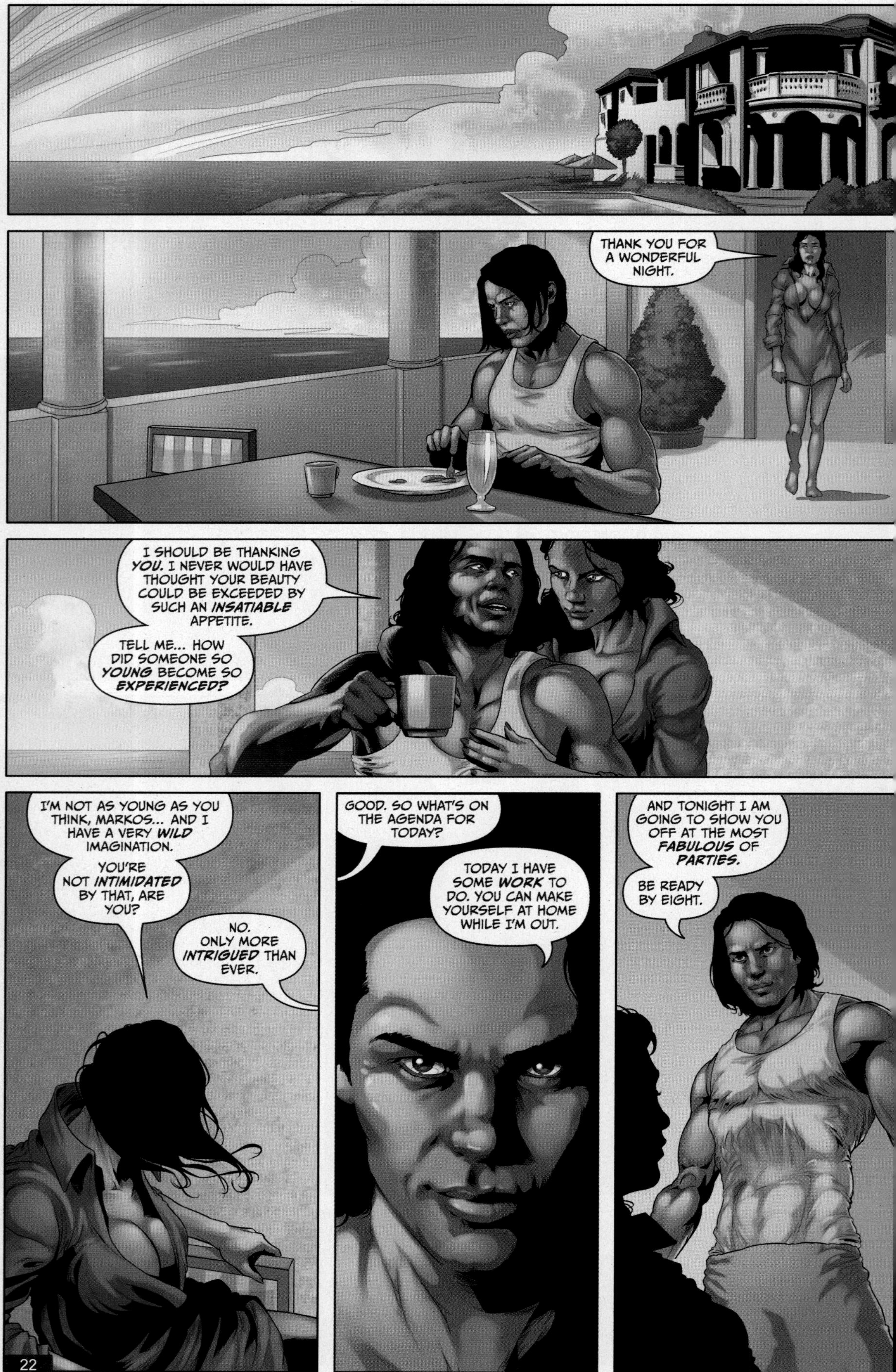
THANK YOU FOR A WONDERFUL NIGHT.
I SHOULD BE THANKING YOU. I NEVER WOULD HAVE THOUGHT YOUR BEAUTY COULD BE EXCEEDED BY SUCH AN INSATIABLE APPETITE.
TELL ME... HOW DID SOMEONE SO YOUNG BECOME SO EXPERIENCED?
I'M NOT AS YOUNG AS YOU THINK, MARKOS... AND I HAVE A VERY WILD IMAGINATION.
YOU'RE NOT INTIMIDATED BY THAT, ARE YOU?
NO. ONLY MORE INTRIGUED THAN EVER.
GOOD. SO WHAT'S ON THE AGENDA FOR TODAY?
TODAY I HAVE SOME WORK TO DO. YOU CAN MAKE YOURSELF AT HOME WHILE I'M OUT.
AND TONIGHT I AM GOING TO SHOW YOU OFF AT THE MOST FABULOUS OF PARTIES.
BE READY BY EIGHT.

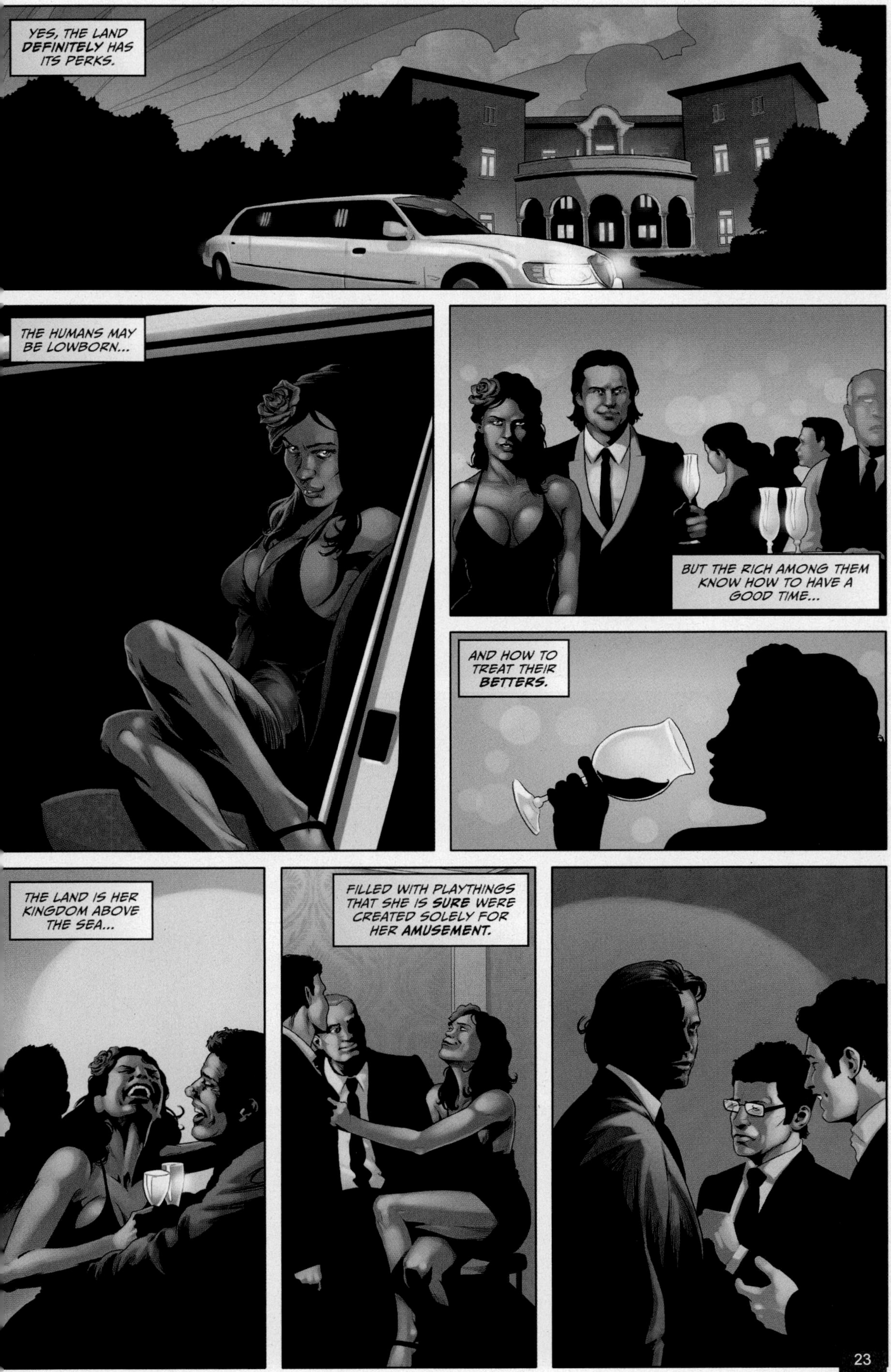
YES, THE LAND DEFINITELY HAS ITS PERKS.
THE HUMANS MAY BE LOWBORN...
BUT THE RICH AMONG THEM KNOW HOW TO HAVE A GOOD TIME...
AND HOW TO TREAT THEIR BETTERS.
THE LAND IS HER KINGDOM ABOVE THE SEA...
FILLED WITH PLAYTHINGS THAT SHE IS SURE WERE CREATED SOLELY FOR HER AMUSEMENT.

COME, MY DEAR. IT'S TIME TO GO.

ALREADY? CAN'T WE STAY, HONEY? I'M HAVING SO MUCH FUN.

MAYBE I CAN STAY AND YOU CAN SEND THE LIMO TO GET ME LATER.

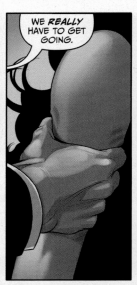
WE REALLY HAVE TO GET GOING.

HEY. TAKE IT EASY.

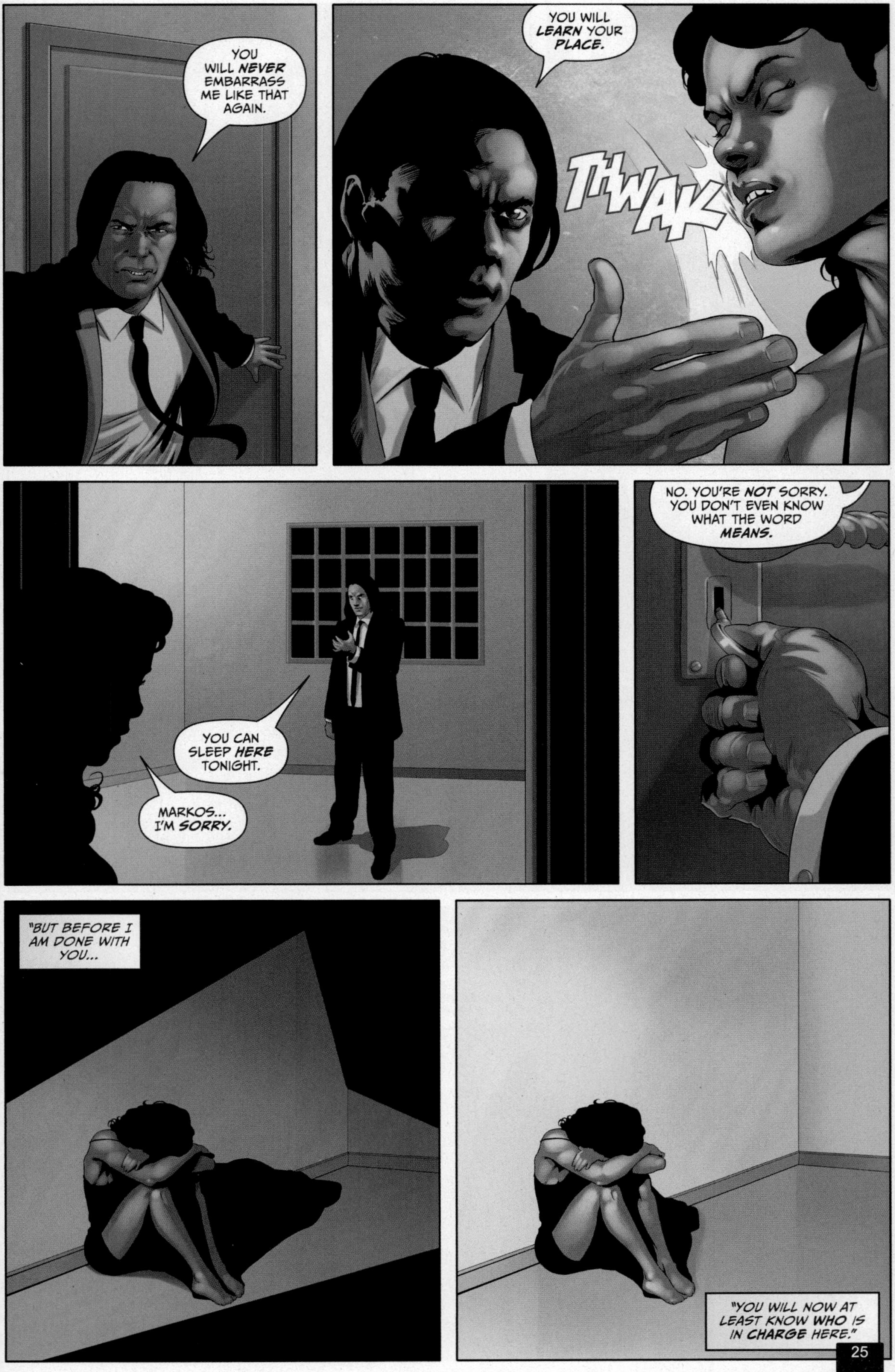
YOU WILL NEVER EMBARRASS ME LIKE THAT AGAIN.
YOU WILL LEARN YOUR PLACE.
THWAK
YOU CAN SLEEP HERE TONIGHT.
MARKOS... I'M SORRY.
NO. YOU'RE NOT SORRY. YOU DON'T EVEN KNOW WHAT THE WORD MEANS.
"BUT BEFORE I AM DONE WITH YOU...
"YOU WILL NOW AT LEAST KNOW WHO IS IN CHARGE HERE."

I'M *SORRY* I HAD TO DO THAT LAST NIGHT, MELENA. YOU HAVE TO UNDERSTAND THAT I AM THE MOST *RESPECTED* MAN ON THIS ISLAND.

PLEASE. SIT DOWN.

YOU SEE, I CAN'T HAVE MY *DATE* ACTING LIKE SOME COMMON *WHORE.*

I'M SORRY. IT WILL NEVER HAPPEN AGAIN.

I SHOULDN'T HAVE DRUNK SO MUCH. I FEEL REALLY HUNGOVER... REALLY *COLD.*

DO YOU THINK I COULD HAVE MY *SHAWL* TO KEEP *WARM?*

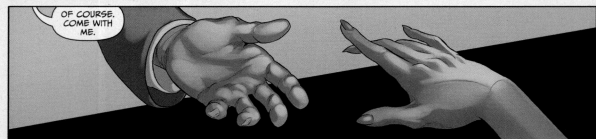

OF COURSE. COME WITH ME.

YOU KNOW MY FATHER WAS A *FISHERMAN.*

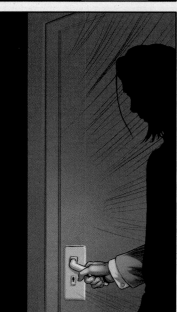

26

I NEVER GOT ALONG WELL WITH HIM. I HATED THE WAY HE ALWAYS *STANK* OF FISH.

I SWORE I WOULD *NEVER* BE A POOR FISHERMAN... THAT I WOULD *MAKE* SOMETHING OF MY LIFE AND NEVER HAVE TO WORRY ABOUT MONEY... NEVER SMELL LIKE *FISH.*

BUT I DID LOVE HIS *STORIES.*

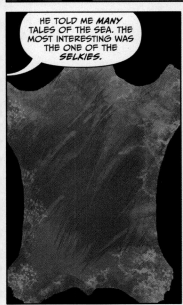

HE TOLD ME *MANY* TALES OF THE SEA. THE MOST INTERESTING WAS THE ONE OF THE *SELKIES.*

WHEN I SAW YOU AND YOUR SISTERS ON THE BEACH I HAD MY *SUSPICIONS.* AND WHEN I CHECKED THE HOTEL AND FOUND OUT YOU WEREN'T STAYING THERE... OR ANYWHERE *ELSE...*

I *KNEW* WHAT YOU WERE.

A SELKIE. A CREATURE OF THE SEA WITH THE POWER TO BECOME *HUMAN.*

I'M *NOT* HUMAN... I'M *HIGHBORN.*

EITHER WAY, YOU'RE GOING TO STAY WITH *ME* NOW.

THE OWNER OF THAT SKIN DIDN'T *OBEY* ME.

SHE NEVER *DID* RETURN TO THE SEA.

MAYBE YOU'LL BE *DIFFERENT.* MAYBE YOU'LL *LISTEN* AND DO EVERYTHING I SAY... AND GET YOUR SKIN *BACK...*

AND SWIM ONCE AGAIN IN THE *SEA*.

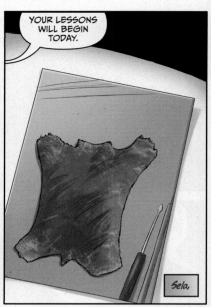

YOUR LESSONS WILL BEGIN TODAY.

Sela,

I know your meeting with Melena did not go well. This was not unexpected.

She was always a strong-willed girl and not prone to listening to good advice. So know she must suffer the consequences of her actions.

The world has become a very dangerous place for Highborns and humans alike. If something is not done many more will suffer the fate of Melena or the humans that suffered through the evil plots of Venus.

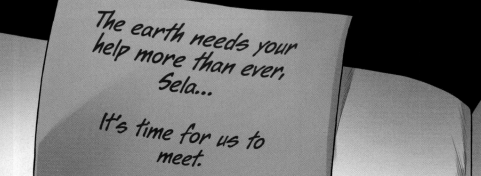

The earth needs your help more than ever, Sela...

It's time for us to meet.

Grimm Fairy Tales

Volume 14

Grimm Fairy Tales

Volume 14

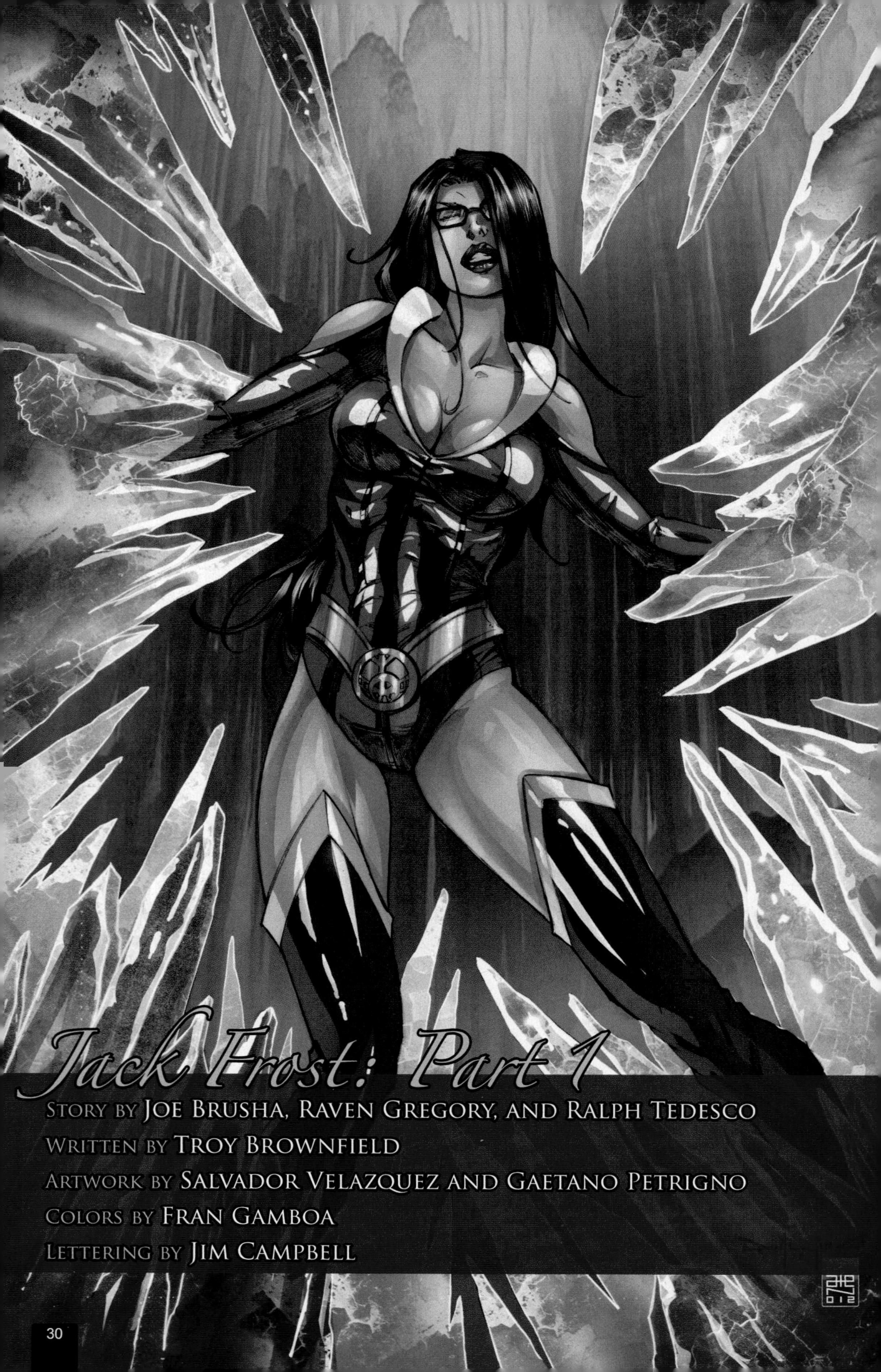
Jack Frost: Part 1
Story by Joe Brusha, Raven Gregory, and Ralph Tedesco
Written by Troy Brownfield
Artwork by Salvador Velazquez and Gaetano Petrigno
Colors by Fran Gamboa
Lettering by Jim Campbell

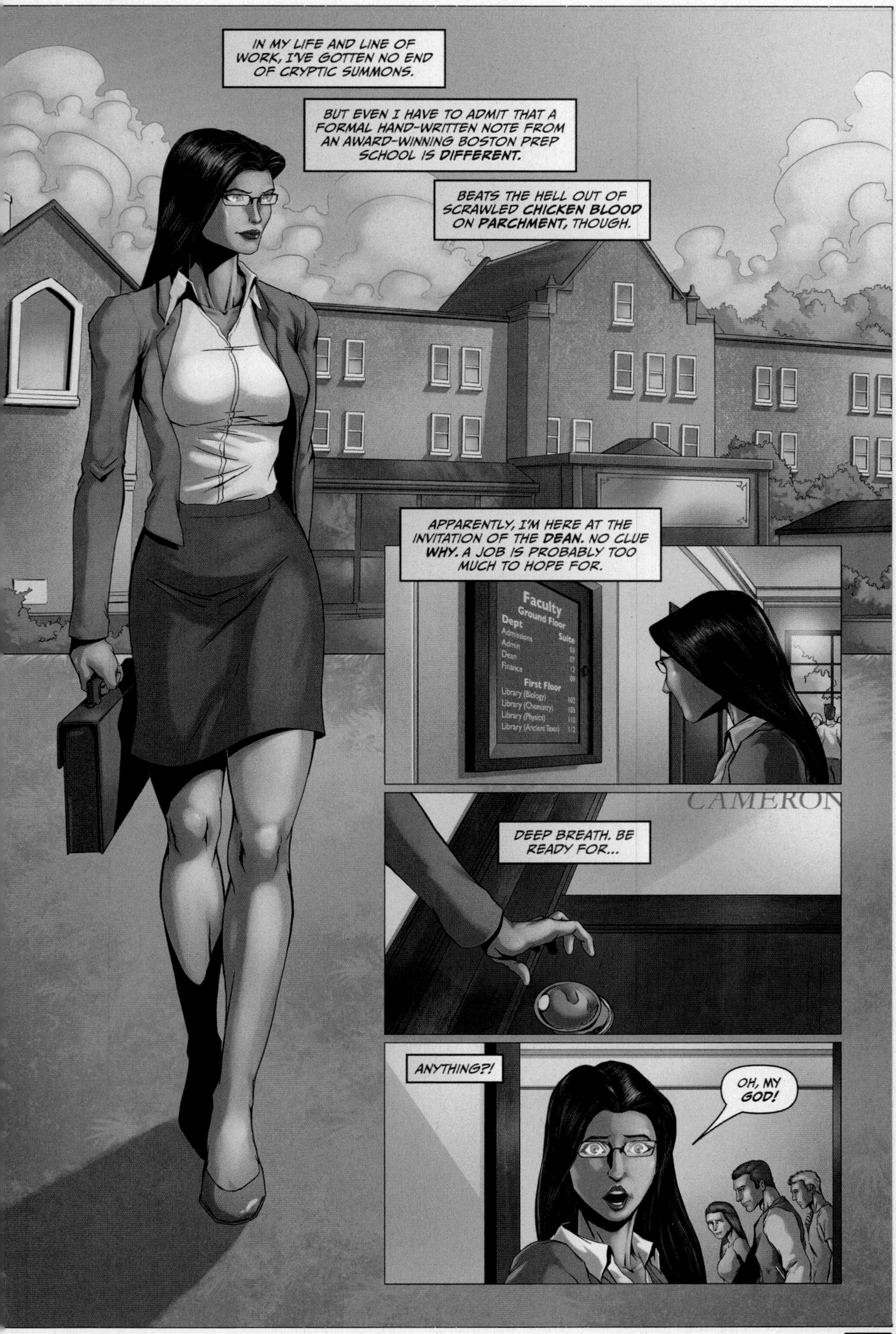

IN MY LIFE AND LINE OF WORK, I'VE GOTTEN NO END OF CRYPTIC SUMMONS.
BUT EVEN I HAVE TO ADMIT THAT A FORMAL HAND-WRITTEN NOTE FROM AN AWARD-WINNING BOSTON PREP SCHOOL IS **DIFFERENT.**
BEATS THE HELL OUT OF SCRAWLED **CHICKEN BLOOD** ON **PARCHMENT,** THOUGH.
APPARENTLY, I'M HERE AT THE INVITATION OF THE **DEAN.** NO CLUE **WHY.** A JOB IS PROBABLY TOO MUCH TO HOPE FOR.
Faculty
Ground Floor
Dept
Suite
Admissions
Admin
Dean
Finance
First Floor
Library (Biology)
Library (Chemistry)
Library (Physics)
Library (Ancient Texts)
CAMERON
DEEP BREATH. BE READY FOR...
ANYTHING?!
OH, MY **GOD!**

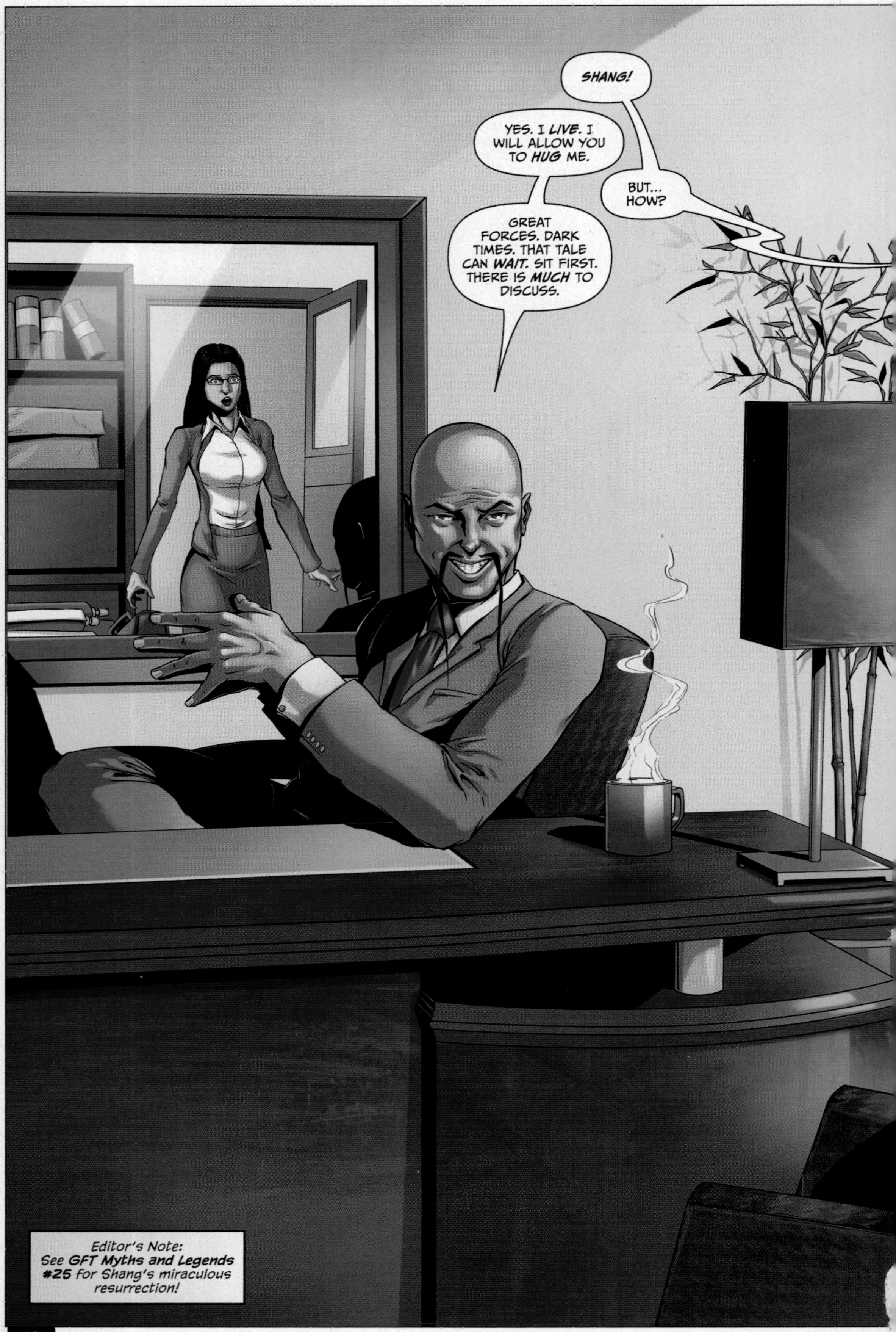
SHANG!
YES. I LIVE. I WILL ALLOW YOU TO HUG ME.
BUT... HOW?
GREAT FORCES. DARK TIMES. THAT TALE CAN WAIT. SIT FIRST. THERE IS MUCH TO DISCUSS.
Editor's Note: See GFT Myths and Legends #25 for Shang's miraculous resurrection!

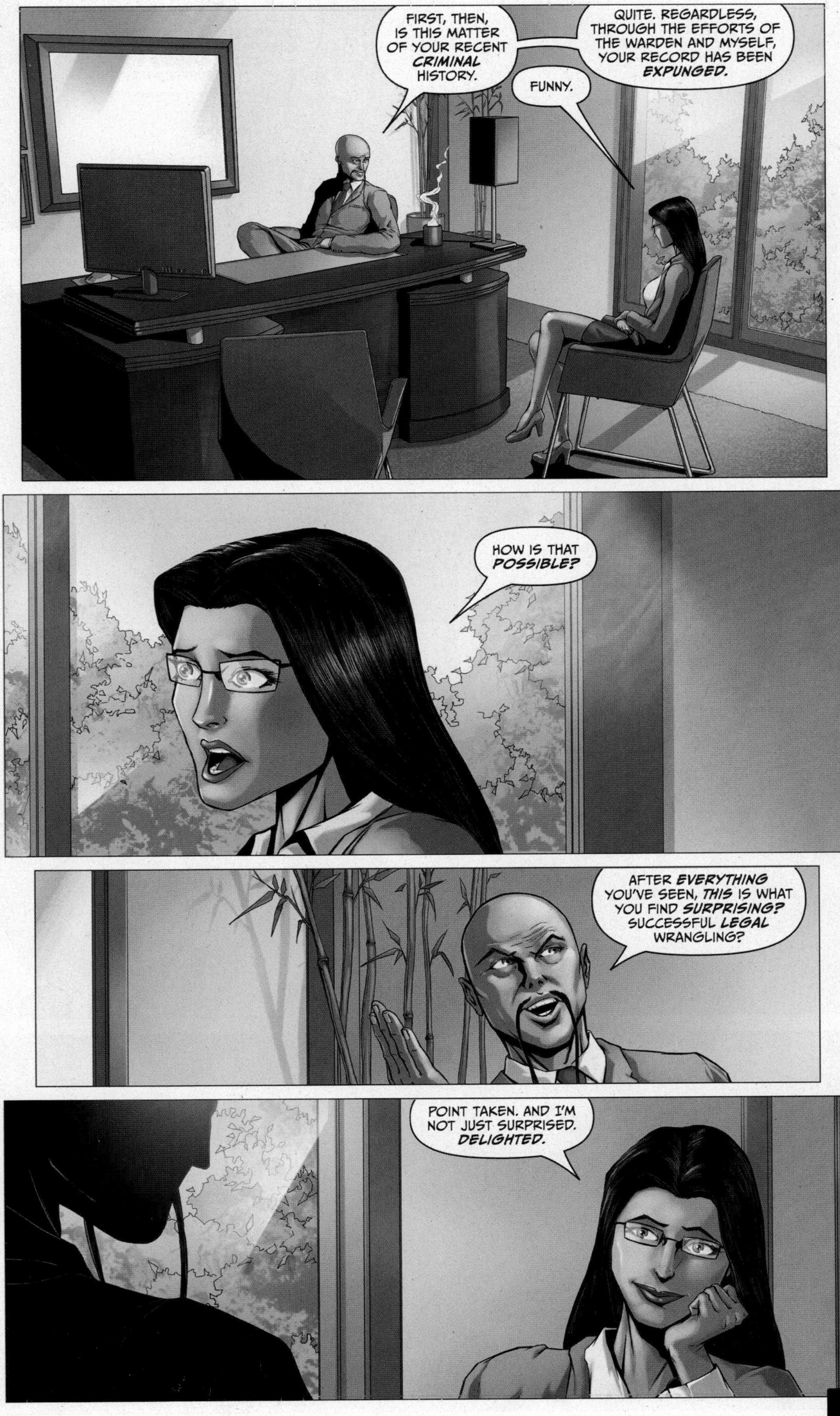
FIRST, THEN, IS THIS MATTER OF YOUR RECENT CRIMINAL HISTORY.
FUNNY.
QUITE. REGARDLESS, THROUGH THE EFFORTS OF THE WARDEN AND MYSELF, YOUR RECORD HAS BEEN EXPUNGED.
HOW IS THAT POSSIBLE?
AFTER EVERYTHING YOU'VE SEEN, THIS IS WHAT YOU FIND SURPRISING? SUCCESSFUL LEGAL WRANGLING?
POINT TAKEN. AND I'M NOT JUST SURPRISED. DELIGHTED.

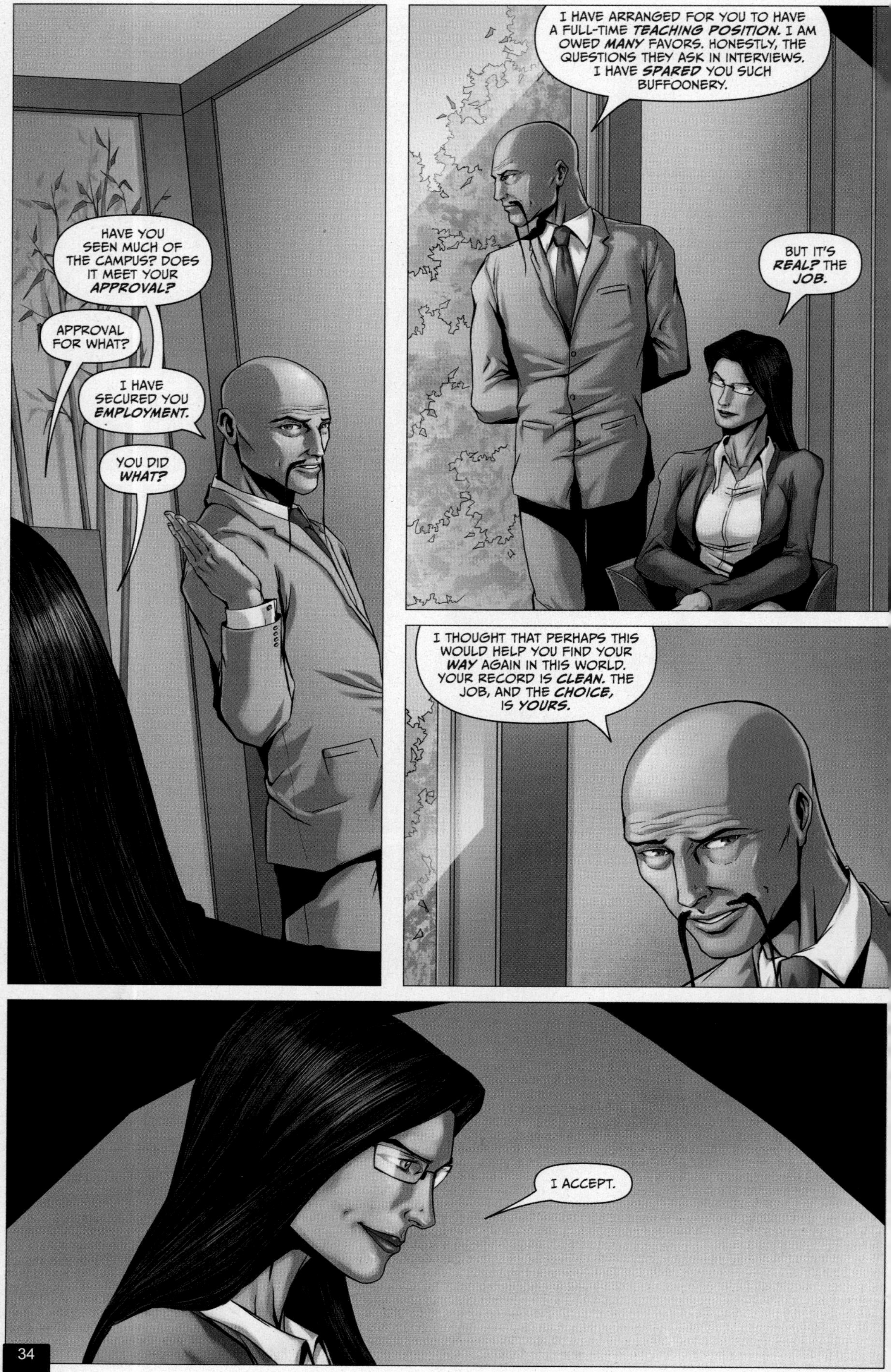
HAVE YOU SEEN MUCH OF THE CAMPUS? DOES IT MEET YOUR APPROVAL?
APPROVAL FOR WHAT?
I HAVE SECURED YOU EMPLOYMENT.
YOU DID WHAT?
I HAVE ARRANGED FOR YOU TO HAVE A FULL-TIME TEACHING POSITION. I AM OWED MANY FAVORS. HONESTLY, THE QUESTIONS THEY ASK IN INTERVIEWS. I HAVE SPARED YOU SUCH BUFFOONERY.
BUT IT'S REAL? THE JOB.
I THOUGHT THAT PERHAPS THIS WOULD HELP YOU FIND YOUR WAY AGAIN IN THIS WORLD. YOUR RECORD IS CLEAN. THE JOB, AND THE CHOICE, IS YOURS.
I ACCEPT.

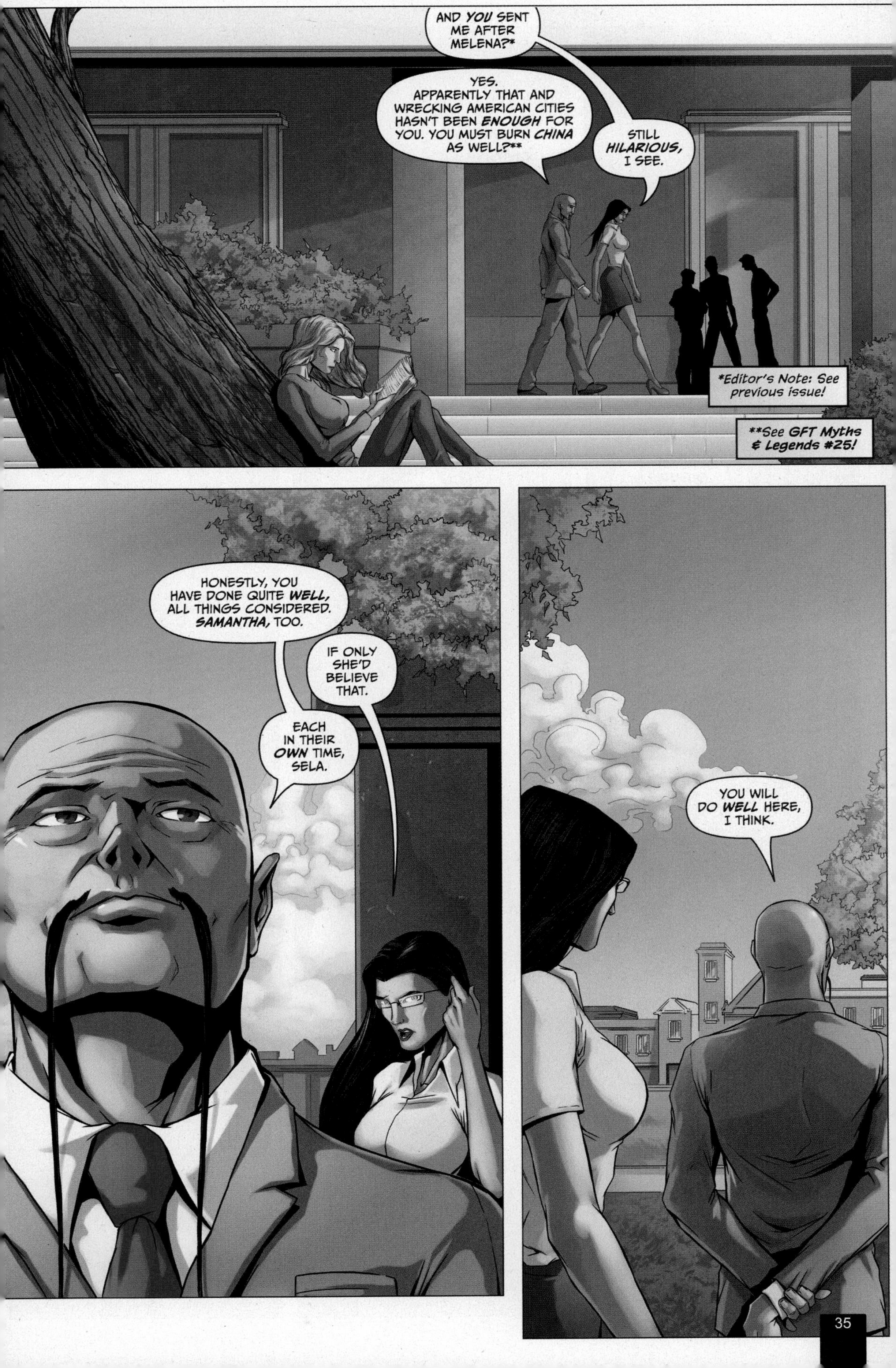
AND YOU SENT ME AFTER MELENA?*
YES. APPARENTLY THAT AND WRECKING AMERICAN CITIES HASN'T BEEN ENOUGH FOR YOU. YOU MUST BURN CHINA AS WELL?**
STILL HILARIOUS, I SEE.
*Editor's Note: See previous issue!
**See GFT Myths & Legends #25!
HONESTLY, YOU HAVE DONE QUITE WELL, ALL THINGS CONSIDERED. SAMANTHA, TOO.
IF ONLY SHE'D BELIEVE THAT.
EACH IN THEIR OWN TIME, SELA.
YOU WILL DO WELL HERE, I THINK.

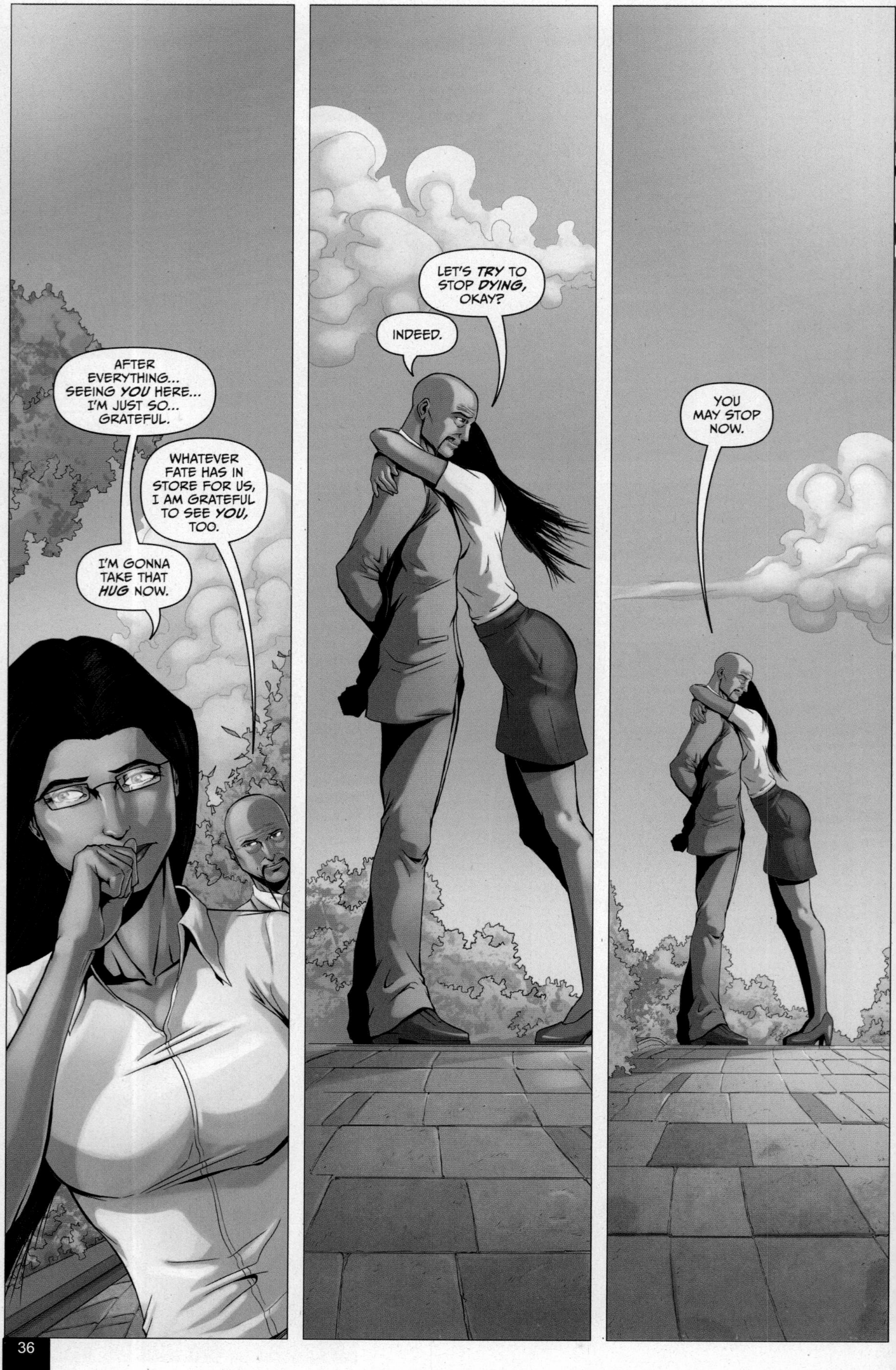
AFTER EVERYTHING... SEEING *YOU* HERE... I'M JUST SO... GRATEFUL.
WHATEVER FATE HAS IN STORE FOR US, I AM GRATEFUL TO SEE *YOU*, TOO.
I'M GONNA TAKE THAT *HUG* NOW.
LET'S *TRY* TO STOP *DYING*, OKAY?
INDEED.
YOU MAY STOP NOW.

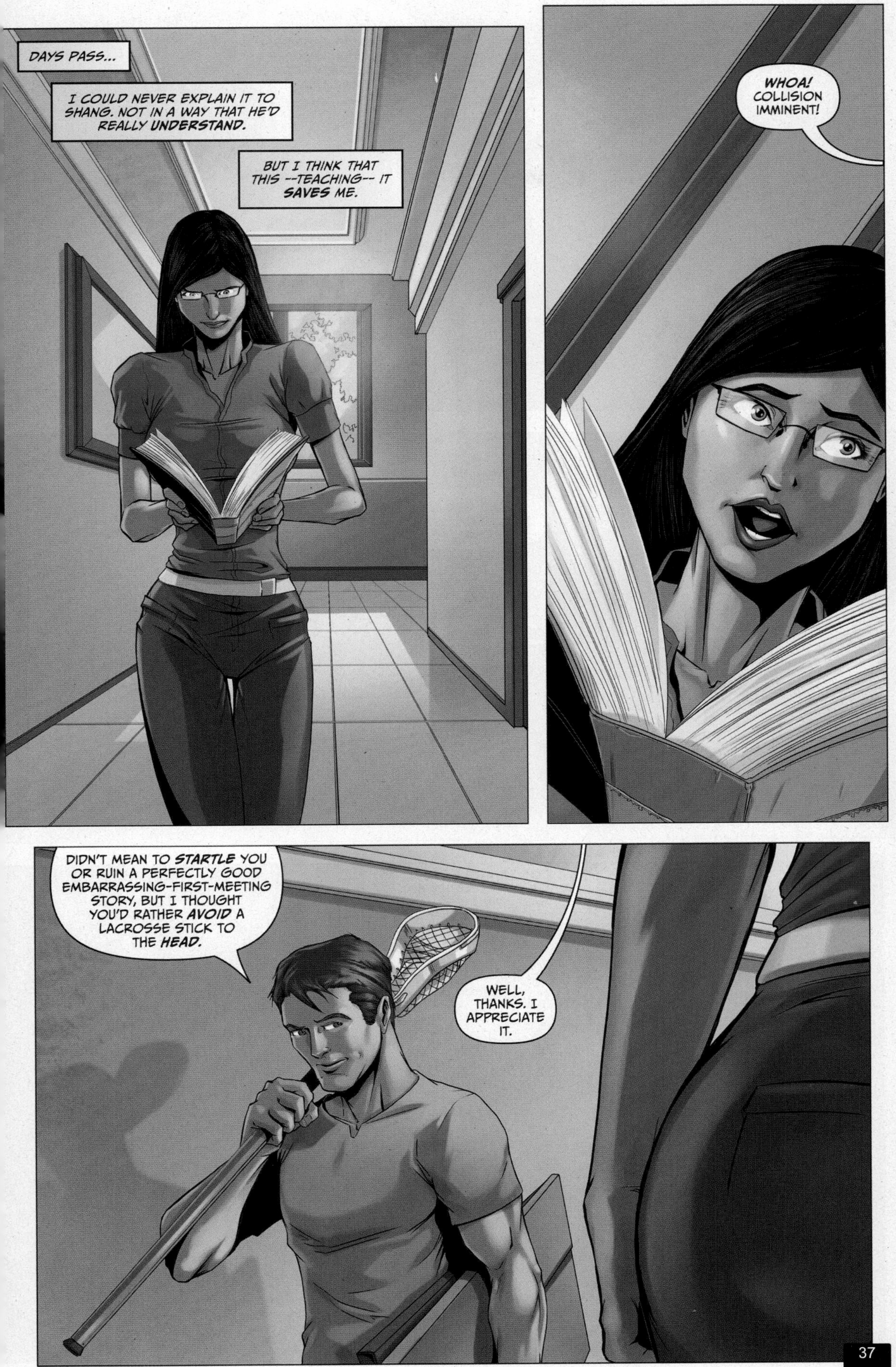
DAYS PASS...
I COULD NEVER EXPLAIN IT TO SHANG. NOT IN A WAY THAT HE'D REALLY UNDERSTAND.
BUT I THINK THAT THIS --TEACHING-- IT SAVES ME.
WHOA! COLLISION IMMINENT!
DIDN'T MEAN TO STARTLE YOU OR RUIN A PERFECTLY GOOD EMBARRASSING-FIRST-MEETING STORY, BUT I THOUGHT YOU'D RATHER AVOID A LACROSSE STICK TO THE HEAD.
WELL, THANKS. I APPRECIATE IT.

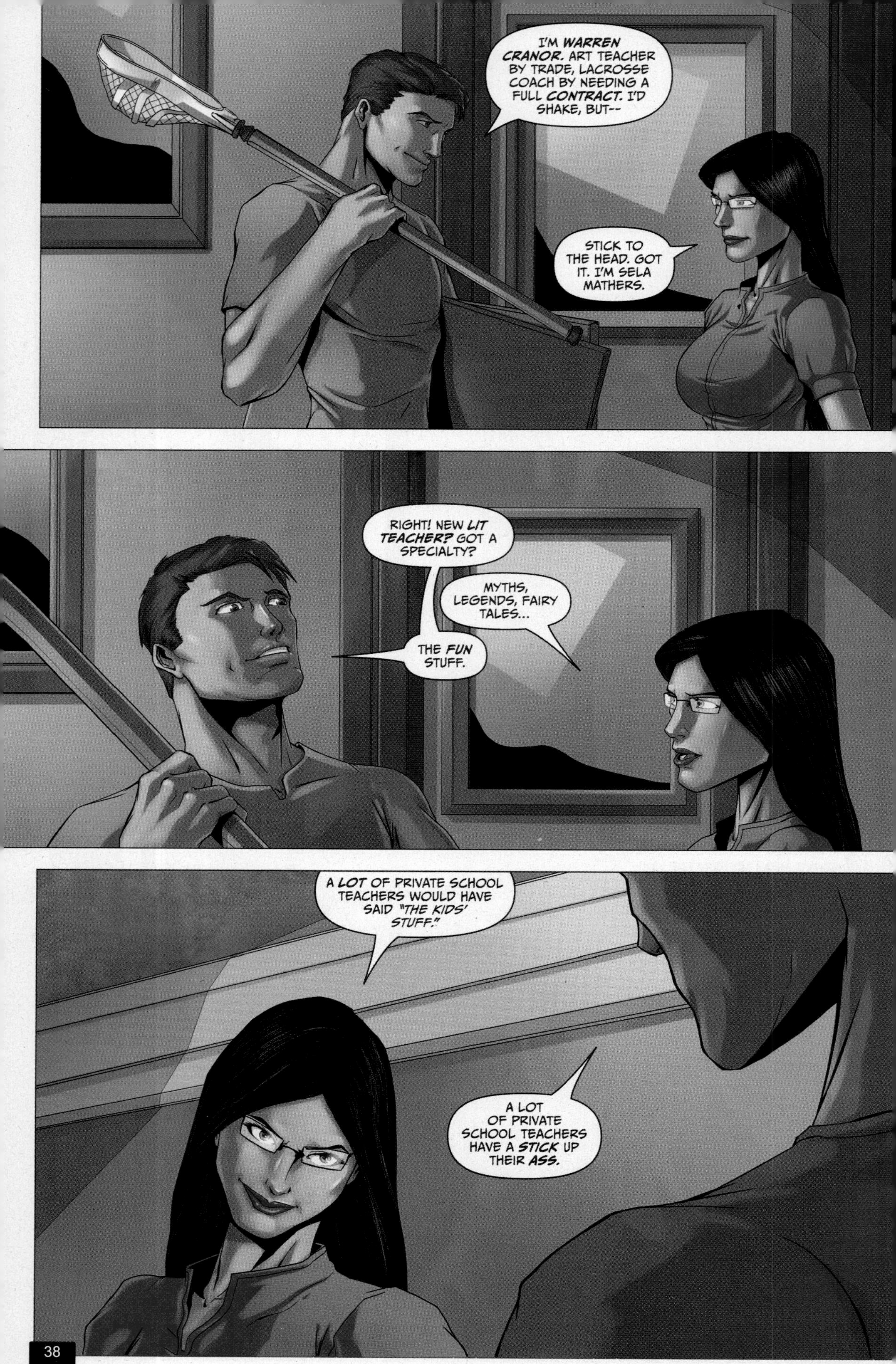
I'M **WARREN CRANOR.** ART TEACHER BY TRADE, LACROSSE COACH BY NEEDING A FULL **CONTRACT.** I'D SHAKE, BUT--
STICK TO THE HEAD. GOT IT. I'M SELA MATHERS.
RIGHT! NEW *LIT TEACHER?* GOT A SPECIALTY?
MYTHS, LEGENDS, FAIRY TALES...
THE *FUN* STUFF.
A *LOT* OF PRIVATE SCHOOL TEACHERS WOULD HAVE SAID *"THE KIDS' STUFF."*
A LOT OF PRIVATE SCHOOL TEACHERS HAVE A *STICK* UP THEIR *ASS.*

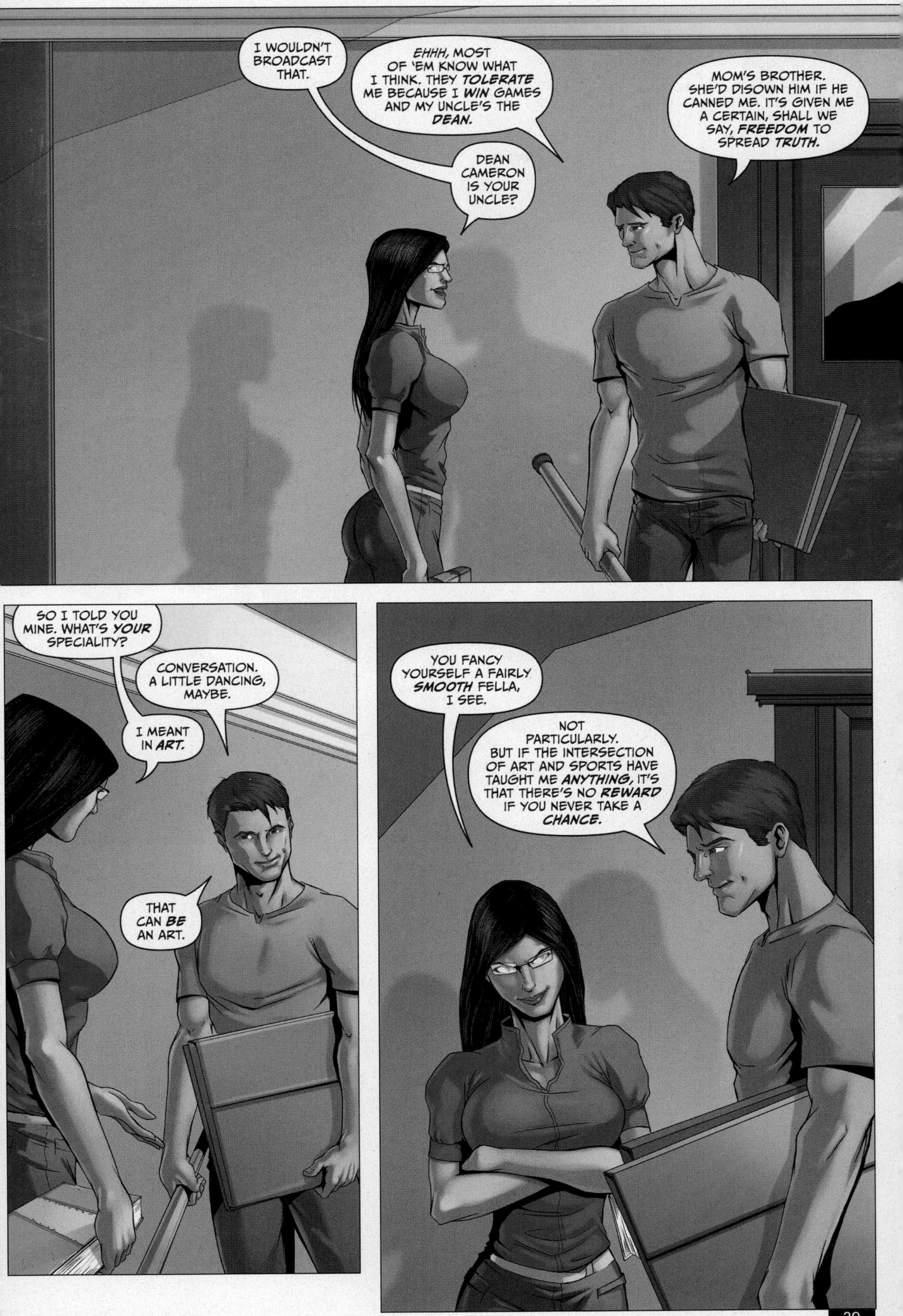
I WOULDN'T BROADCAST THAT.
EHHH, MOST OF 'EM KNOW WHAT I THINK. THEY TOLERATE ME BECAUSE I WIN GAMES AND MY UNCLE'S THE DEAN.
DEAN CAMERON IS YOUR UNCLE?
MOM'S BROTHER. SHE'D DISOWN HIM IF HE CANNED ME. IT'S GIVEN ME A CERTAIN, SHALL WE SAY, FREEDOM TO SPREAD TRUTH.
SO I TOLD YOU MINE. WHAT'S YOUR SPECIALITY?
CONVERSATION. A LITTLE DANCING, MAYBE.
I MEANT IN ART.
THAT CAN BE AN ART.
YOU FANCY YOURSELF A FAIRLY SMOOTH FELLA, I SEE.
NOT PARTICULARLY. BUT IF THE INTERSECTION OF ART AND SPORTS HAVE TAUGHT ME ANYTHING, IT'S THAT THERE'S NO REWARD IF YOU NEVER TAKE A CHANCE.

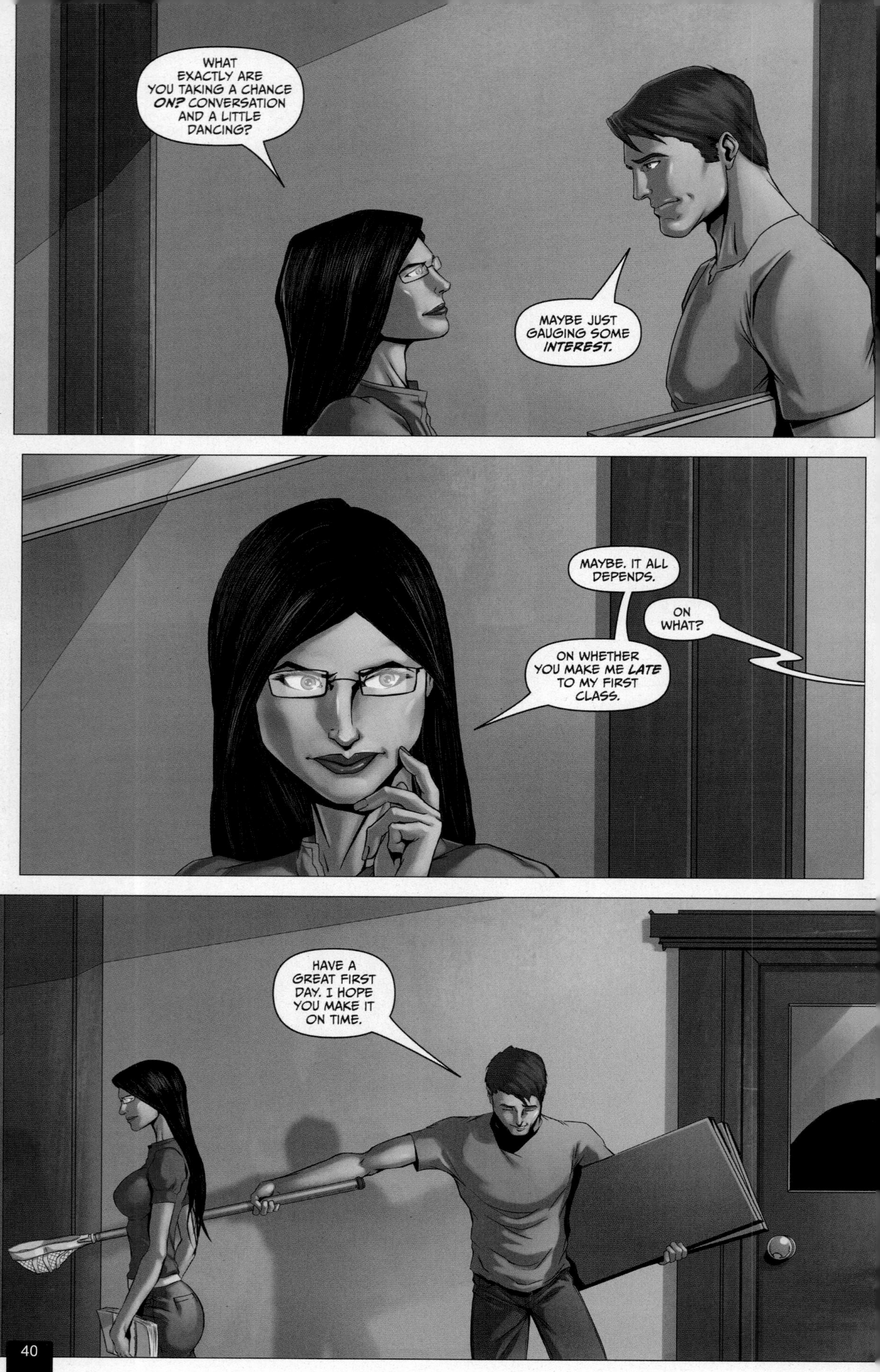
WHAT EXACTLY ARE YOU TAKING A CHANCE ON? CONVERSATION AND A LITTLE DANCING?
MAYBE JUST GAUGING SOME INTEREST.
MAYBE. IT ALL DEPENDS.
ON WHAT?
ON WHETHER YOU MAKE ME LATE TO MY FIRST CLASS.
HAVE A GREAT FIRST DAY. I HOPE YOU MAKE IT ON TIME.

CLASSES START SMOOTH (AND ON TIME). I CAN TELL RIGHT AWAY THAT THE JUNIOR ENGLISH CLASS HAS IT ON THE BALL. INCLUDING THE FOUR LACROSSE PLAYERS I HAVE.

SALINGER
HARPER LEE
VONNEGUT
POE
TWAIN

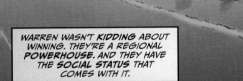

WARREN WASN'T KIDDING ABOUT WINNING. THEY'RE A REGIONAL POWERHOUSE. AND THEY HAVE THE SOCIAL STATUS THAT COMES WITH IT.

I'VE ALREADY HEARD THINGS ABOUT HOW SOME OF THEM ACT, BUT I CAN'T TELL YET IF IT'S NORMAL TEENAGE IDIOTIC BEHAVIOR OR SOMETHING WORSE.

AS SUSPICIOUS AND PARANOID AS MY LIFE HAS MADE ME, I STILL WOULDN'T HAVE LEAPED TO THAT CONCLUSION RIGHT AWAY.

NOT UNTIL I READ ABOUT THE SUICIDE.

41

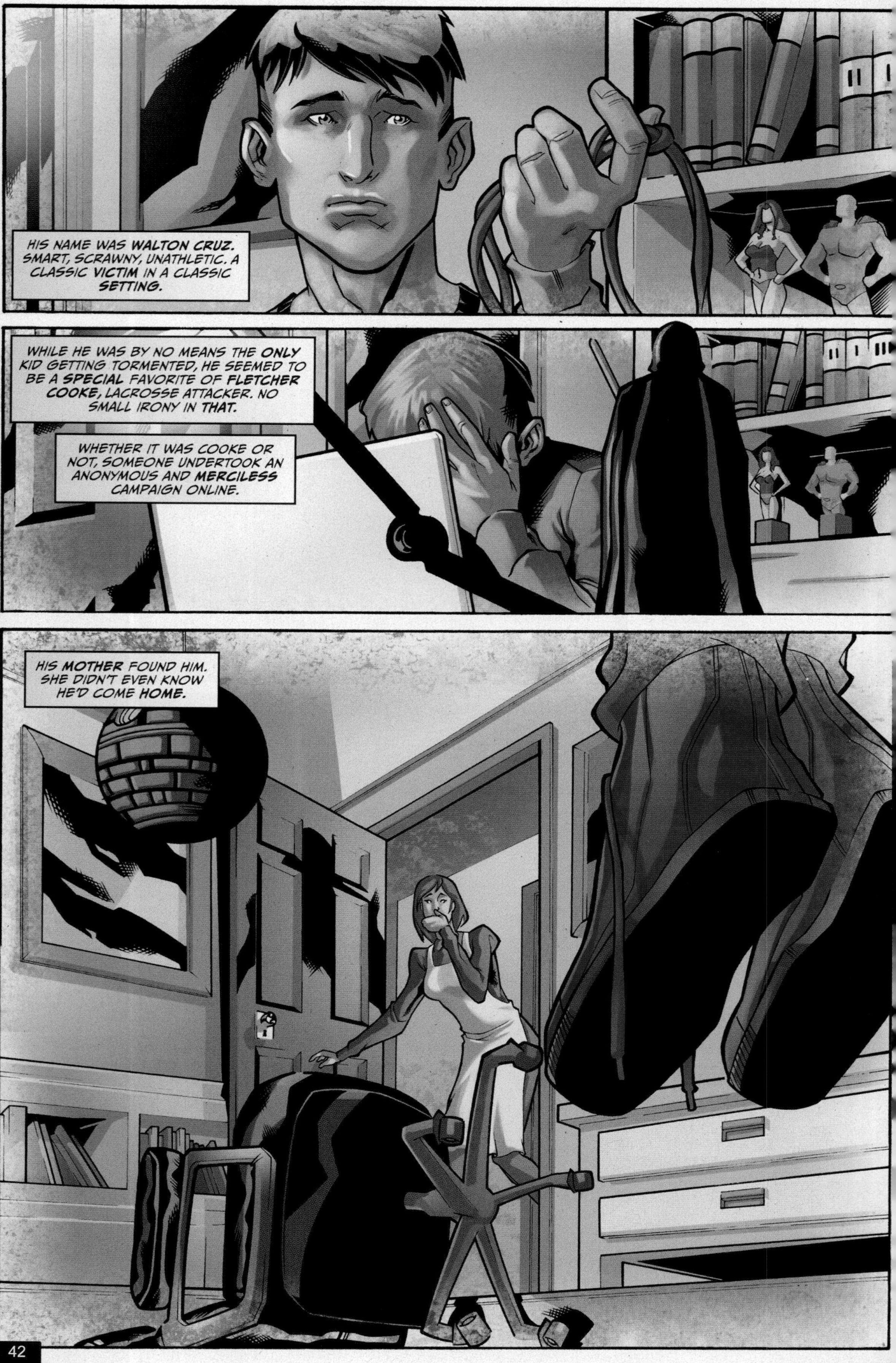
HIS NAME WAS WALTON CRUZ. SMART, SCRAWNY, UNATHLETIC. A CLASSIC VICTIM IN A CLASSIC SETTING.
WHILE HE WAS BY NO MEANS THE ONLY KID GETTING TORMENTED, HE SEEMED TO BE A SPECIAL FAVORITE OF FLETCHER COOKE, LACROSSE ATTACKER. NO SMALL IRONY IN THAT.
WHETHER IT WAS COOKE OR NOT, SOMEONE UNDERTOOK AN ANONYMOUS AND MERCILESS CAMPAIGN ONLINE.
HIS MOTHER FOUND HIM. SHE DIDN'T EVEN KNOW HE'D COME HOME.

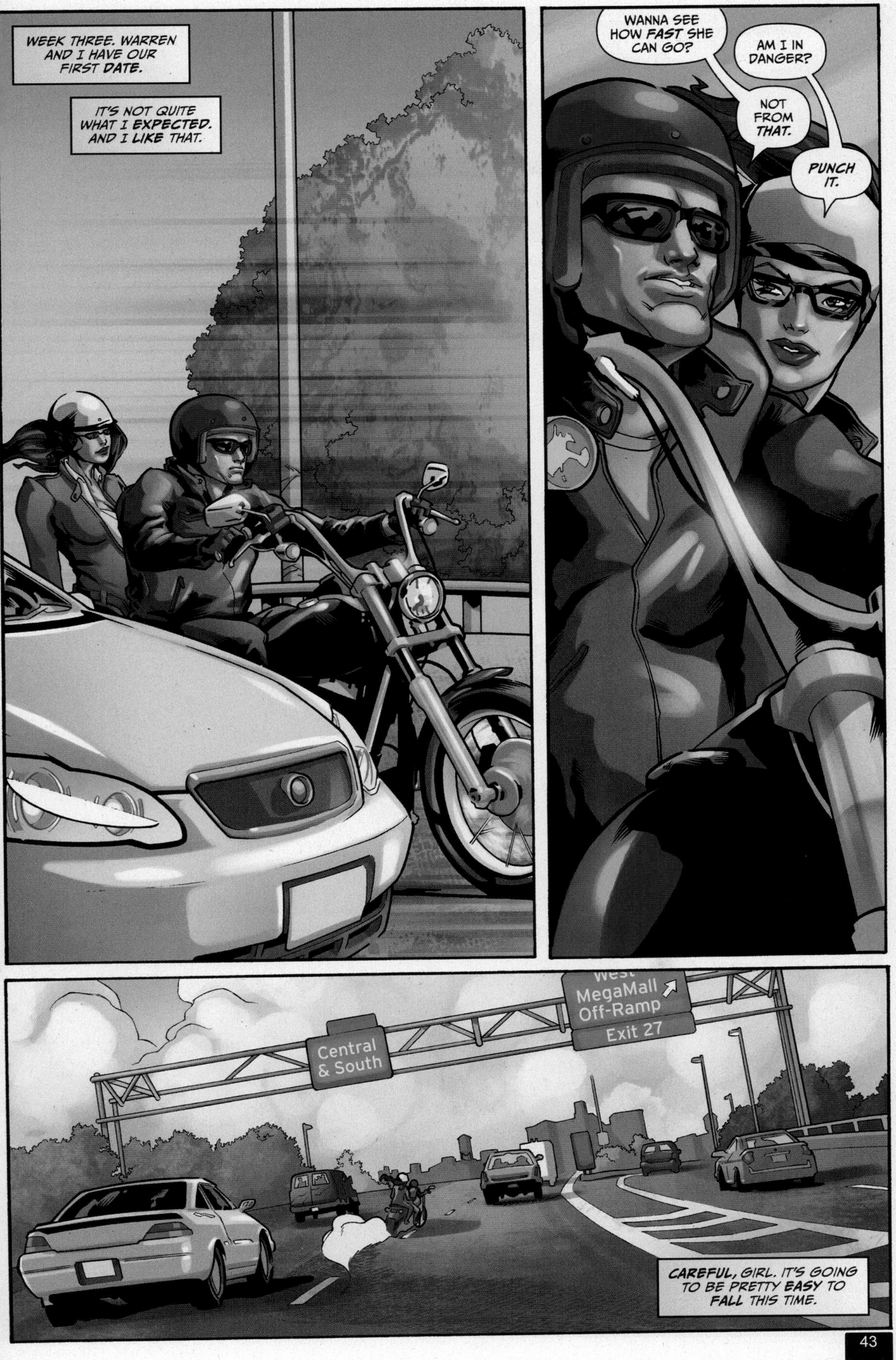
WEEK THREE. WARREN AND I HAVE OUR FIRST DATE.
IT'S NOT QUITE WHAT I EXPECTED. AND I LIKE THAT.
WANNA SEE HOW FAST SHE CAN GO?
AM I IN DANGER?
NOT FROM THAT.
PUNCH IT.
Central & South
MegaMall Off-Ramp
Exit 27
CAREFUL, GIRL. IT'S GOING TO BE PRETTY EASY TO FALL THIS TIME.

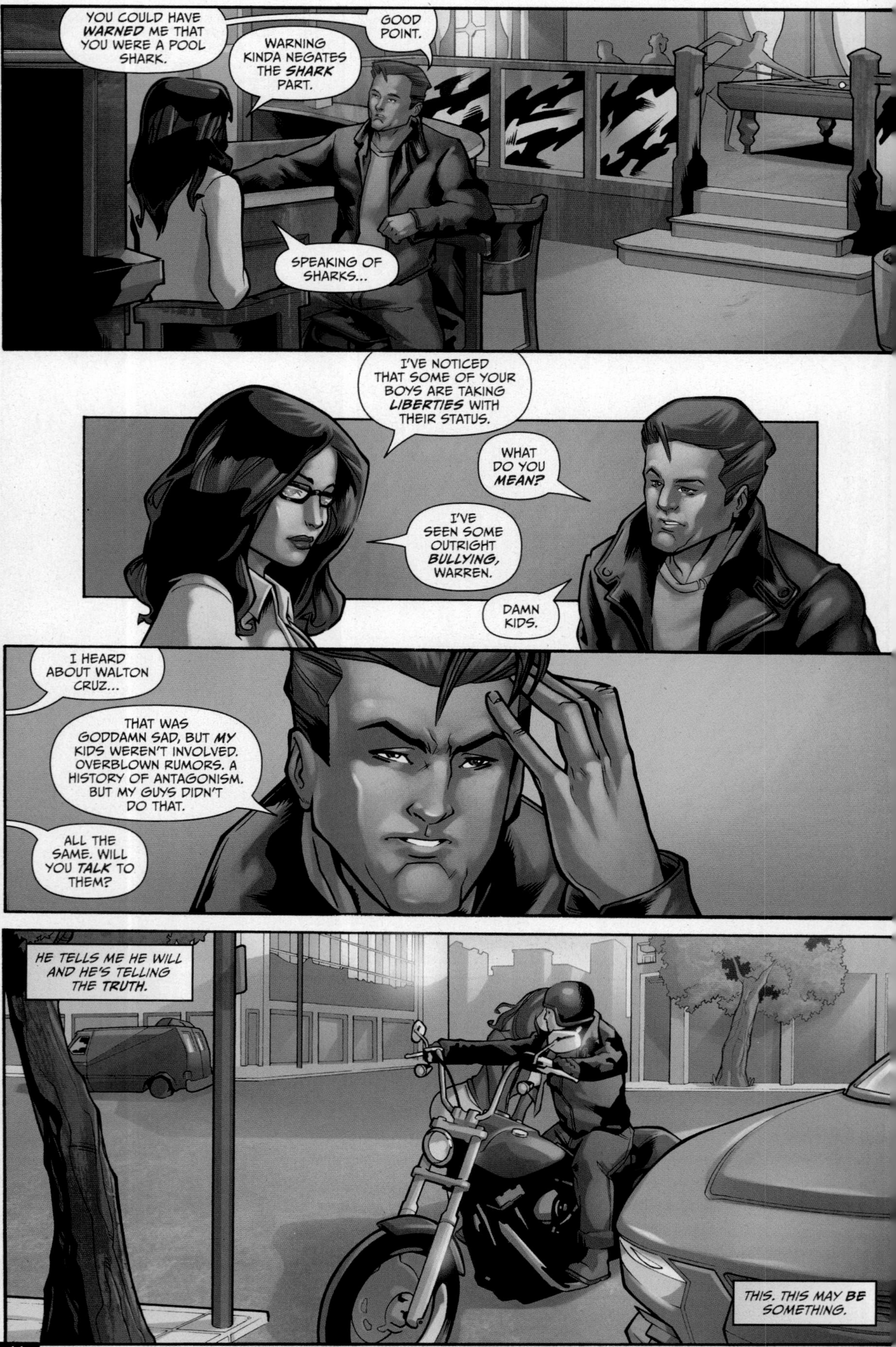

YOU COULD HAVE WARNED ME THAT YOU WERE A POOL SHARK.
GOOD POINT.
WARNING KINDA NEGATES THE SHARK PART.
SPEAKING OF SHARKS...
I'VE NOTICED THAT SOME OF YOUR BOYS ARE TAKING LIBERTIES WITH THEIR STATUS.
WHAT DO YOU MEAN?
I'VE SEEN SOME OUTRIGHT BULLYING, WARREN.
DAMN KIDS.
I HEARD ABOUT WALTON CRUZ...
THAT WAS GODDAMN SAD, BUT MY KIDS WEREN'T INVOLVED. OVERBLOWN RUMORS. A HISTORY OF ANTAGONISM. BUT MY GUYS DIDN'T DO THAT.
ALL THE SAME. WILL YOU TALK TO THEM?
HE TELLS ME HE WILL AND HE'S TELLING THE TRUTH.
THIS. THIS MAY BE SOMETHING.

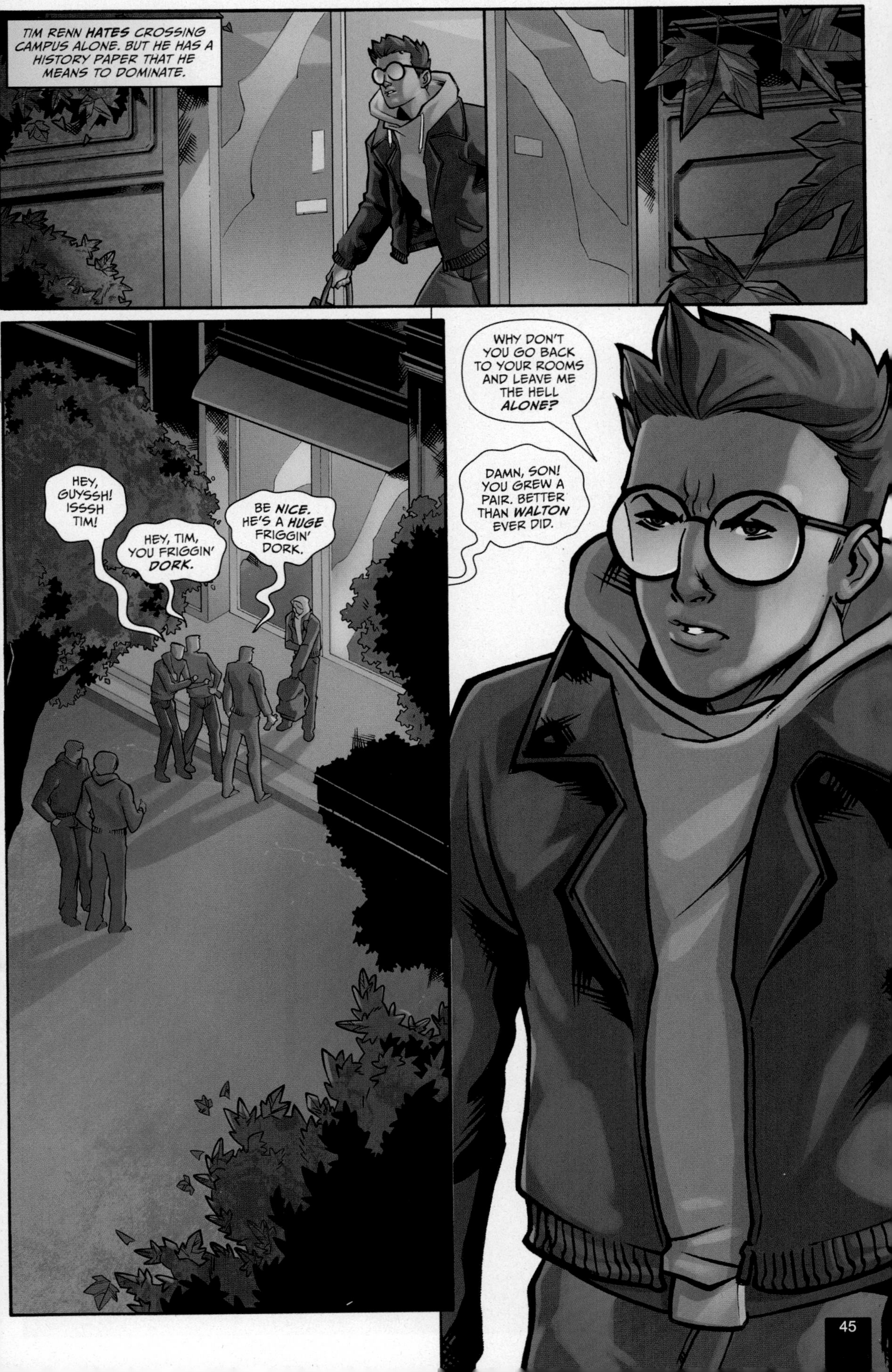

TIM RENN **HATES** CROSSING CAMPUS ALONE. BUT HE HAS A HISTORY PAPER THAT HE MEANS TO DOMINATE.
HEY, GUYSSH! ISSSH TIM!
HEY, TIM, YOU FRIGGIN' **DORK.**
BE **NICE.** HE'S A **HUGE** FRIGGIN' DORK.
WHY DON'T YOU GO BACK TO YOUR ROOMS AND LEAVE ME THE HELL **ALONE?**
DAMN, SON! YOU GREW A PAIR. BETTER THAN **WALTON** EVER DID.

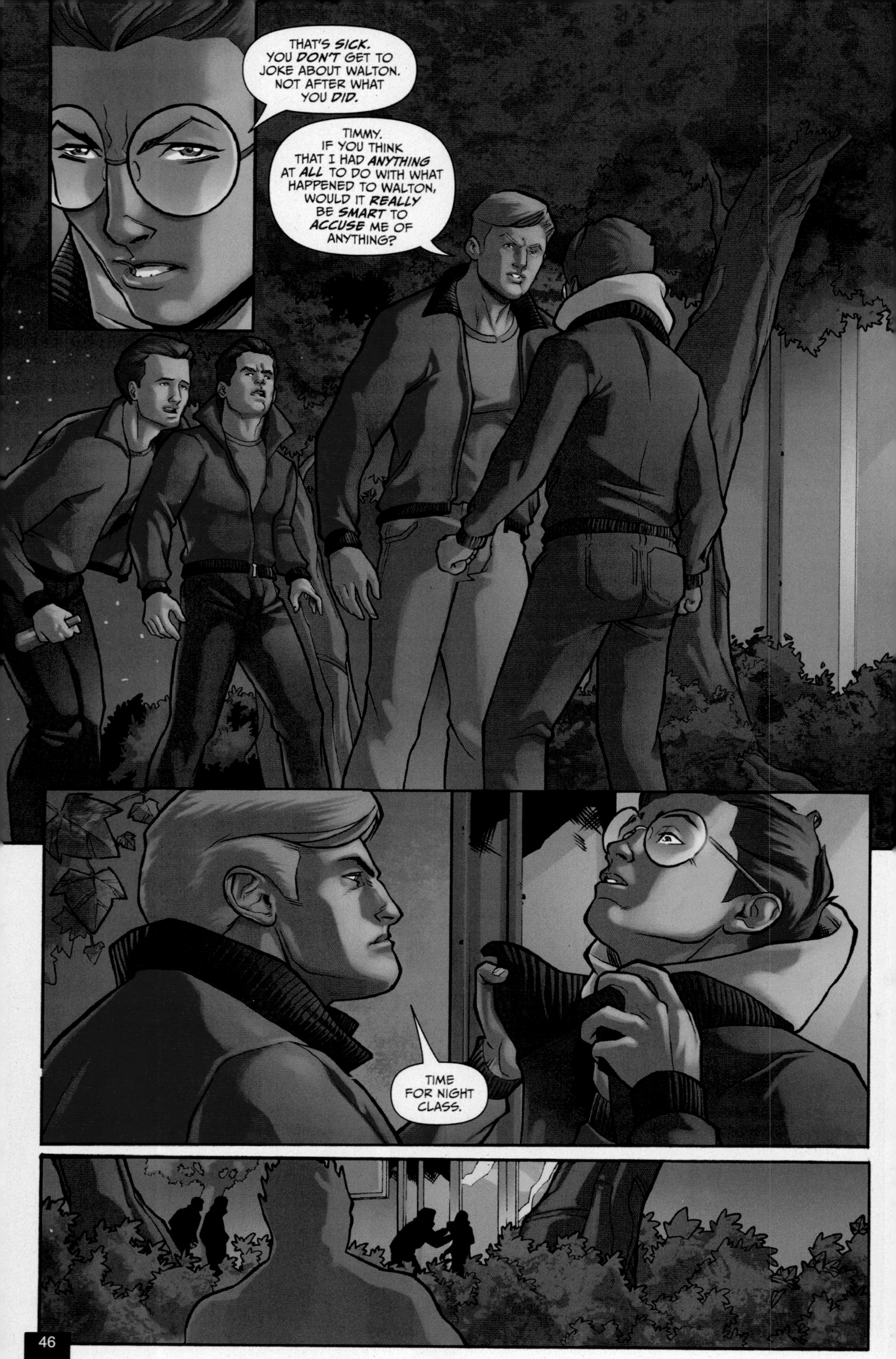
THAT'S SICK. YOU DON'T GET TO JOKE ABOUT WALTON. NOT AFTER WHAT YOU DID.
TIMMY. IF YOU THINK THAT I HAD ANYTHING AT ALL TO DO WITH WHAT HAPPENED TO WALTON, WOULD IT REALLY BE SMART TO ACCUSE ME OF ANYTHING?
TIME FOR NIGHT CLASS.

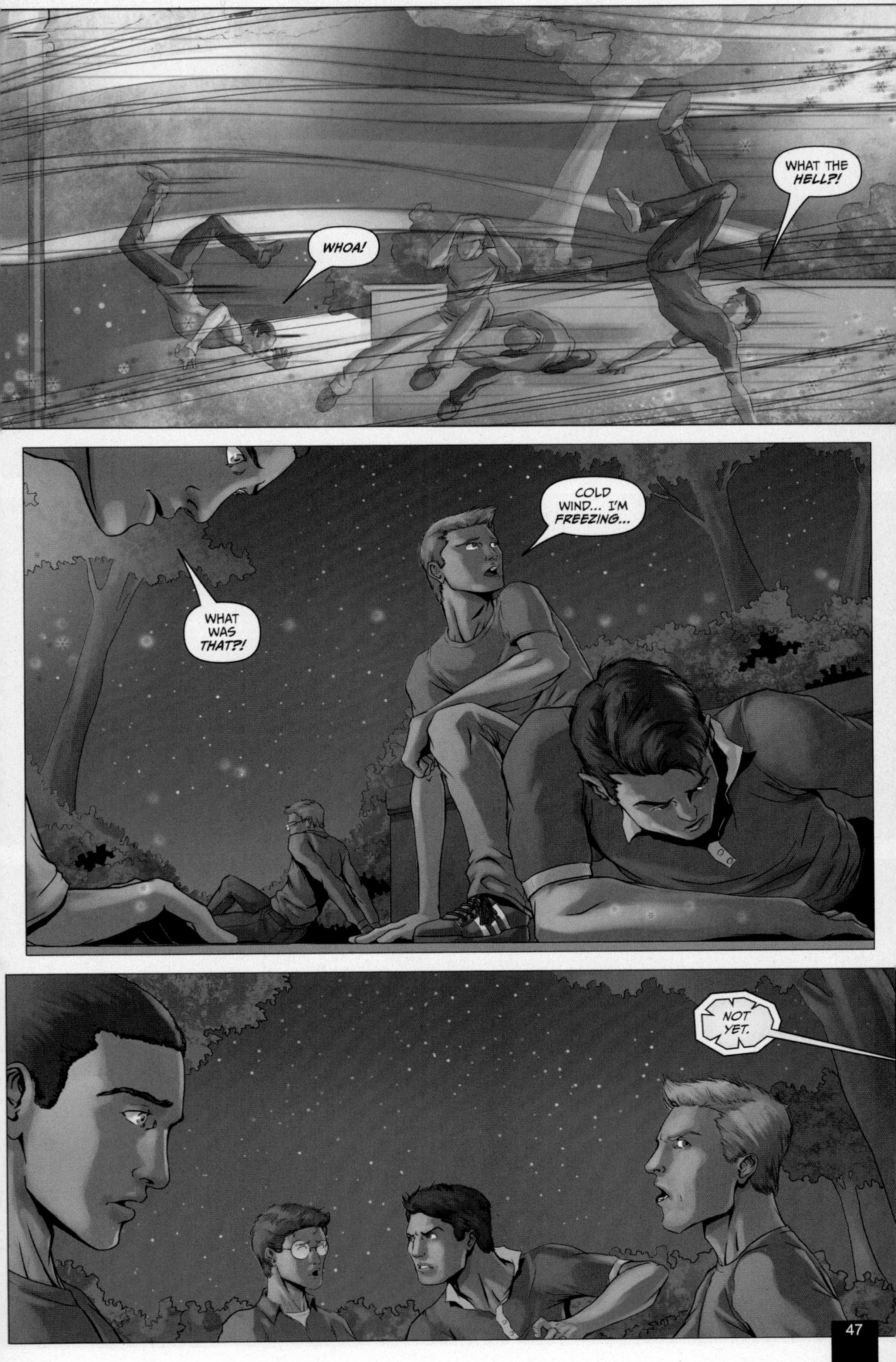
WHOA!
WHAT THE HELL?!
WHAT WAS THAT?!
COLD WIND... I'M FREEZING...
NOT YET.

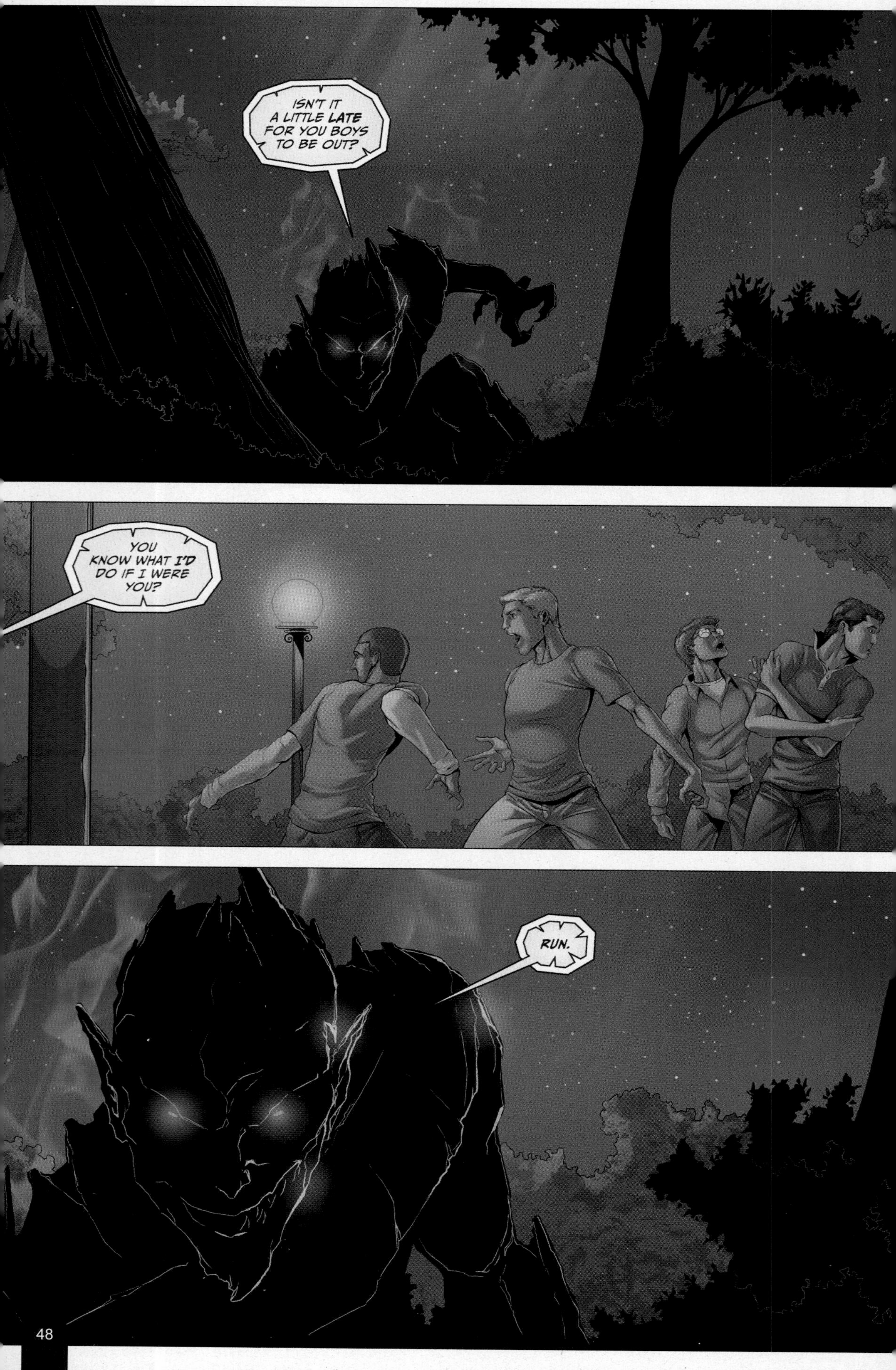
ISN'T IT A LITTLE LATE FOR YOU BOYS TO BE OUT?
YOU KNOW WHAT I'D DO IF I WERE YOU?
RUN.

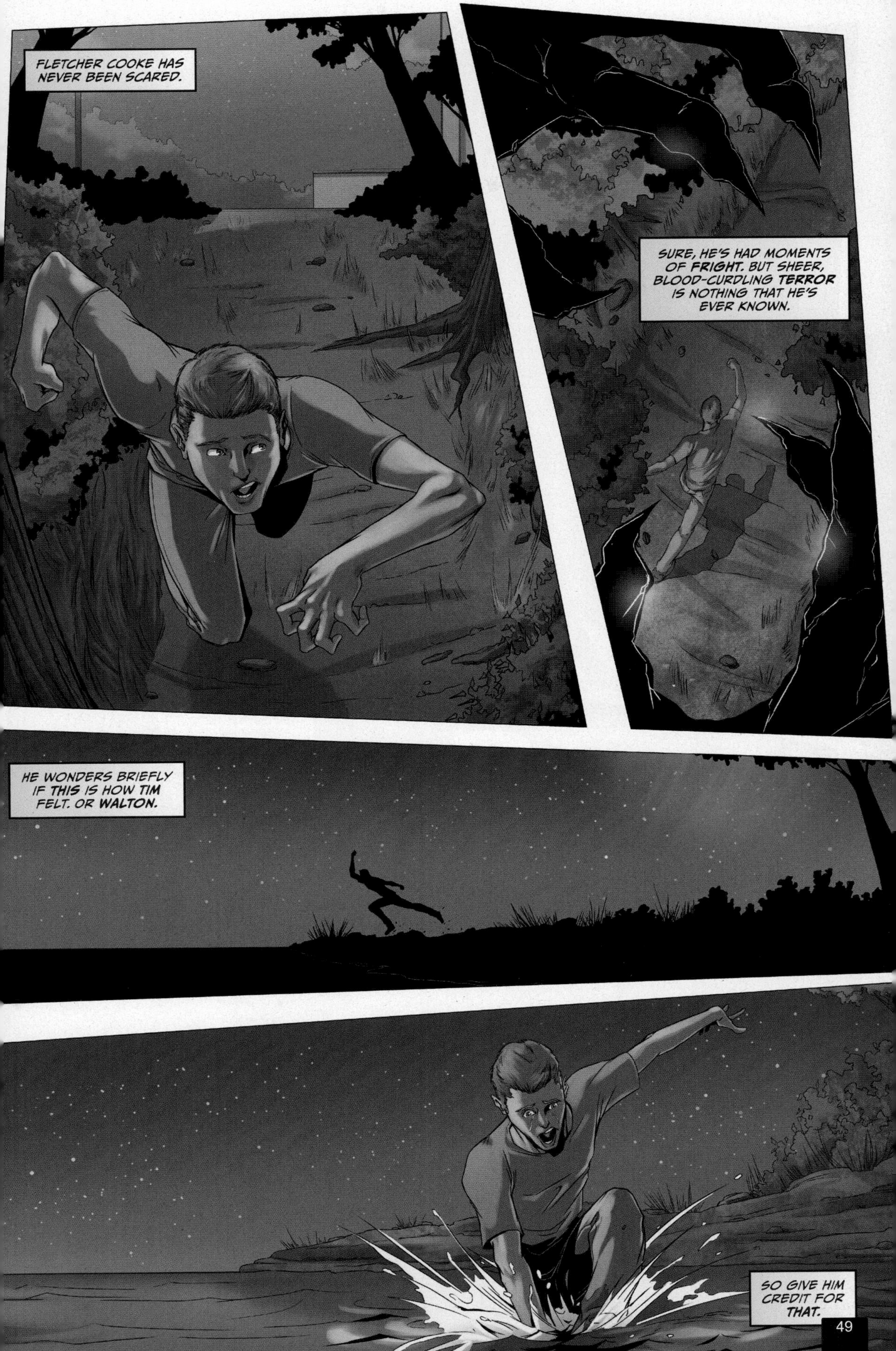
FLETCHER COOKE HAS NEVER BEEN SCARED.
SURE, HE'S HAD MOMENTS OF FRIGHT. BUT SHEER, BLOOD-CURDLING TERROR IS NOTHING THAT HE'S EVER KNOWN.
HE WONDERS BRIEFLY IF THIS IS HOW TIM FELT. OR WALTON.
SO GIVE HIM CREDIT FOR THAT.

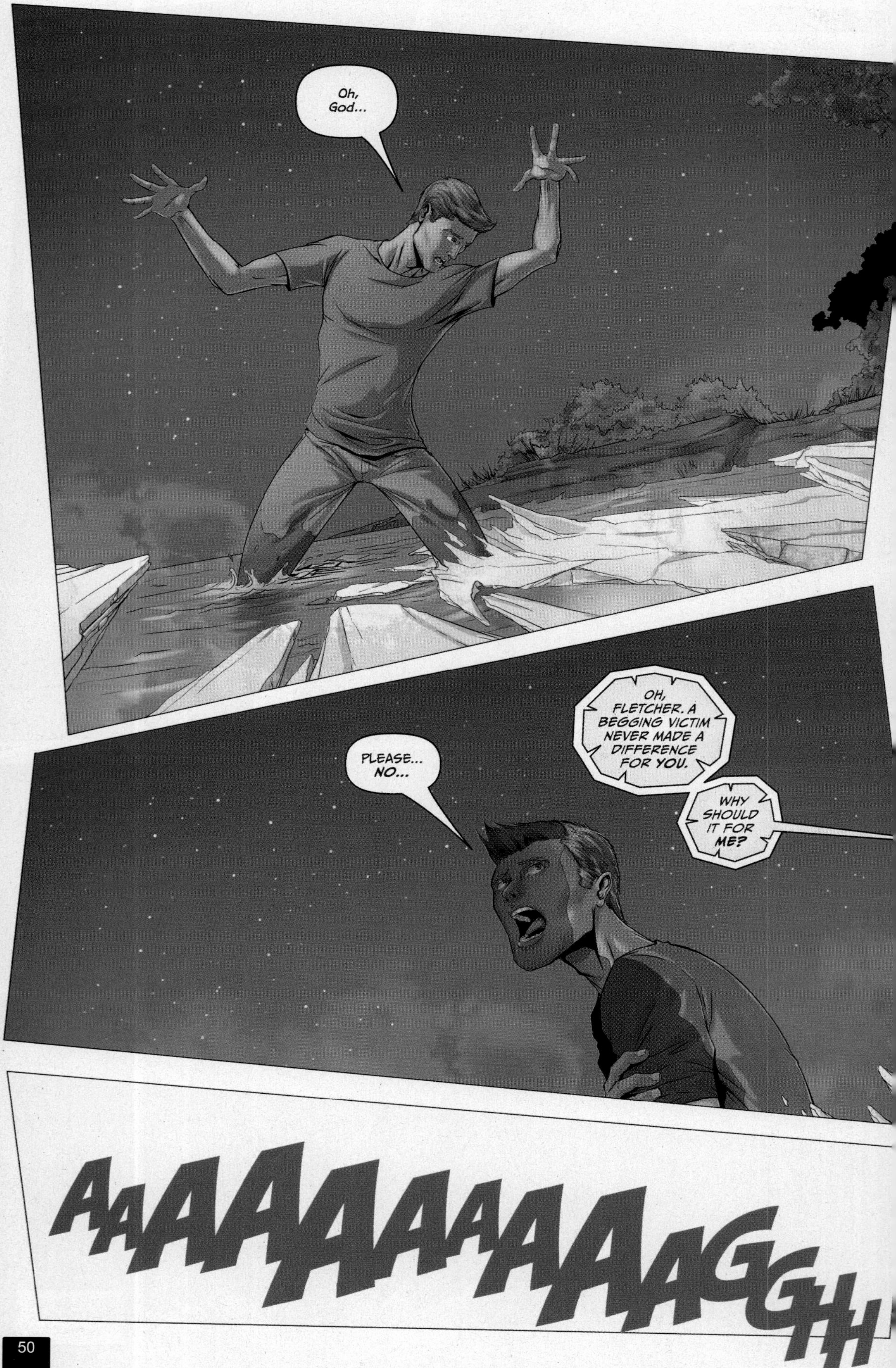

Oh, God...
PLEASE... NO...
OH, FLETCHER. A BEGGING VICTIM NEVER MADE A DIFFERENCE FOR YOU.
WHY SHOULD IT FOR ME?
AAAAAAAAAAAAGGHH

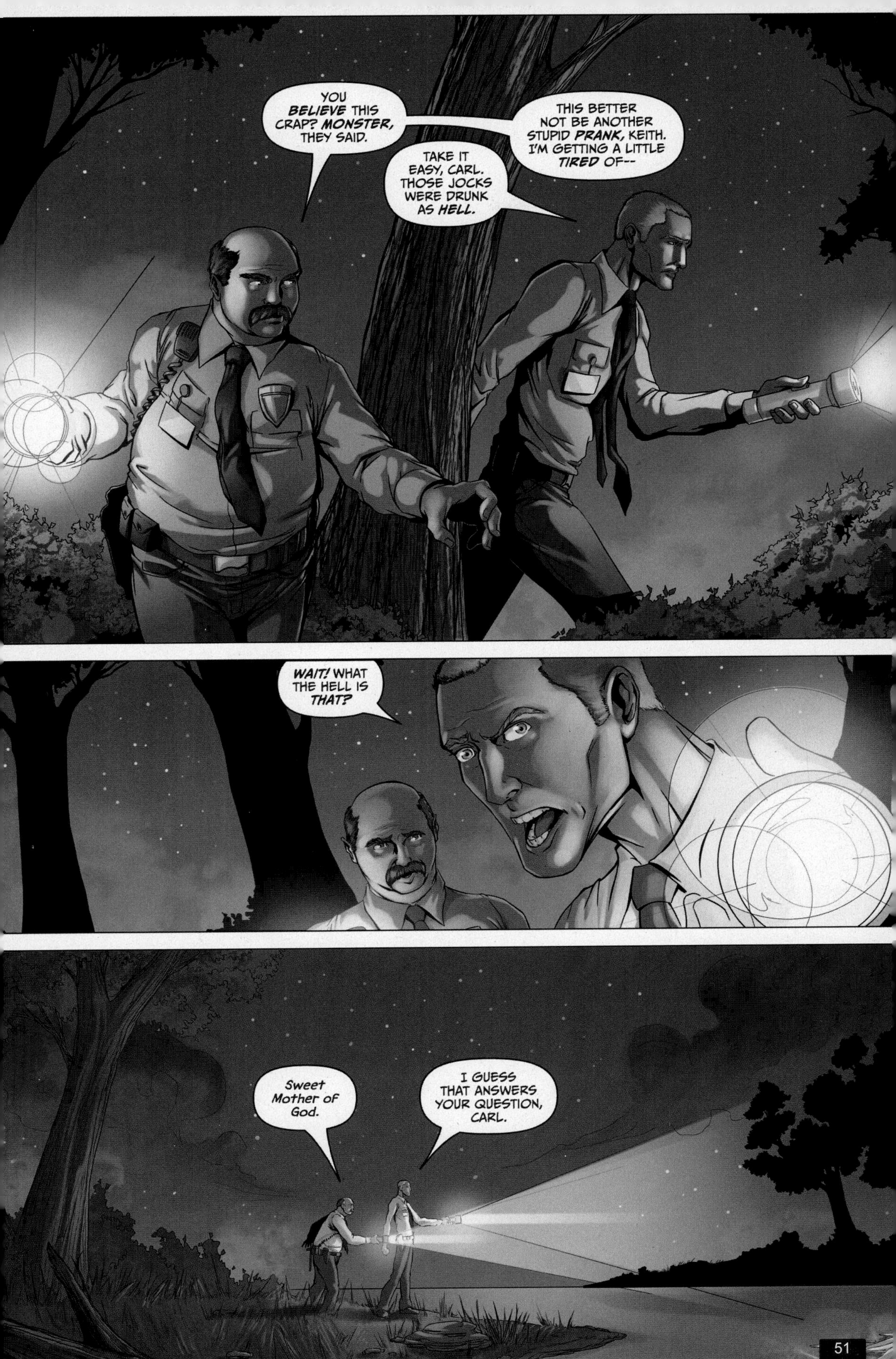
YOU BELIEVE THIS CRAP? MONSTER, THEY SAID.
THIS BETTER NOT BE ANOTHER STUPID PRANK, KEITH. I'M GETTING A LITTLE TIRED OF--
TAKE IT EASY, CARL. THOSE JOCKS WERE DRUNK AS HELL.
WAIT! WHAT THE HELL IS THAT?
Sweet Mother of God.
I GUESS THAT ANSWERS YOUR QUESTION, CARL.

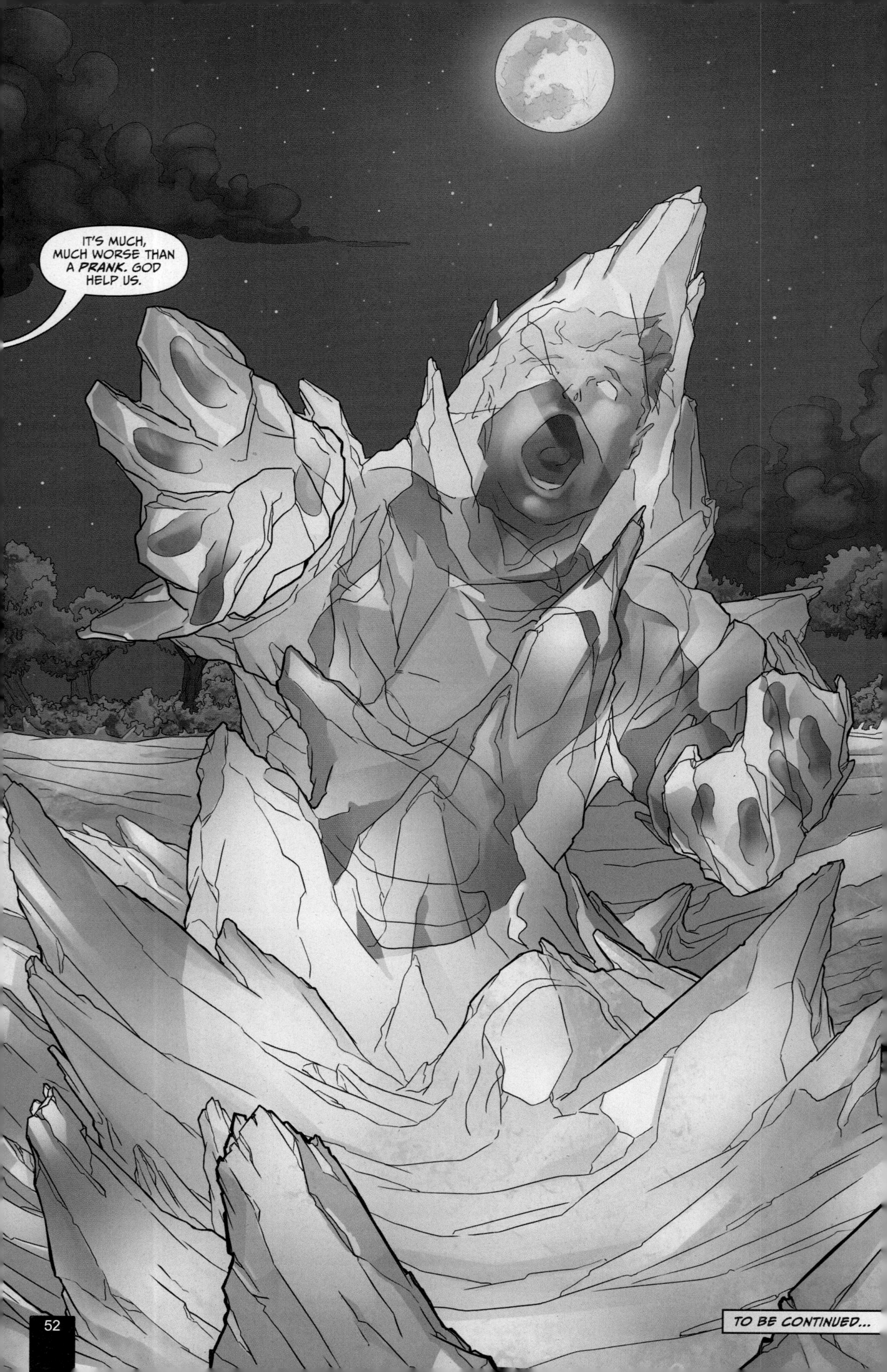
IT'S MUCH, MUCH WORSE THAN A PRANK. GOD HELP US.
TO BE CONTINUED...

Grimm Fairy Tales

Volume 14

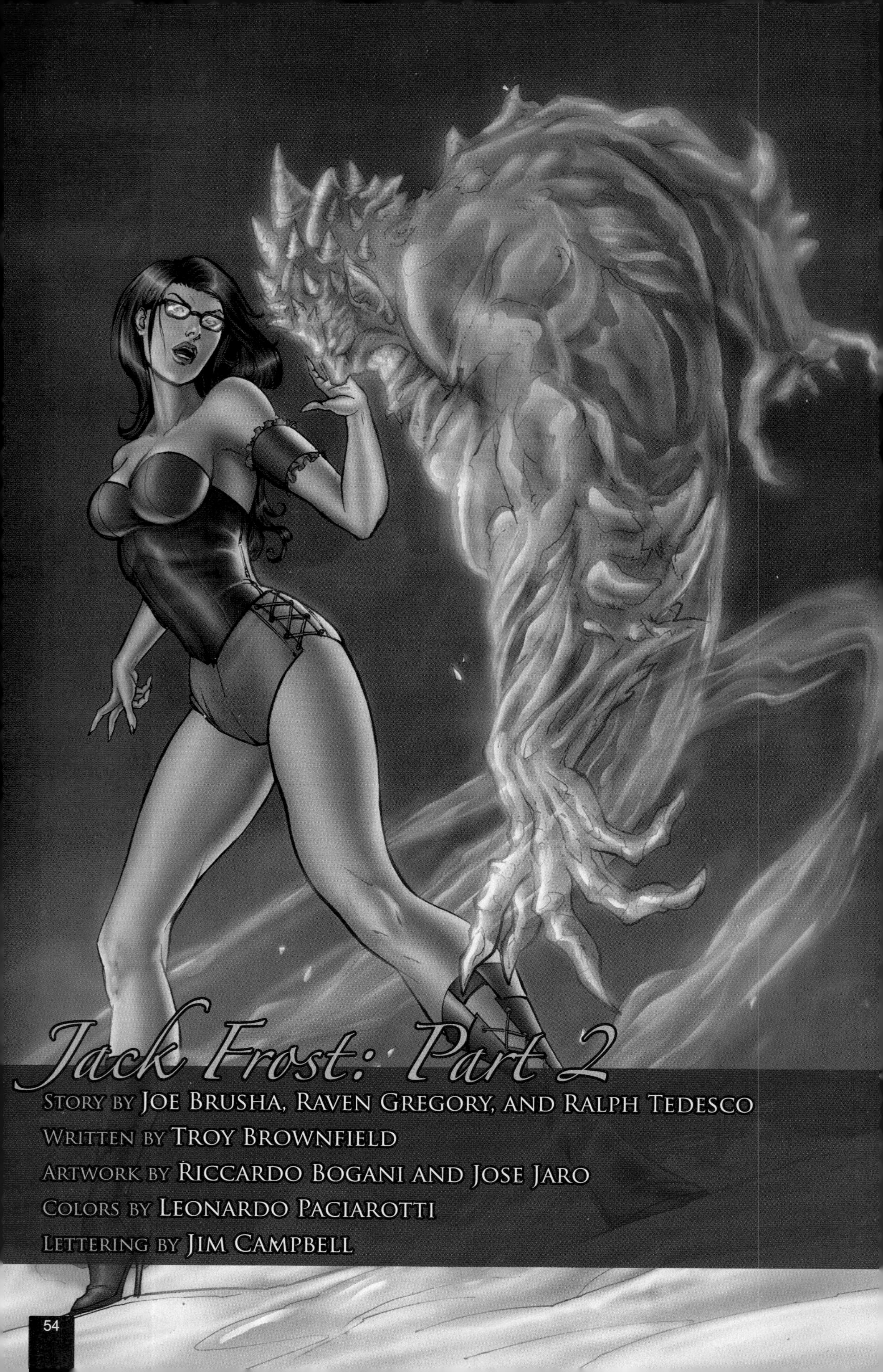
Jack Frost: Part 2
Story by Joe Brusha, Raven Gregory, and Ralph Tedesco
Written by Troy Brownfield
Artwork by Riccardo Bogani and Jose Jaro
Colors by Leonardo Paciarotti
Lettering by Jim Campbell

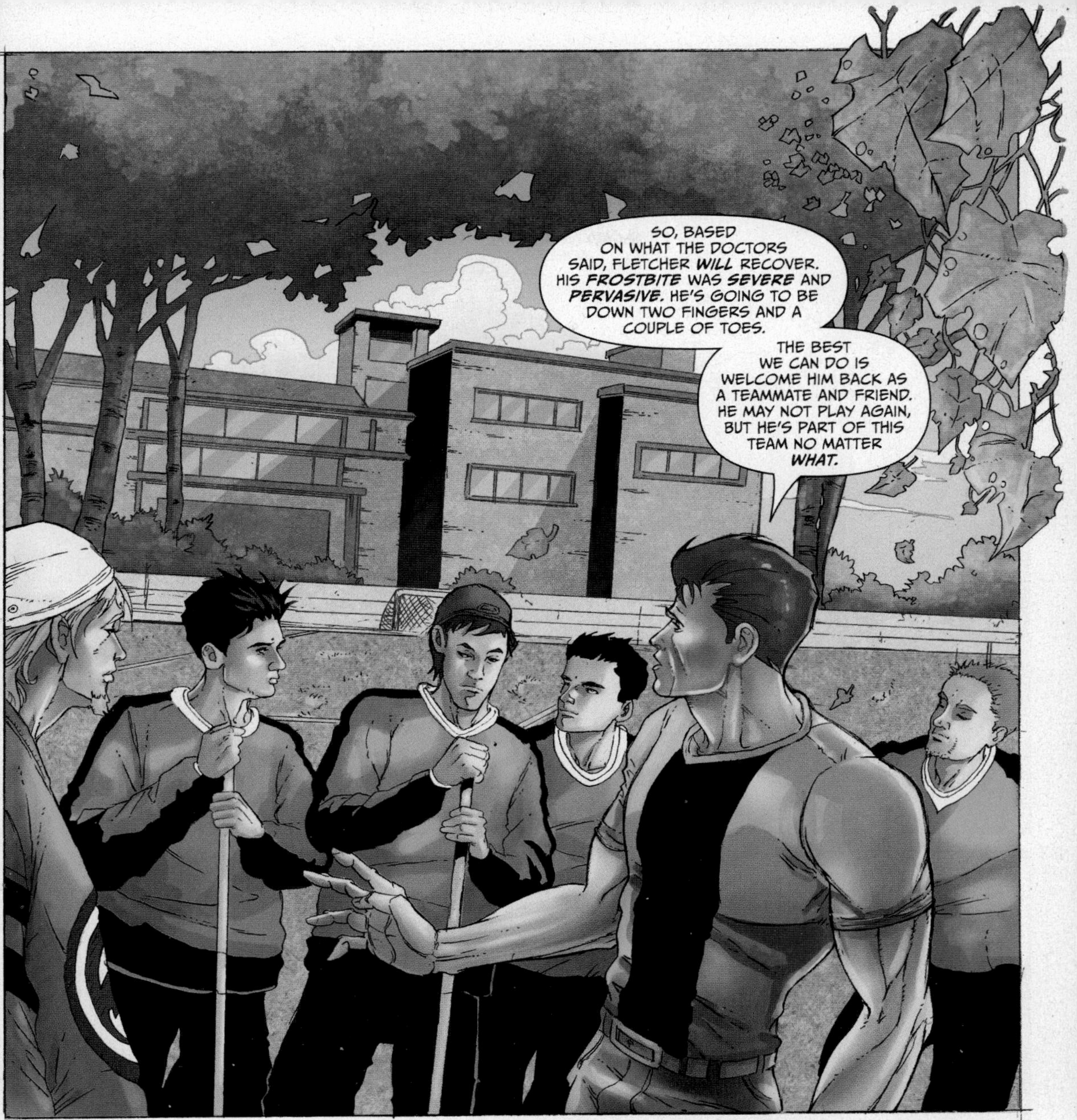
SO, BASED ON WHAT THE DOCTORS SAID, FLETCHER WILL RECOVER. HIS FROSTBITE WAS SEVERE AND PERVASIVE. HE'S GOING TO BE DOWN TWO FINGERS AND A COUPLE OF TOES.
THE BEST WE CAN DO IS WELCOME HIM BACK AS A TEAMMATE AND FRIEND. HE MAY NOT PLAY AGAIN, BUT HE'S PART OF THIS TEAM NO MATTER WHAT.

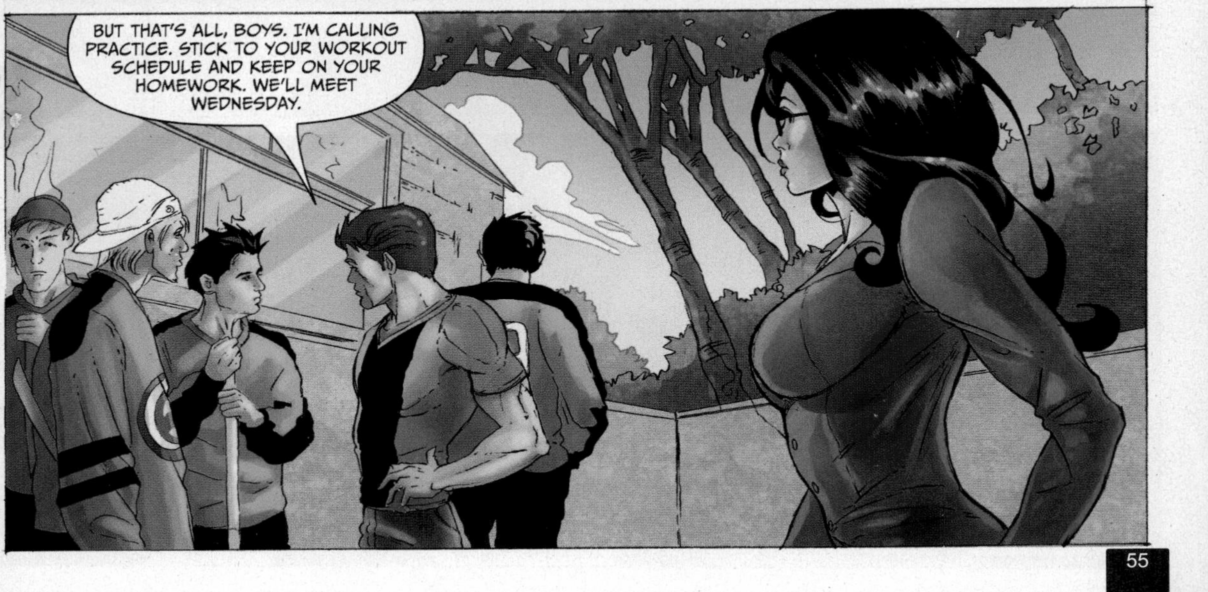
BUT THAT'S ALL, BOYS. I'M CALLING PRACTICE. STICK TO YOUR WORKOUT SCHEDULE AND KEEP ON YOUR HOMEWORK. WE'LL MEET WEDNESDAY.

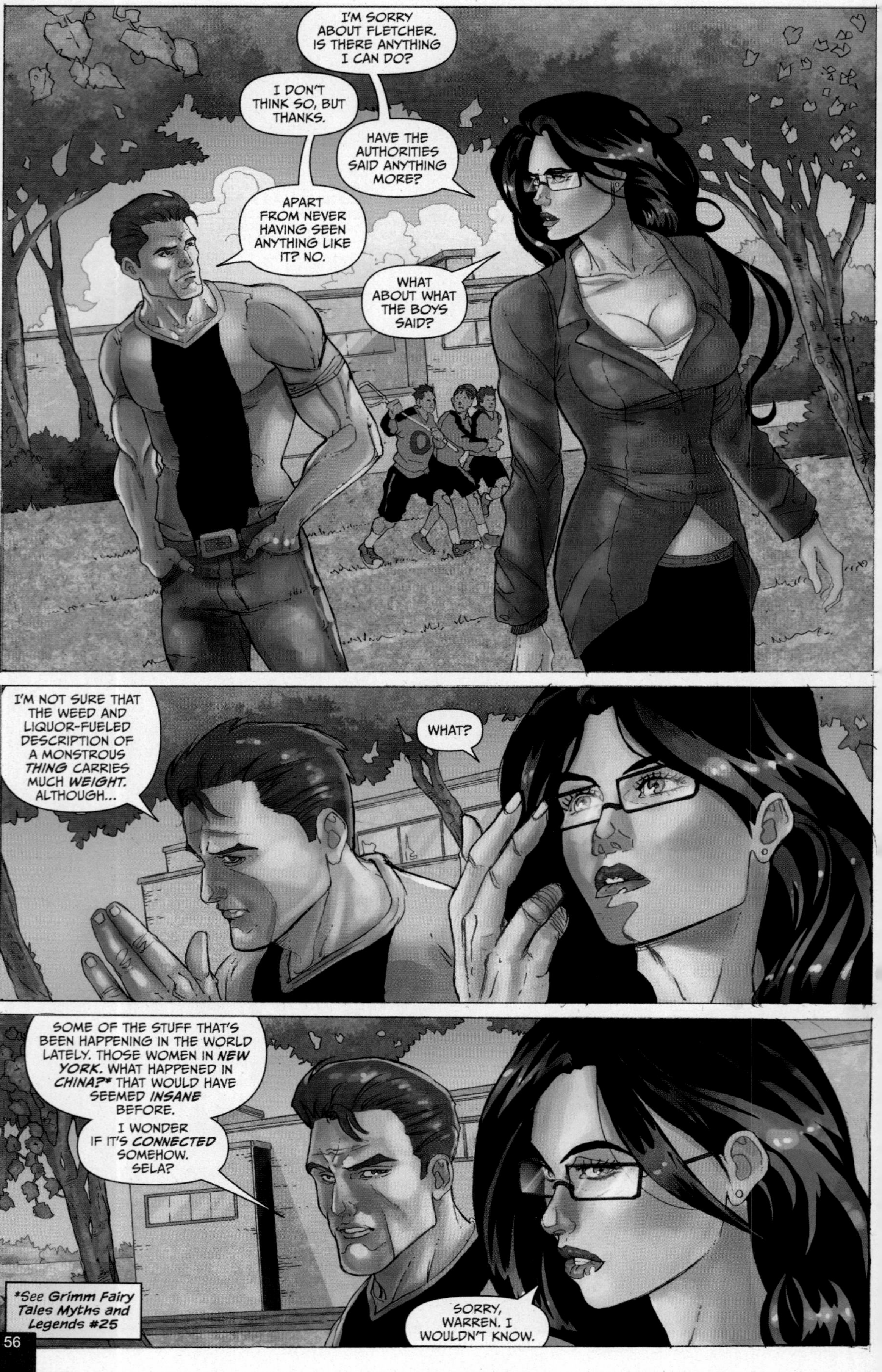
I'M SORRY ABOUT FLETCHER. IS THERE ANYTHING I CAN DO?
I DON'T THINK SO, BUT THANKS.
HAVE THE AUTHORITIES SAID ANYTHING MORE?
APART FROM NEVER HAVING SEEN ANYTHING LIKE IT? NO.
WHAT ABOUT WHAT THE BOYS SAID?
I'M NOT SURE THAT THE WEED AND LIQUOR-FUELED DESCRIPTION OF A MONSTROUS *THING* CARRIES MUCH *WEIGHT*. ALTHOUGH...
WHAT?
SOME OF THE STUFF THAT'S BEEN HAPPENING IN THE WORLD LATELY. THOSE WOMEN IN *NEW YORK*. WHAT HAPPENED IN *CHINA?** THAT WOULD HAVE SEEMED *INSANE* BEFORE.
I WONDER IF IT'S *CONNECTED* SOMEHOW. SELA?
*See Grimm Fairy Tales Myths and Legends #25
SORRY, WARREN. I WOULDN'T KNOW.

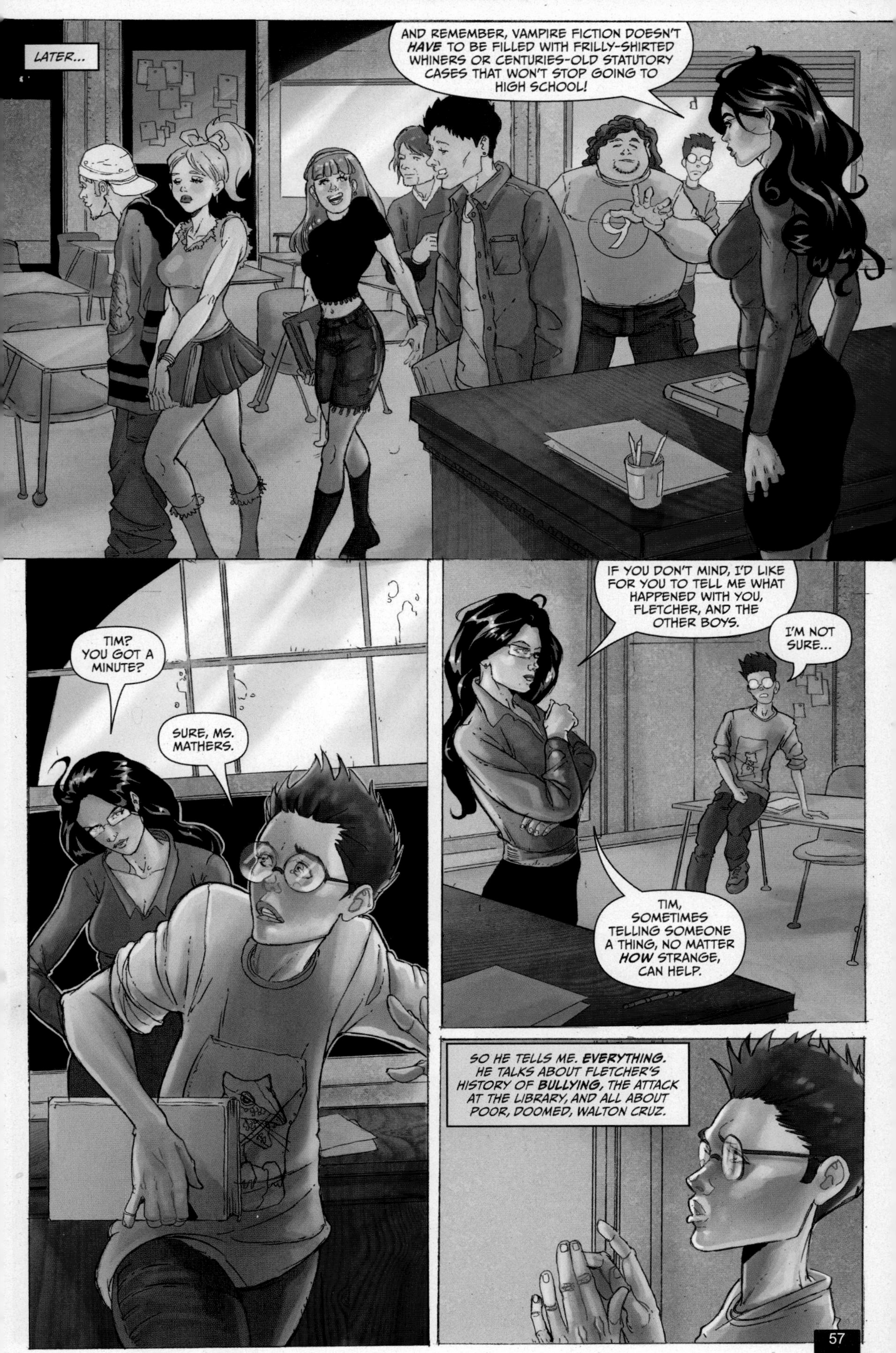
LATER...
AND REMEMBER, VAMPIRE FICTION DOESN'T *HAVE* TO BE FILLED WITH FRILLY-SHIRTED WHINERS OR CENTURIES-OLD STATUTORY CASES THAT WON'T STOP GOING TO HIGH SCHOOL!
TIM? YOU GOT A MINUTE?
SURE, MS. MATHERS.
IF YOU DON'T MIND, I'D LIKE FOR YOU TO TELL ME WHAT HAPPENED WITH YOU, FLETCHER, AND THE OTHER BOYS.
I'M NOT SURE...
TIM, SOMETIMES TELLING SOMEONE A THING, NO MATTER *HOW* STRANGE, CAN HELP.
SO HE TELLS ME. **EVERYTHING.** HE TALKS ABOUT FLETCHER'S HISTORY OF **BULLYING**, THE ATTACK AT THE LIBRARY, AND ALL ABOUT POOR, DOOMED, WALTON CRUZ.

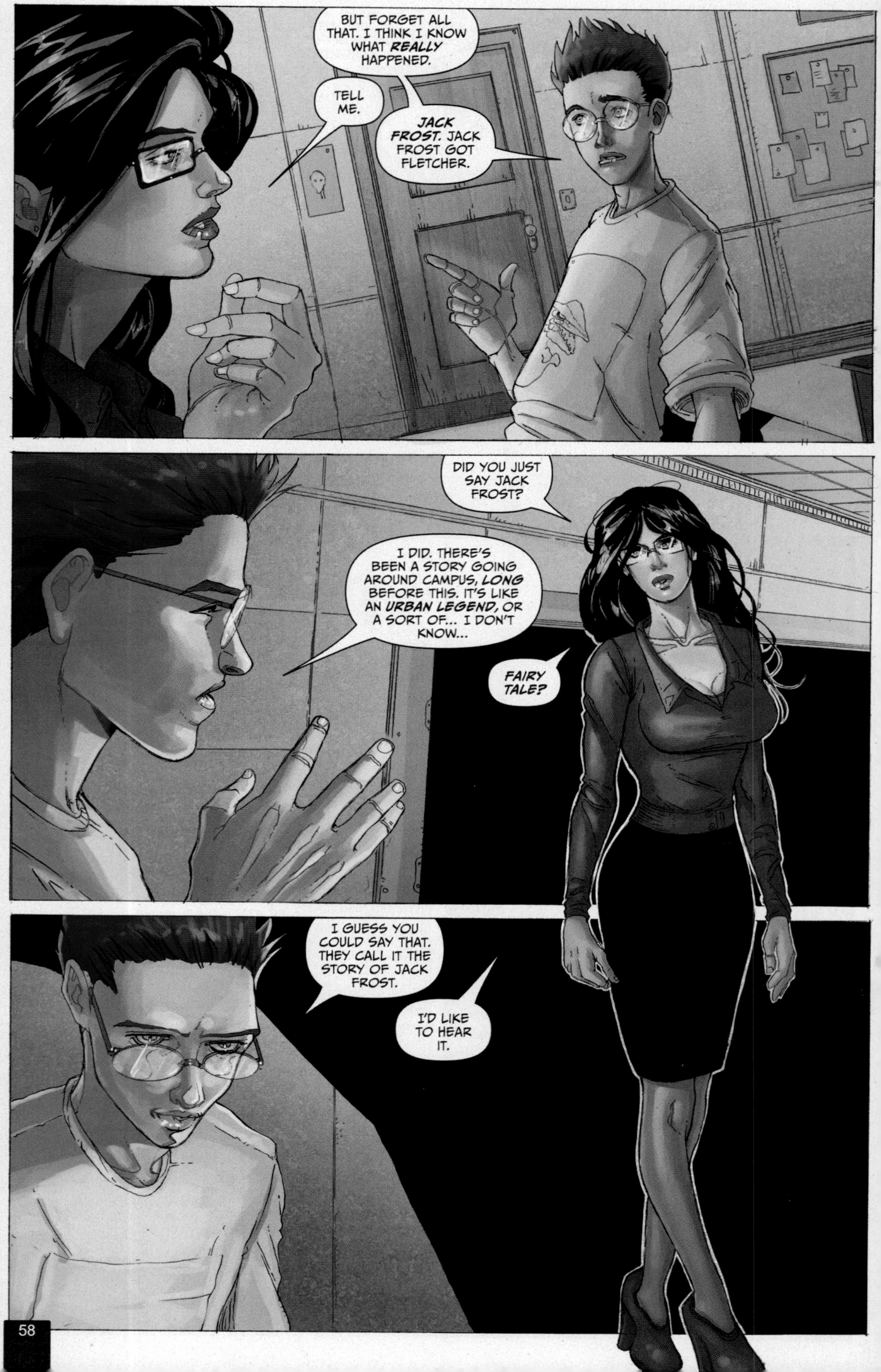
BUT FORGET ALL THAT. I THINK I KNOW WHAT **REALLY** HAPPENED.
TELL ME.
JACK FROST. JACK FROST GOT FLETCHER.
DID YOU JUST SAY JACK FROST?
I DID. THERE'S BEEN A STORY GOING AROUND CAMPUS, **LONG** BEFORE THIS. IT'S LIKE AN **URBAN LEGEND**, OR A SORT OF... I DON'T KNOW...
FAIRY TALE?
I GUESS YOU COULD SAY THAT. THEY CALL IT THE STORY OF JACK FROST.
I'D LIKE TO HEAR IT.

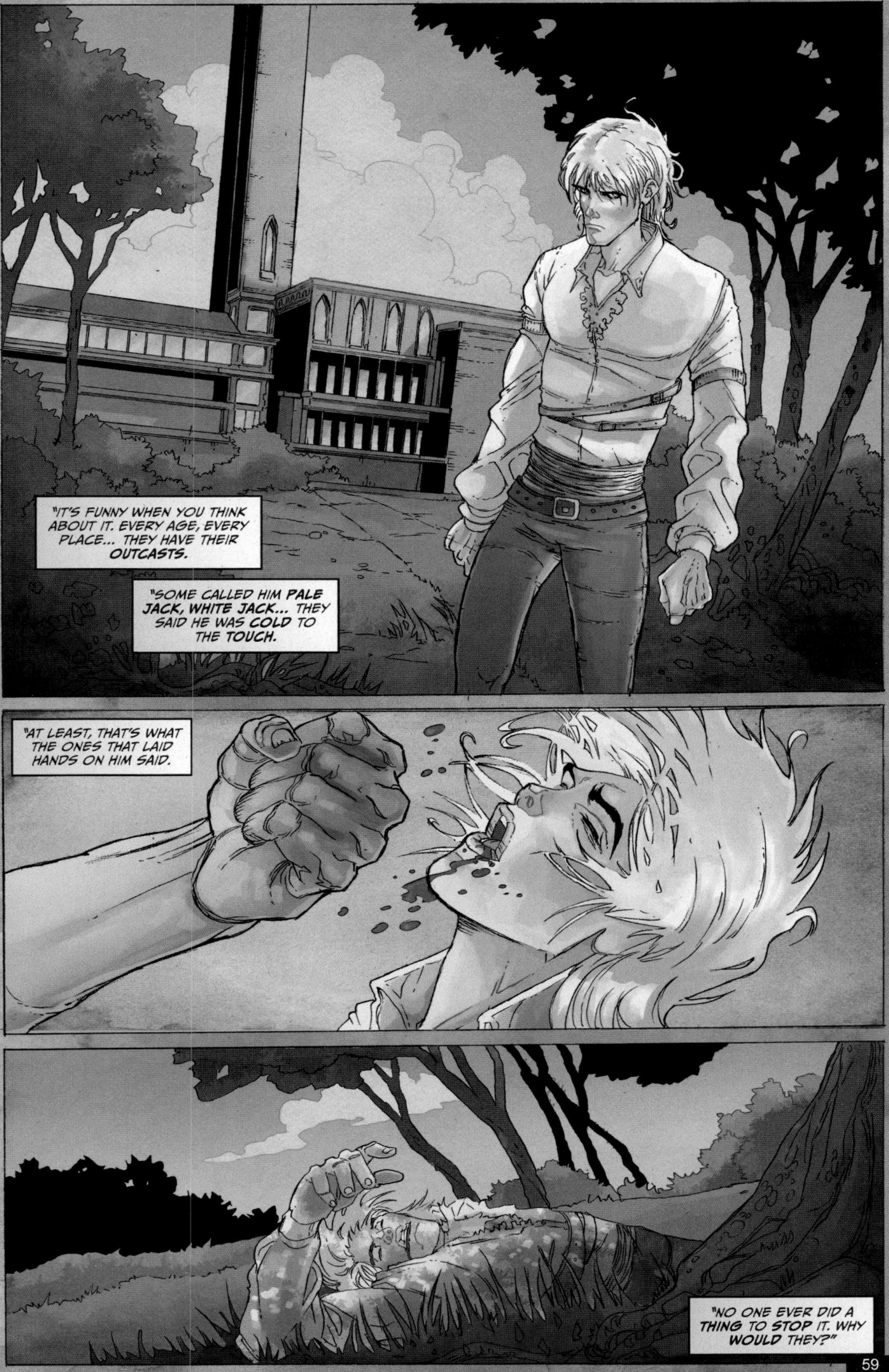
"IT'S FUNNY WHEN YOU THINK ABOUT IT. EVERY AGE, EVERY PLACE... THEY HAVE THEIR OUTCASTS.
"SOME CALLED HIM PALE JACK, WHITE JACK... THEY SAID HE WAS COLD TO THE TOUCH.
"AT LEAST, THAT'S WHAT THE ONES THAT LAID HANDS ON HIM SAID.
"NO ONE EVER DID A THING TO STOP IT. WHY WOULD THEY?"

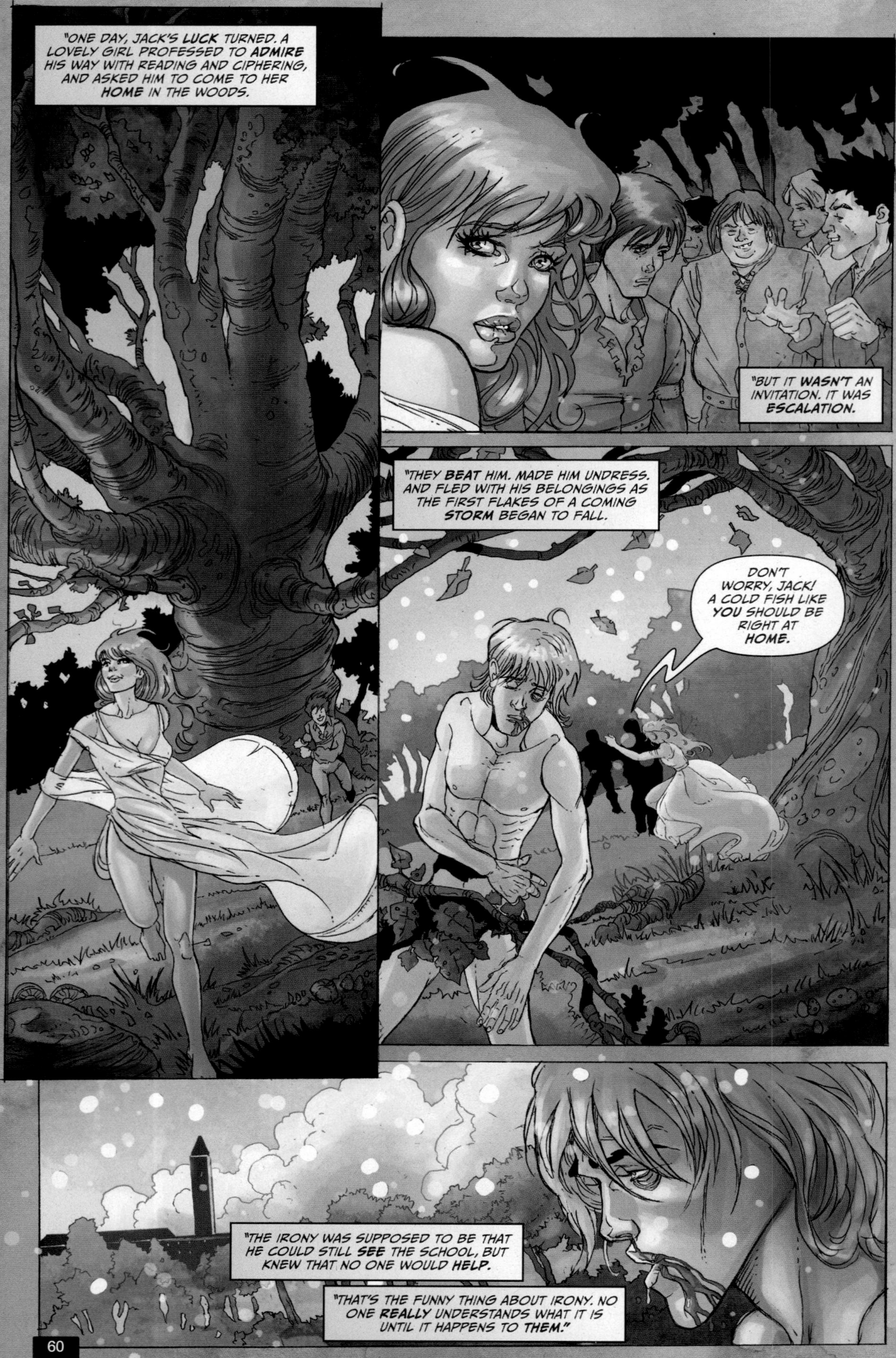

"ONE DAY, JACK'S LUCK TURNED. A LOVELY GIRL PROFESSED TO ADMIRE HIS WAY WITH READING AND CIPHERING, AND ASKED HIM TO COME TO HER HOME IN THE WOODS.
"BUT IT WASN'T AN INVITATION. IT WAS ESCALATION.
"THEY BEAT HIM. MADE HIM UNDRESS. AND FLED WITH HIS BELONGINGS AS THE FIRST FLAKES OF A COMING STORM BEGAN TO FALL.
DON'T WORRY, JACK! A COLD FISH LIKE YOU SHOULD BE RIGHT AT HOME.
"THE IRONY WAS SUPPOSED TO BE THAT HE COULD STILL SEE THE SCHOOL, BUT KNEW THAT NO ONE WOULD HELP.
"THAT'S THE FUNNY THING ABOUT IRONY. NO ONE REALLY UNDERSTANDS WHAT IT IS UNTIL IT HAPPENS TO THEM."

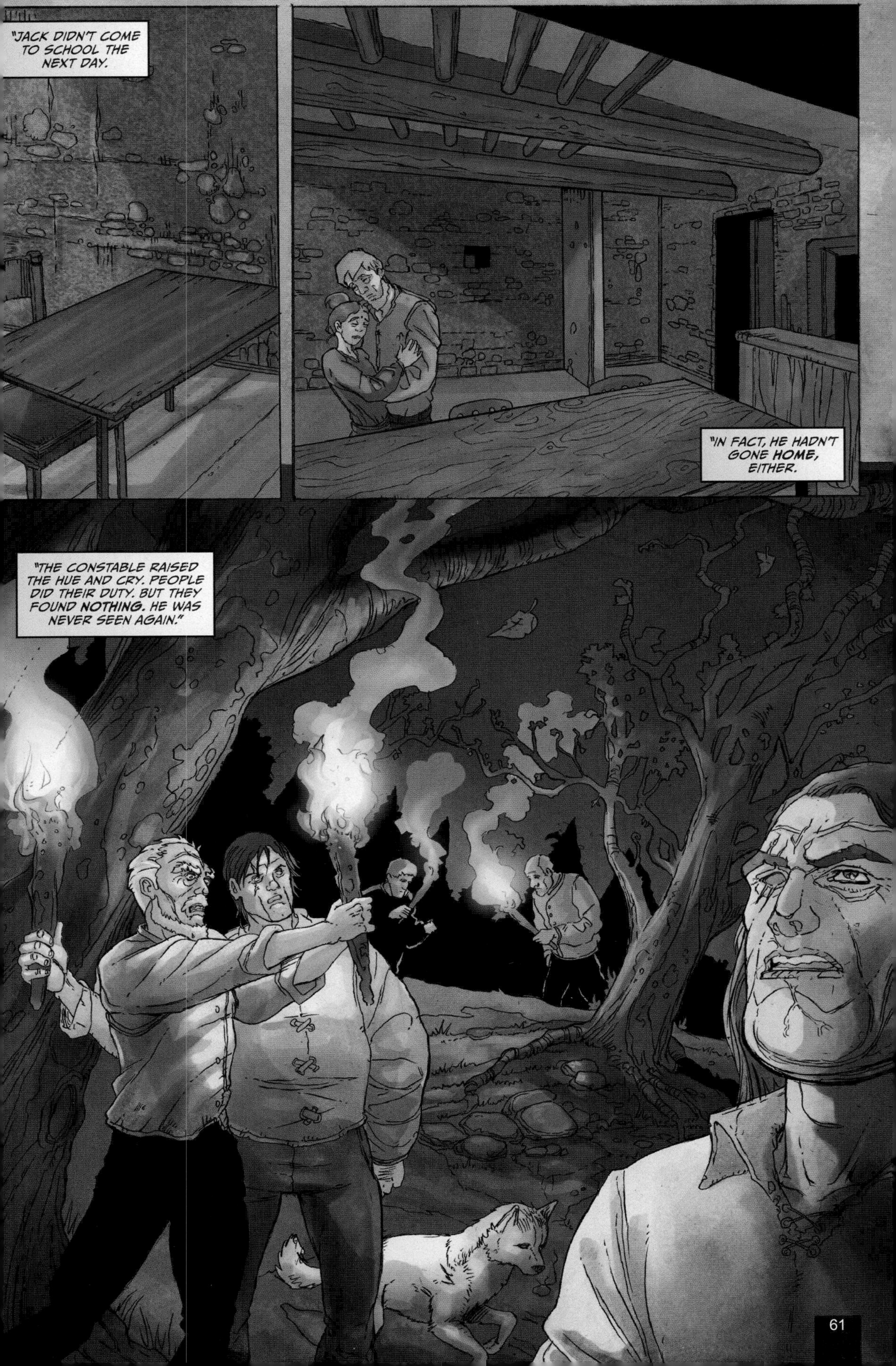
"JACK DIDN'T COME TO SCHOOL THE NEXT DAY.
"IN FACT, HE HADN'T GONE HOME, EITHER.
"THE CONSTABLE RAISED THE HUE AND CRY. PEOPLE DID THEIR DUTY. BUT THEY FOUND NOTHING. HE WAS NEVER SEEN AGAIN."

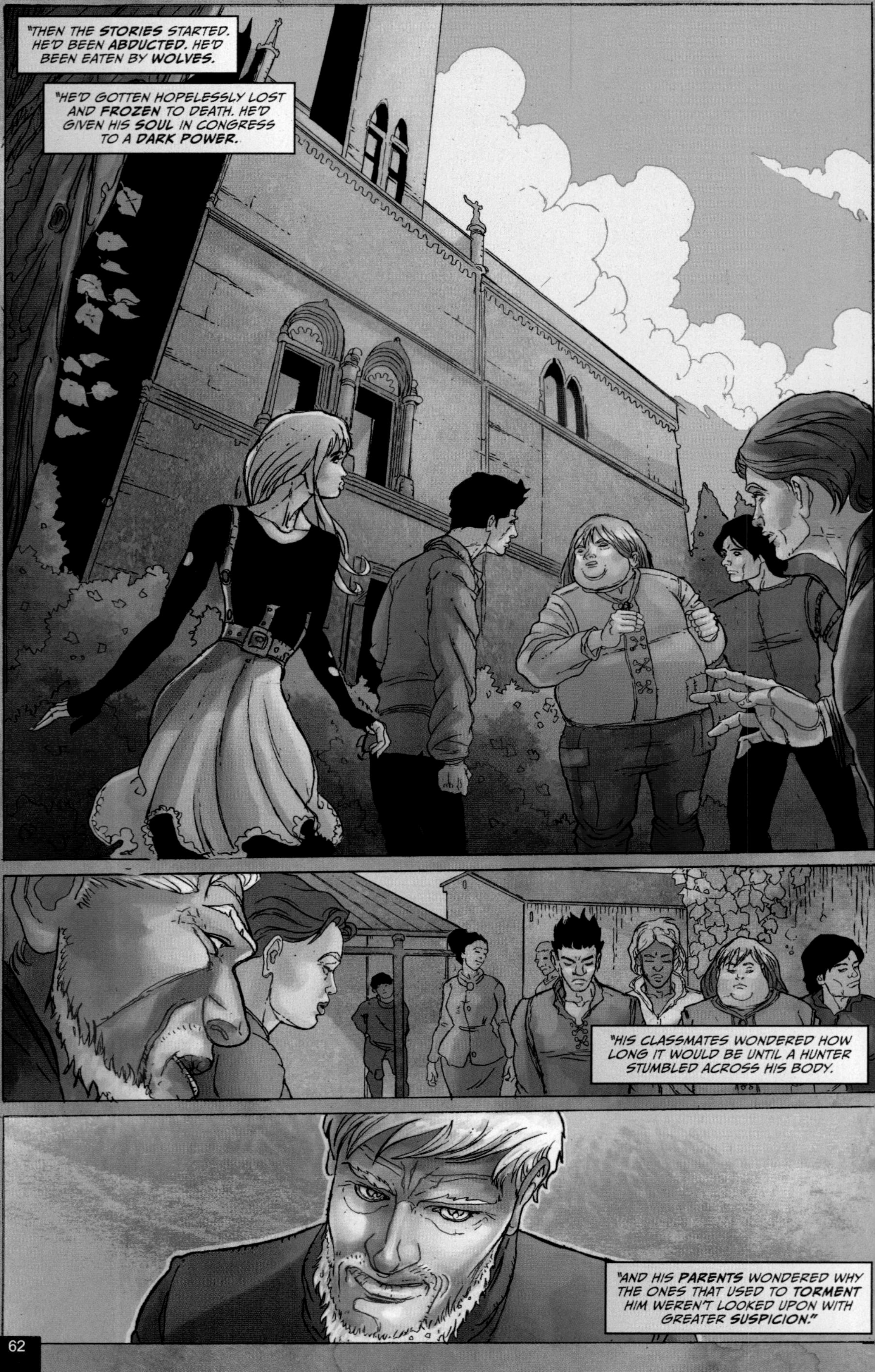
"THEN THE STORIES STARTED. HE'D BEEN ABDUCTED. HE'D BEEN EATEN BY WOLVES.
"HE'D GOTTEN HOPELESSLY LOST AND FROZEN TO DEATH. HE'D GIVEN HIS SOUL IN CONGRESS TO A DARK POWER.
"HIS CLASSMATES WONDERED HOW LONG IT WOULD BE UNTIL A HUNTER STUMBLED ACROSS HIS BODY.
"AND HIS PARENTS WONDERED WHY THE ONES THAT USED TO TORMENT HIM WEREN'T LOOKED UPON WITH GREATER SUSPICION."

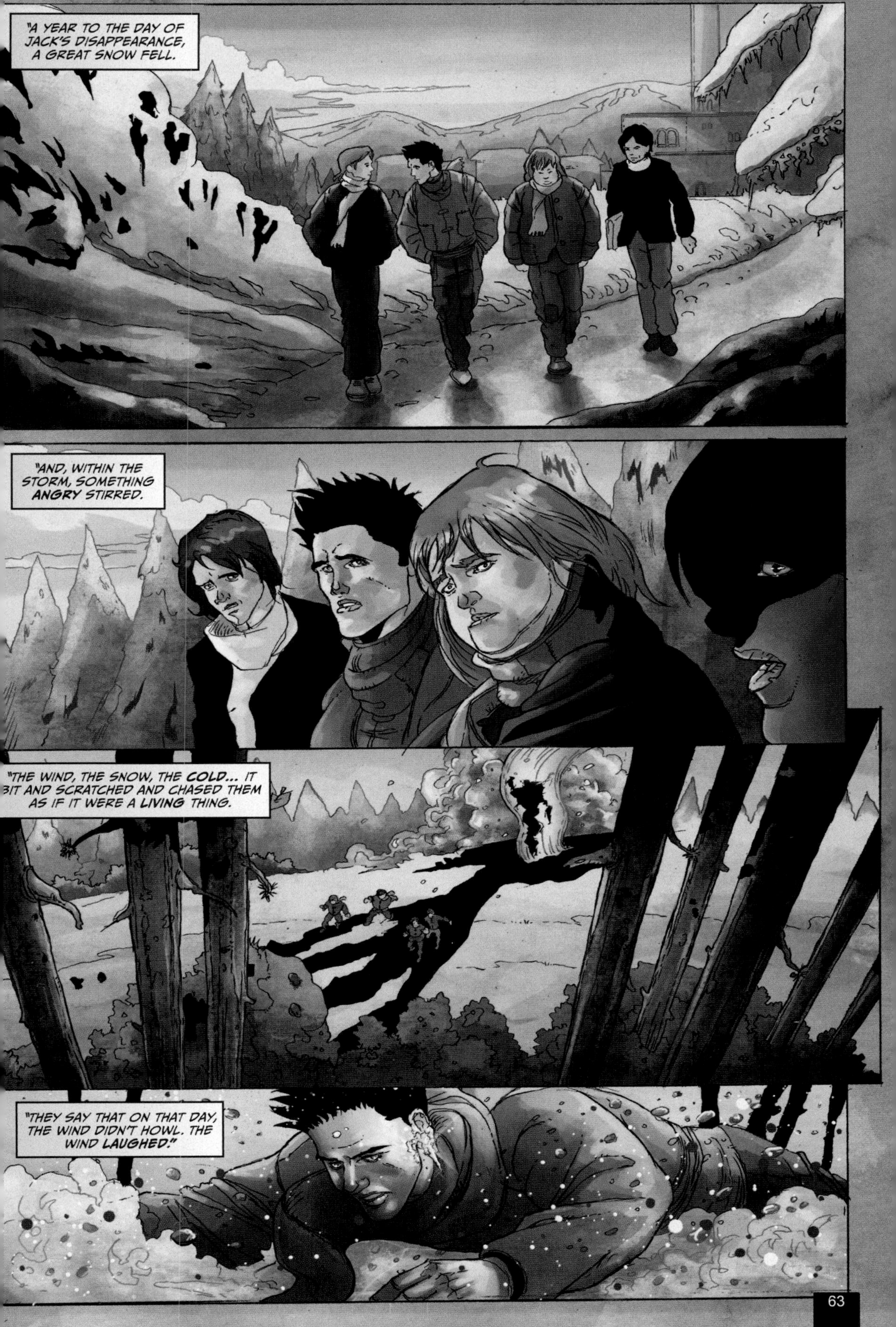
"A YEAR TO THE DAY OF JACK'S DISAPPEARANCE, A GREAT SNOW FELL.
"AND, WITHIN THE STORM, SOMETHING ANGRY STIRRED.
"THE WIND, THE SNOW, THE COLD... IT BIT AND SCRATCHED AND CHASED THEM AS IF IT WERE A LIVING THING.
"THEY SAY THAT ON THAT DAY, THE WIND DIDN'T HOWL. THE WIND LAUGHED."

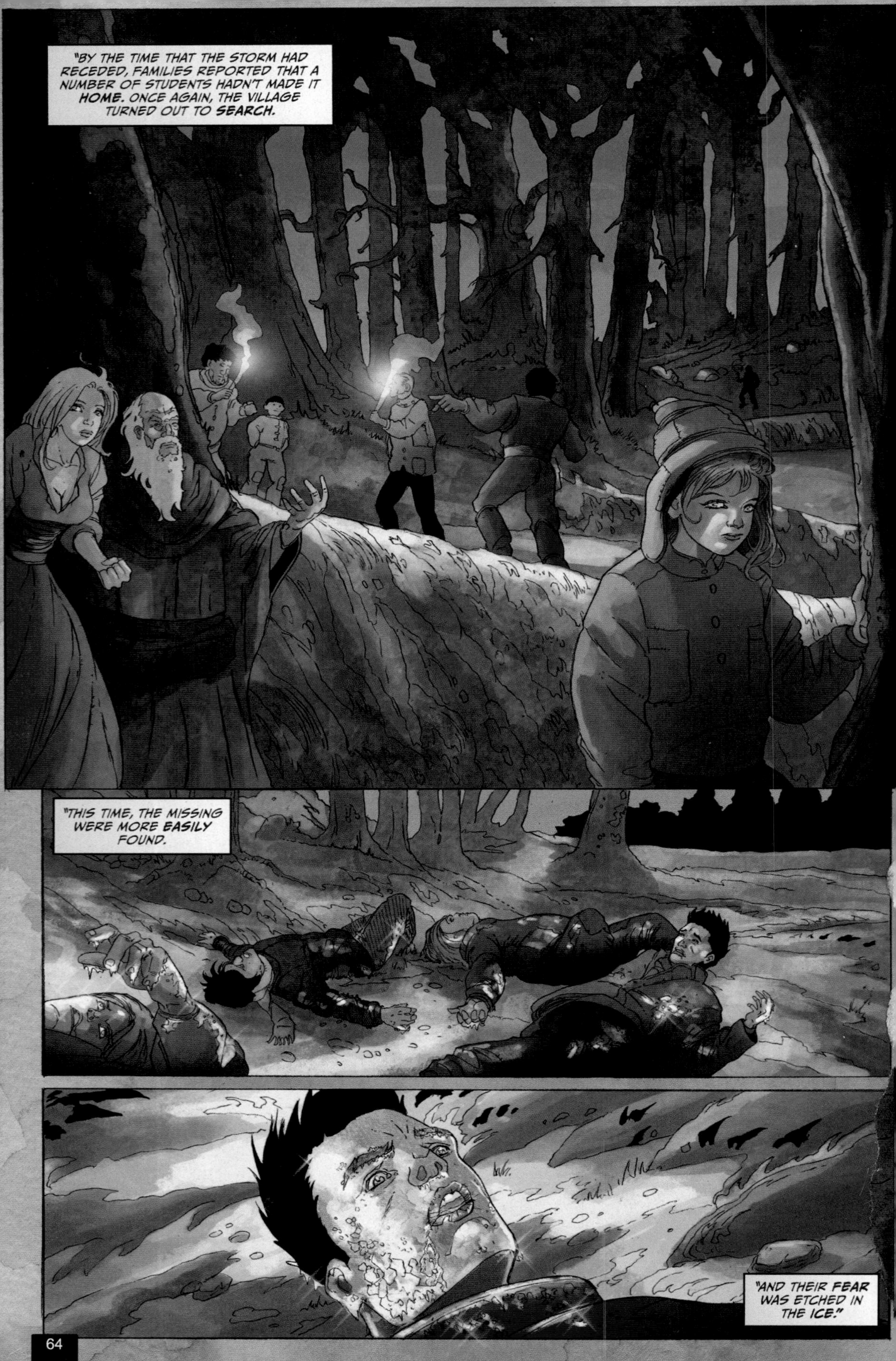
"BY THE TIME THAT THE STORM HAD RECEDED, FAMILIES REPORTED THAT A NUMBER OF STUDENTS HADN'T MADE IT HOME. ONCE AGAIN, THE VILLAGE TURNED OUT TO SEARCH.
"THIS TIME, THE MISSING WERE MORE EASILY FOUND.
"AND THEIR FEAR WAS ETCHED IN THE ICE."

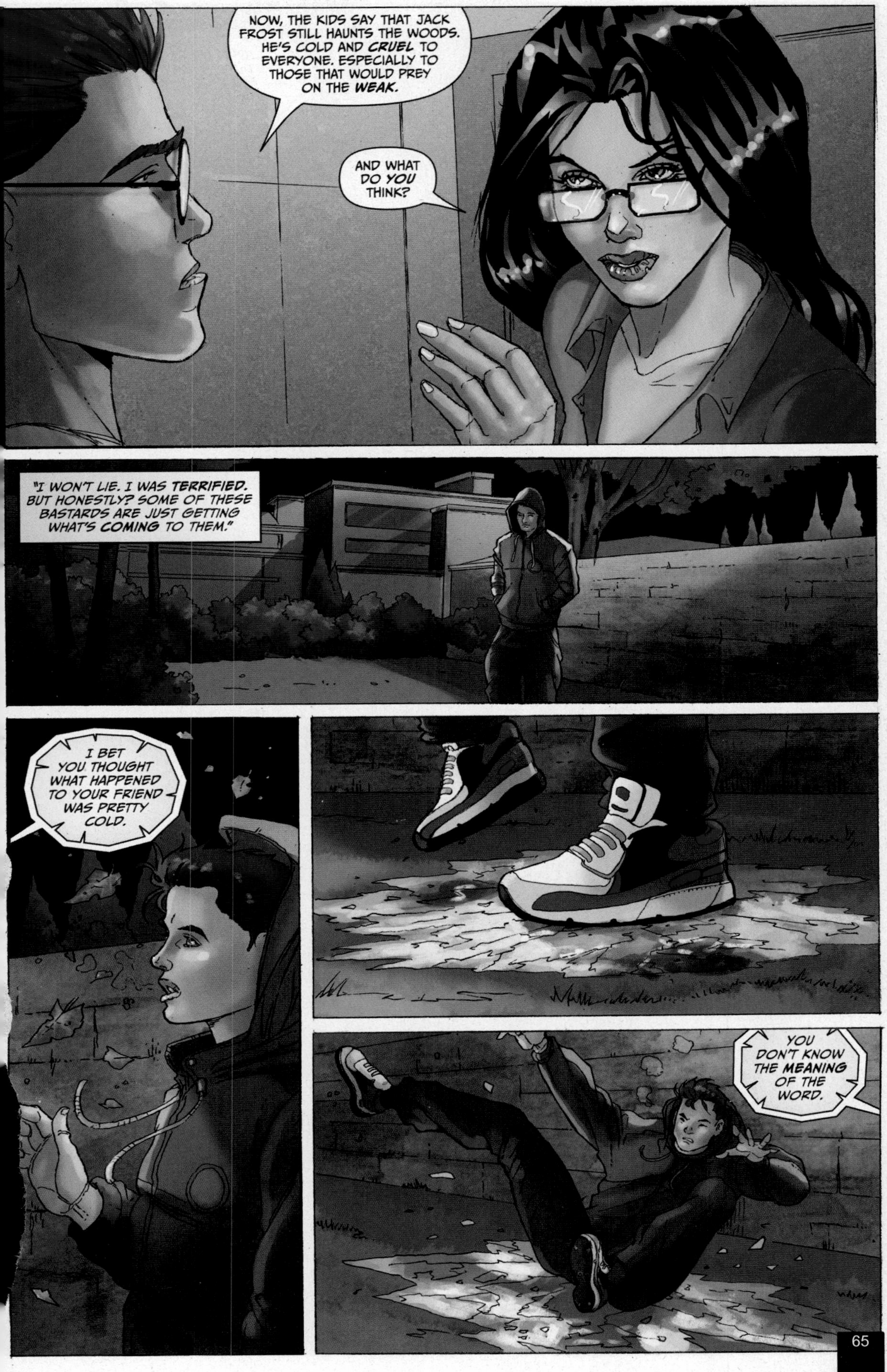
NOW, THE KIDS SAY THAT JACK FROST STILL HAUNTS THE WOODS. HE'S COLD AND *CRUEL* TO EVERYONE. ESPECIALLY TO THOSE THAT WOULD PREY ON THE *WEAK.*
AND WHAT DO *YOU* THINK?
"I WON'T LIE. I WAS *TERRIFIED.* BUT HONESTLY? SOME OF THESE BASTARDS ARE JUST GETTING WHAT'S *COMING* TO THEM."
I BET YOU THOUGHT WHAT HAPPENED TO YOUR FRIEND WAS PRETTY COLD.
YOU DON'T KNOW THE *MEANING* OF THE WORD.

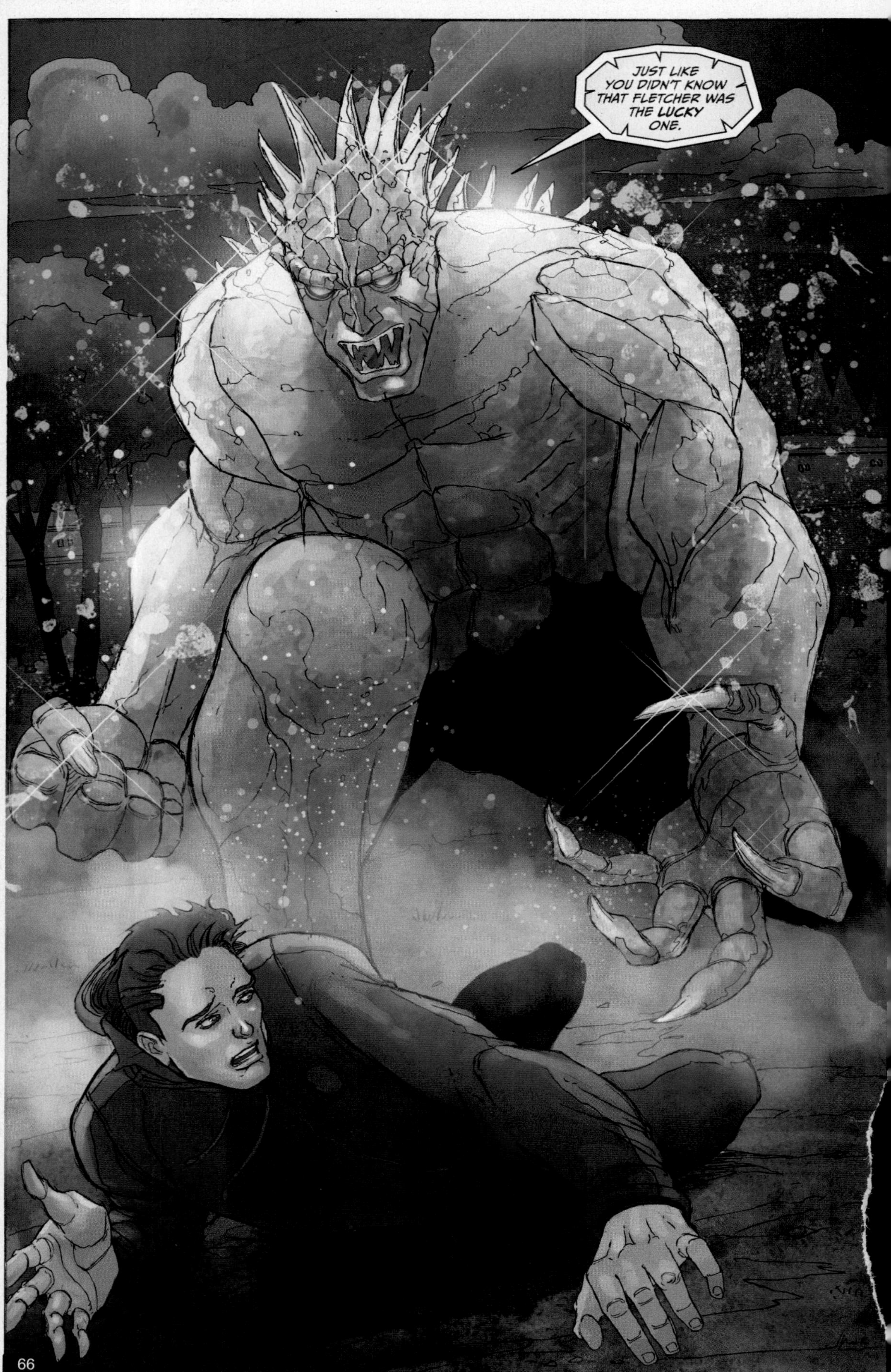
JUST LIKE YOU DIDN'T KNOW THAT FLETCHER WAS THE LUCKY ONE.

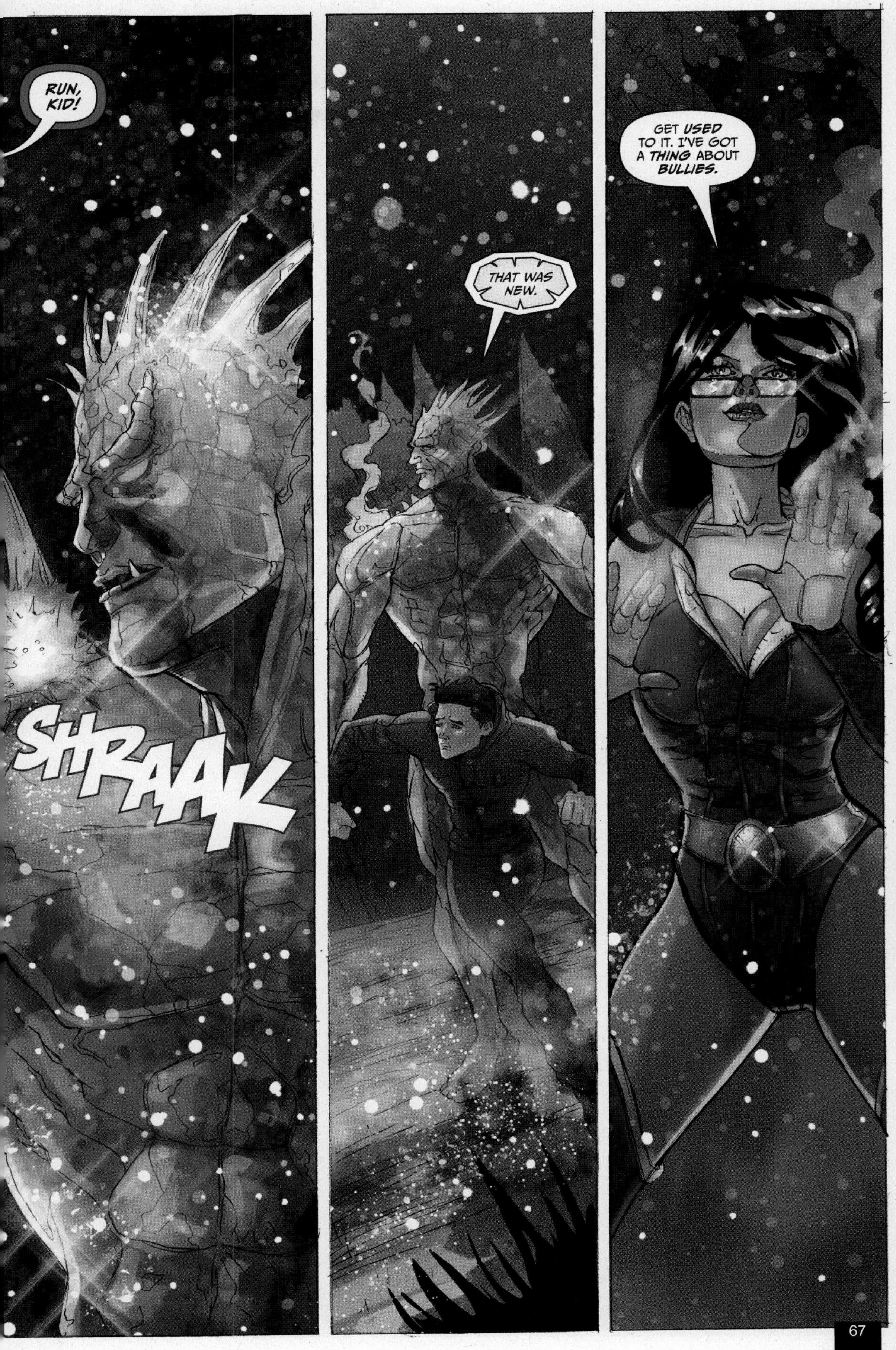
RUN, KID!
SHRAAK
THAT WAS NEW.
GET USED TO IT. I'VE GOT A THING ABOUT BULLIES.

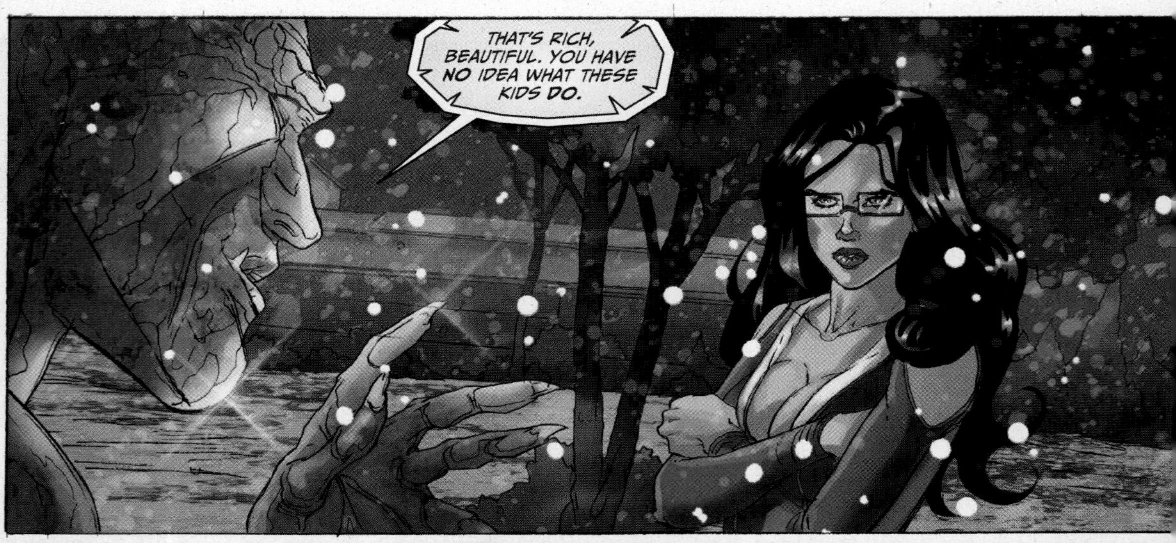
THAT'S RICH, BEAUTIFUL. YOU HAVE NO IDEA WHAT THESE KIDS DO.

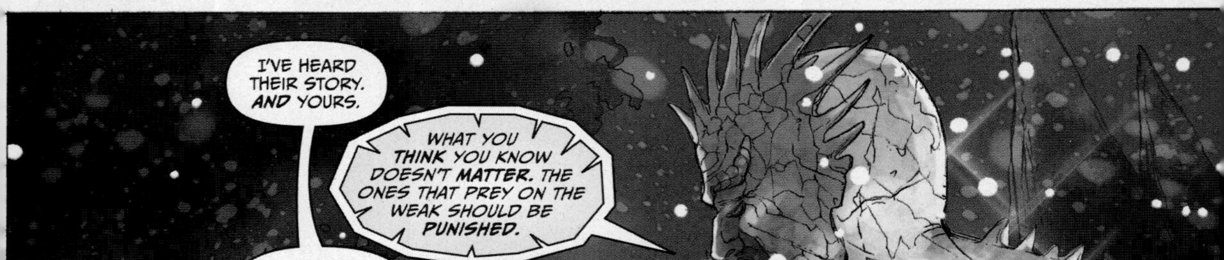
I'VE HEARD THEIR STORY. AND YOURS.
WHAT YOU THINK YOU KNOW DOESN'T MATTER. THE ONES THAT PREY ON THE WEAK SHOULD BE PUNISHED.
MAYBE. AND MAYBE THAT ISN'T FOR YOU TO SAY. I DRAW THE LINE AT FROZEN CHILDREN.

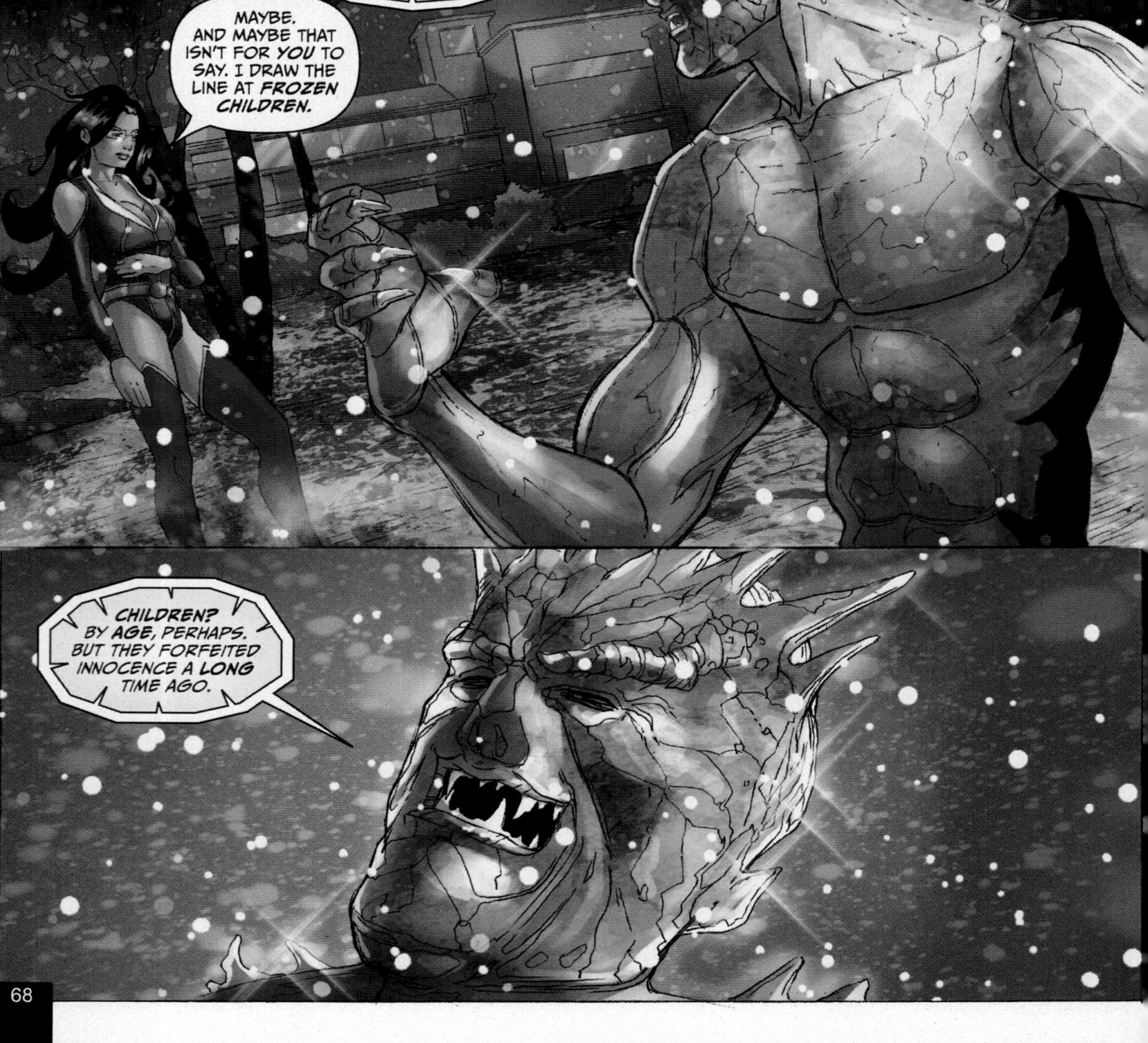
CHILDREN? BY AGE, PERHAPS. BUT THEY FORFEITED INNOCENCE A LONG TIME AGO.

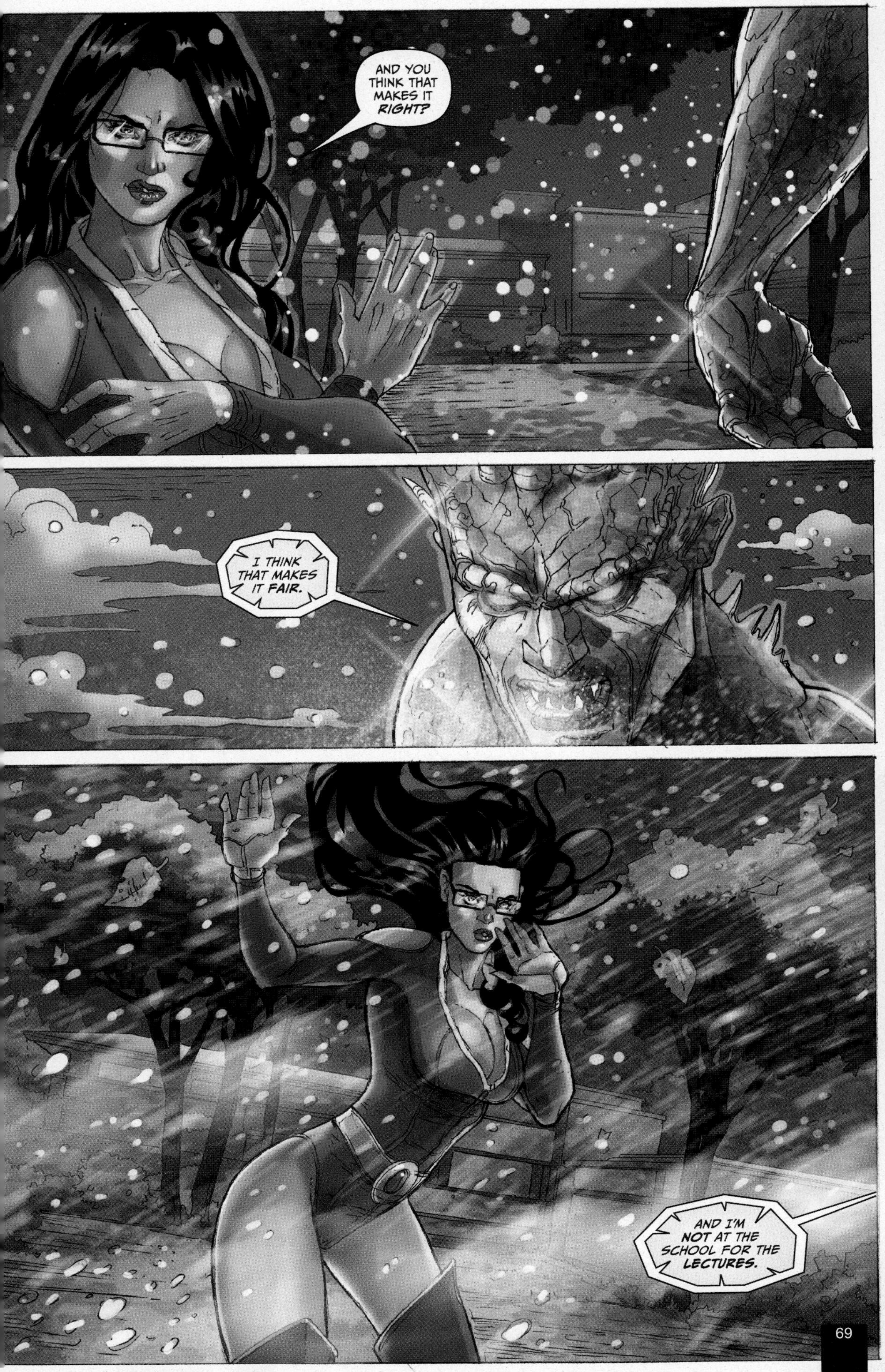
AND YOU THINK THAT MAKES IT RIGHT?
I THINK THAT MAKES IT FAIR.
AND I'M NOT AT THE SCHOOL FOR THE LECTURES.

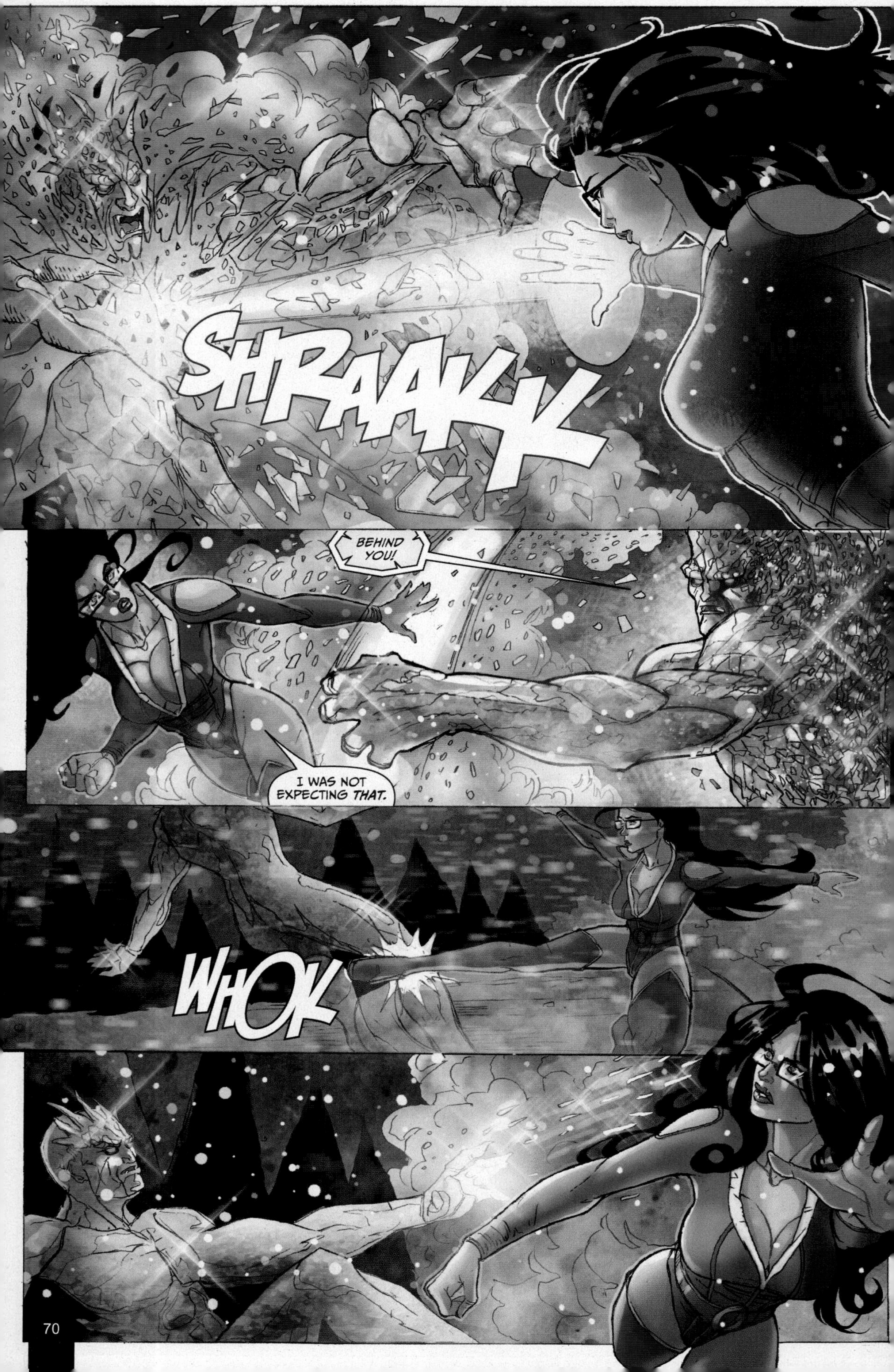
SHRAAKK
BEHIND YOU!
I WAS NOT EXPECTING THAT.
WHOK

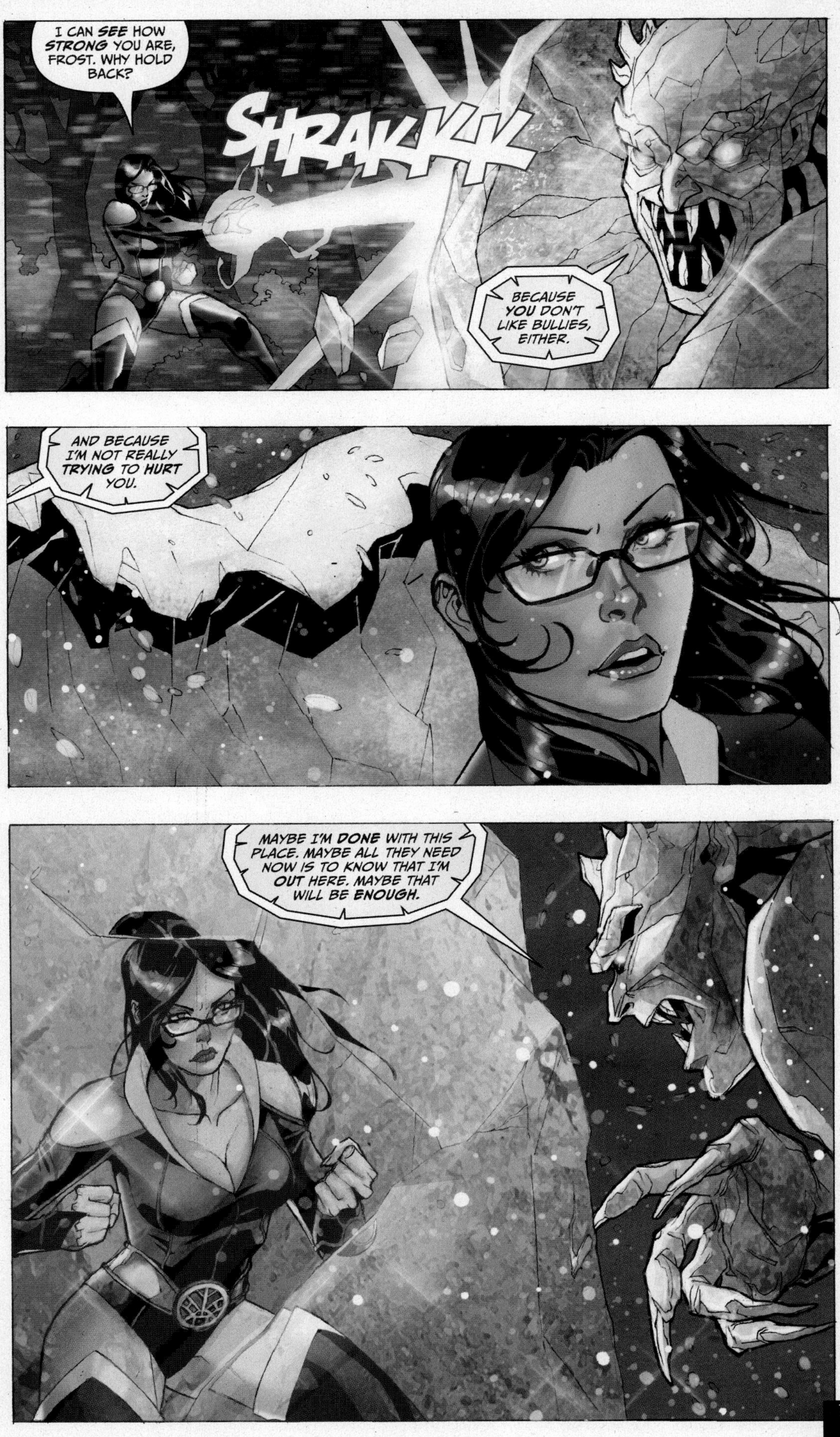

I CAN SEE HOW STRONG YOU ARE, FROST. WHY HOLD BACK?
SHRAKKK
BECAUSE YOU DON'T LIKE BULLIES, EITHER.
AND BECAUSE I'M NOT REALLY TRYING TO HURT YOU.
MAYBE I'M DONE WITH THIS PLACE. MAYBE ALL THEY NEED NOW IS TO KNOW THAT I'M OUT HERE. MAYBE THAT WILL BE ENOUGH.

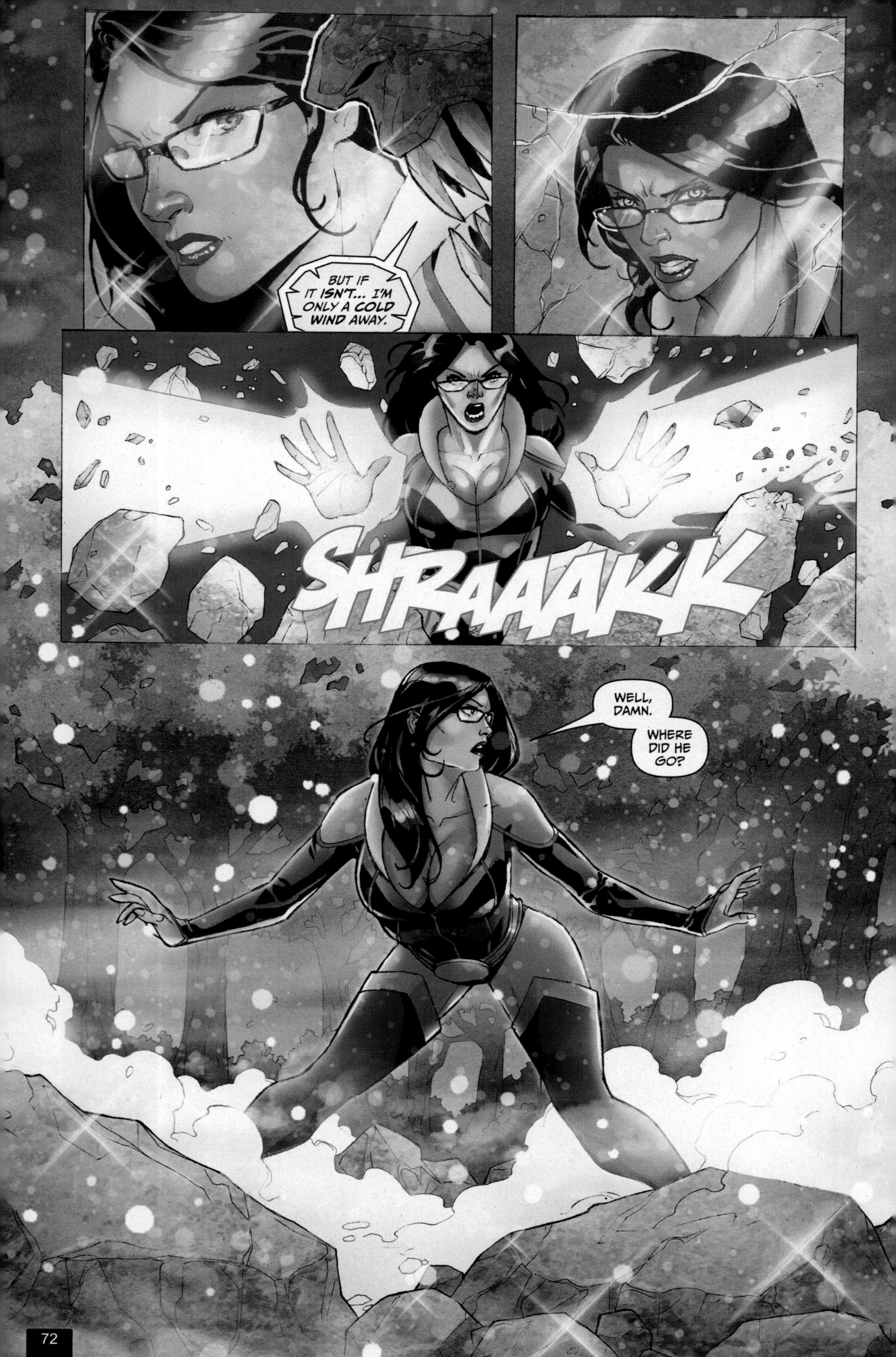
BUT IF IT ISN'T... I'M ONLY A COLD WIND AWAY.
SHRAAAKK
WELL, DAMN.
WHERE DID HE GO?

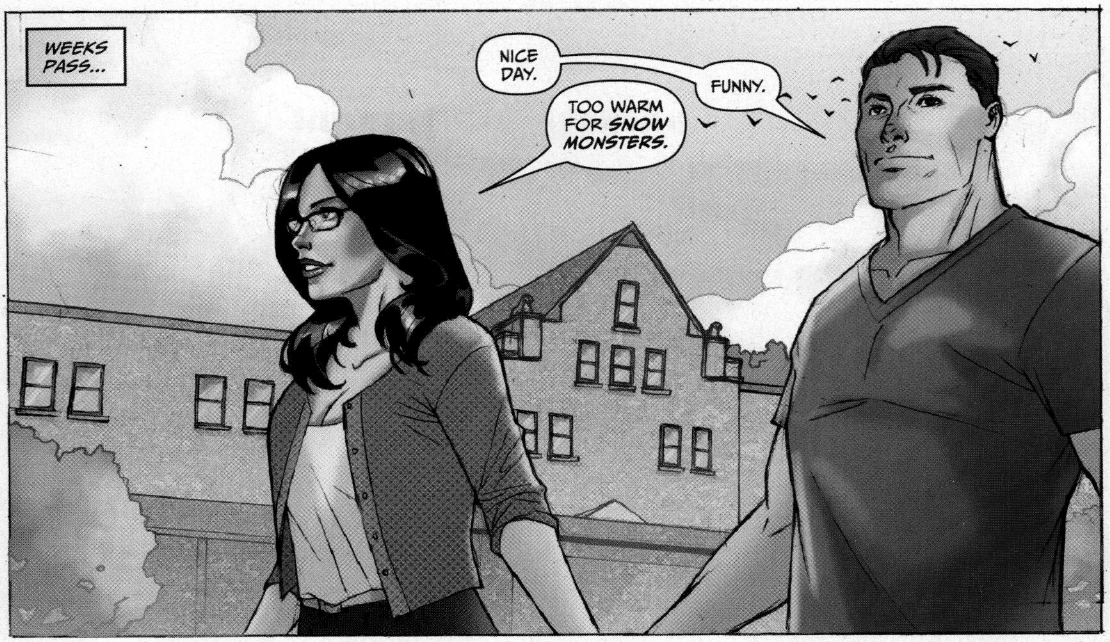
WEEKS PASS...
NICE DAY.
FUNNY.
TOO WARM FOR SNOW MONSTERS.

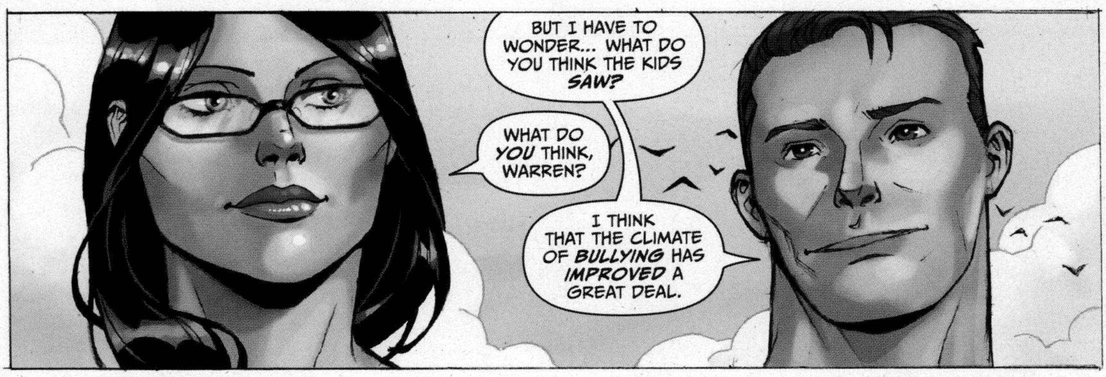
BUT I HAVE TO WONDER... WHAT DO YOU THINK THE KIDS SAW?
WHAT DO YOU THINK, WARREN?
I THINK THAT THE CLIMATE OF BULLYING HAS IMPROVED A GREAT DEAL.

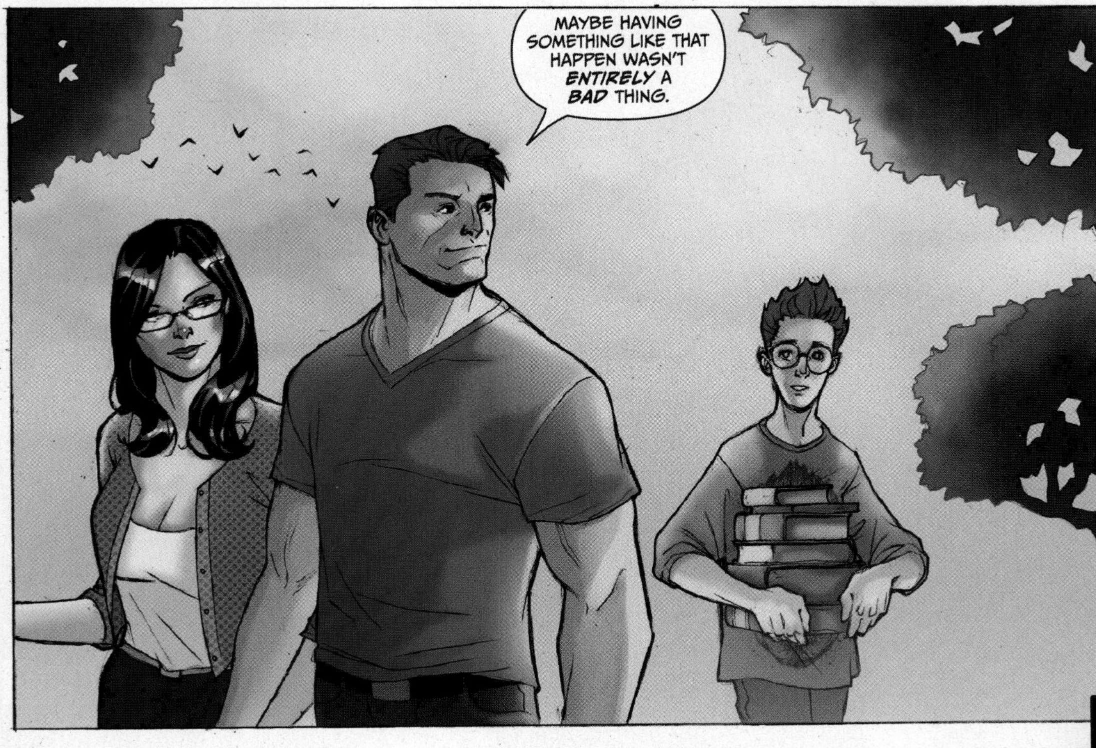
MAYBE HAVING SOMETHING LIKE THAT HAPPEN WASN'T ENTIRELY A BAD THING.

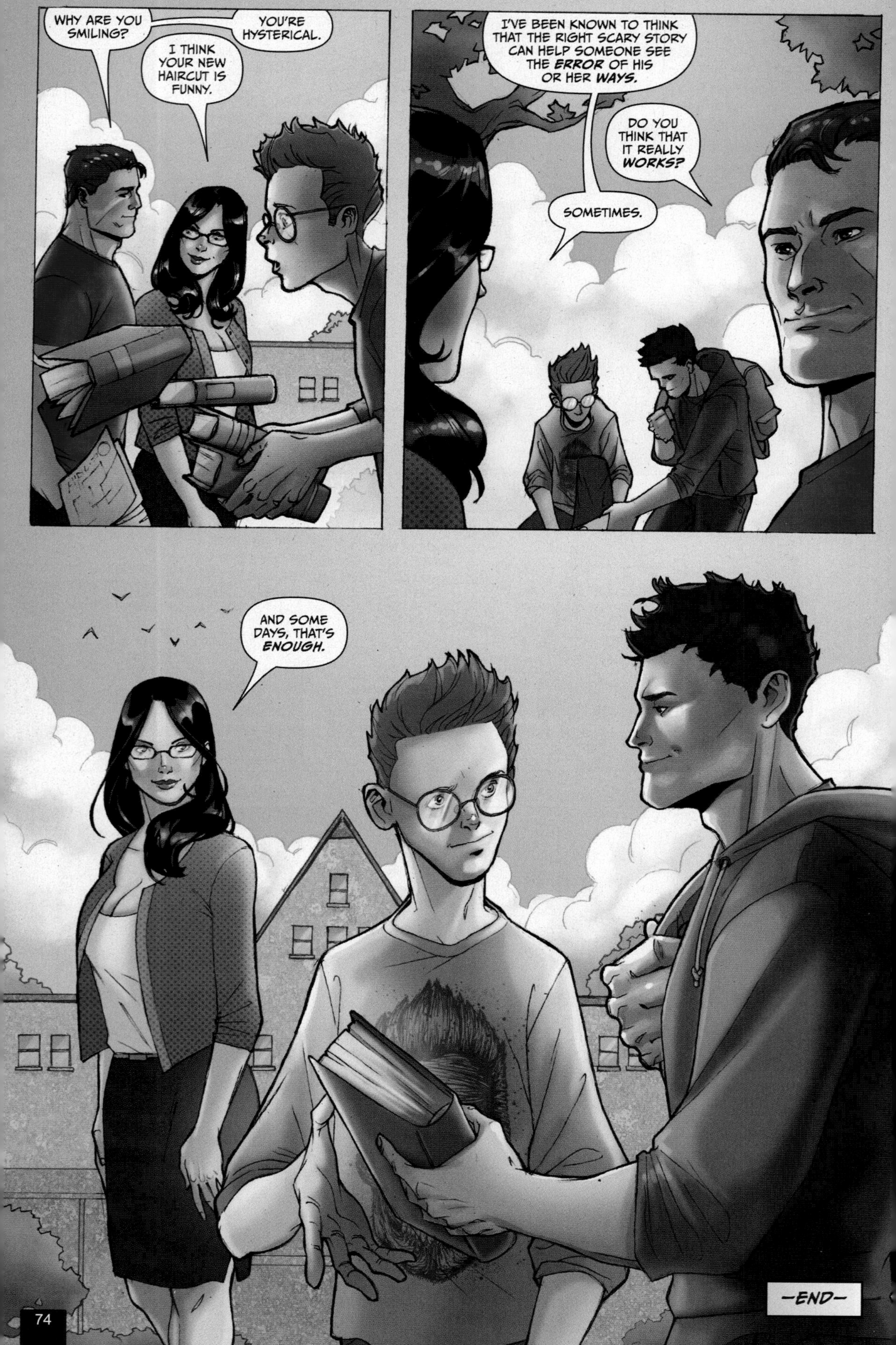
WHY ARE YOU SMILING?
YOU'RE HYSTERICAL.
I THINK YOUR NEW HAIRCUT IS FUNNY.
I'VE BEEN KNOWN TO THINK THAT THE RIGHT SCARY STORY CAN HELP SOMEONE SEE THE ERROR OF HIS OR HER WAYS.
DO YOU THINK THAT IT REALLY WORKS?
SOMETIMES.
AND SOME DAYS, THAT'S ENOUGH.
—END—

Grimm Fairy Tales
Volume 14

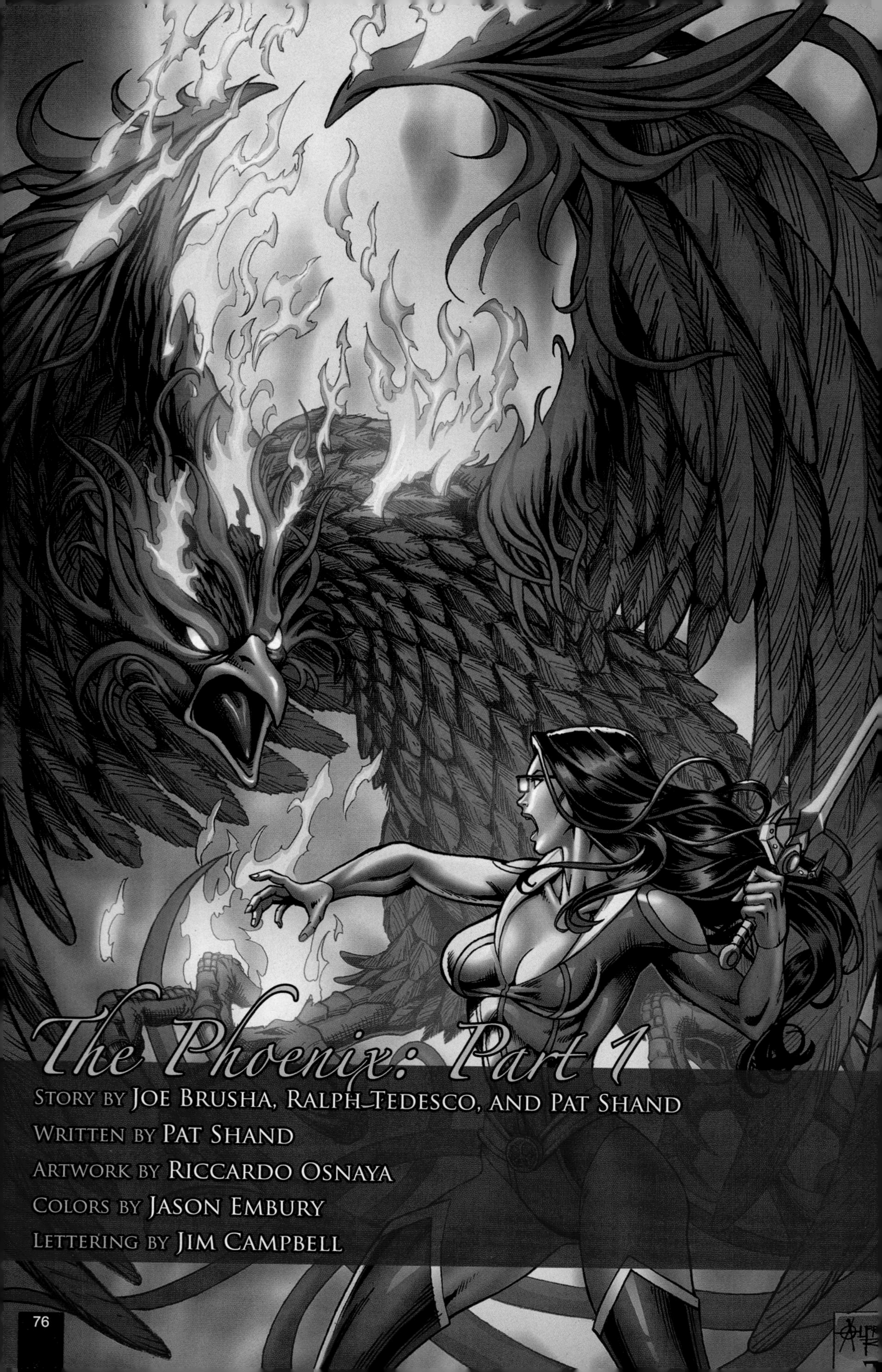
The Phoenix: Part 1
Story by Joe Brusha, Ralph Tedesco, and Pat Shand
Written by Pat Shand
Artwork by Riccardo Osnaya
Colors by Jason Embury
Lettering by Jim Campbell

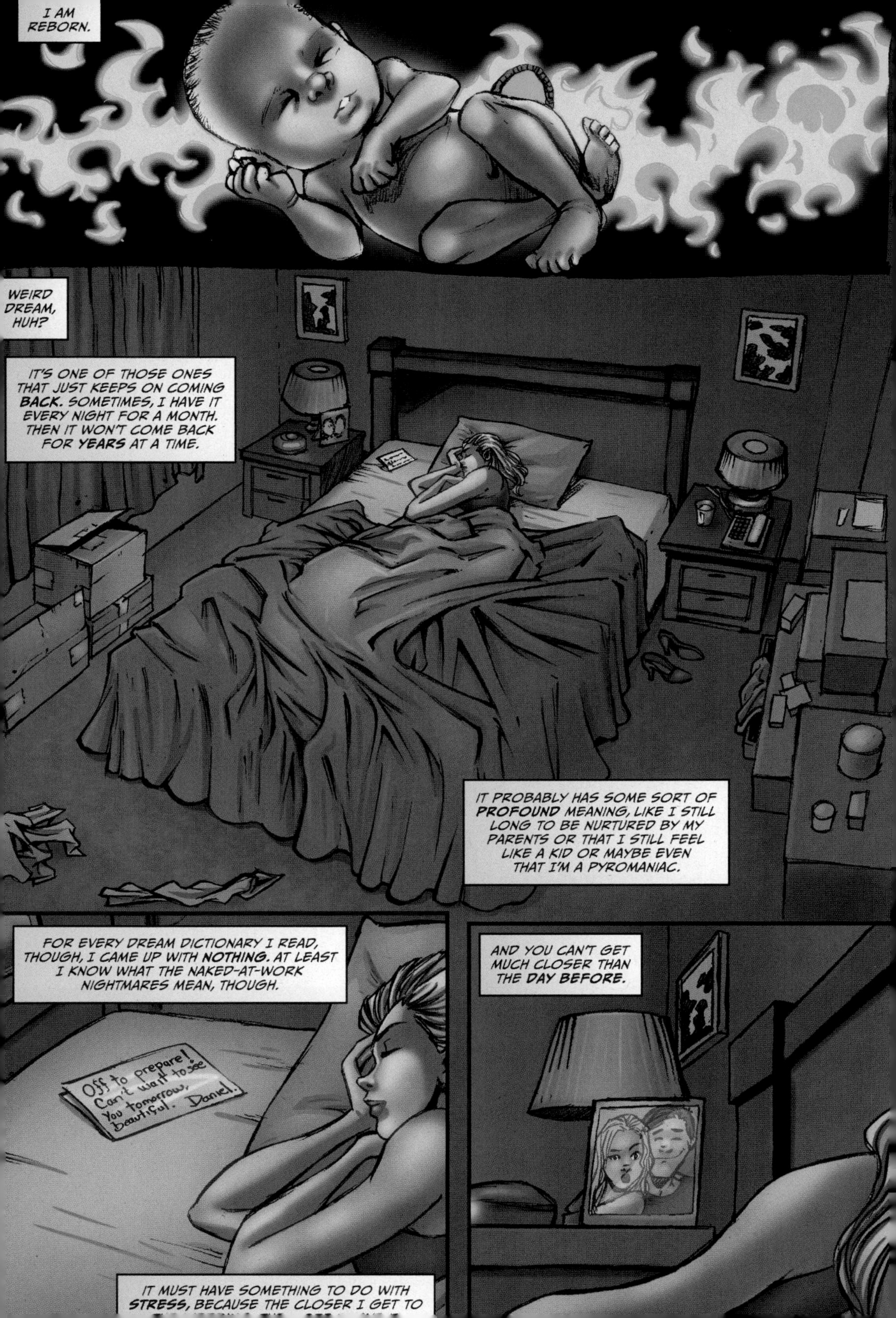

I AM REBORN.
WEIRD DREAM, HUH?
IT'S ONE OF THOSE ONES THAT JUST KEEPS ON COMING BACK. SOMETIMES, I HAVE IT EVERY NIGHT FOR A MONTH. THEN IT WON'T COME BACK FOR YEARS AT A TIME.
IT PROBABLY HAS SOME SORT OF PROFOUND MEANING, LIKE I STILL LONG TO BE NURTURED BY MY PARENTS OR THAT I STILL FEEL LIKE A KID OR MAYBE EVEN THAT I'M A PYROMANIAC.
FOR EVERY DREAM DICTIONARY I READ, THOUGH, I CAME UP WITH NOTHING. AT LEAST I KNOW WHAT THE NAKED-AT-WORK NIGHTMARES MEAN, THOUGH.
Off to prepare! Can't wait to see you tomorrow, beautiful. Daniel.
IT MUST HAVE SOMETHING TO DO WITH STRESS, BECAUSE THE CLOSER I GET TO
AND YOU CAN'T GET MUCH CLOSER THAN THE DAY BEFORE.

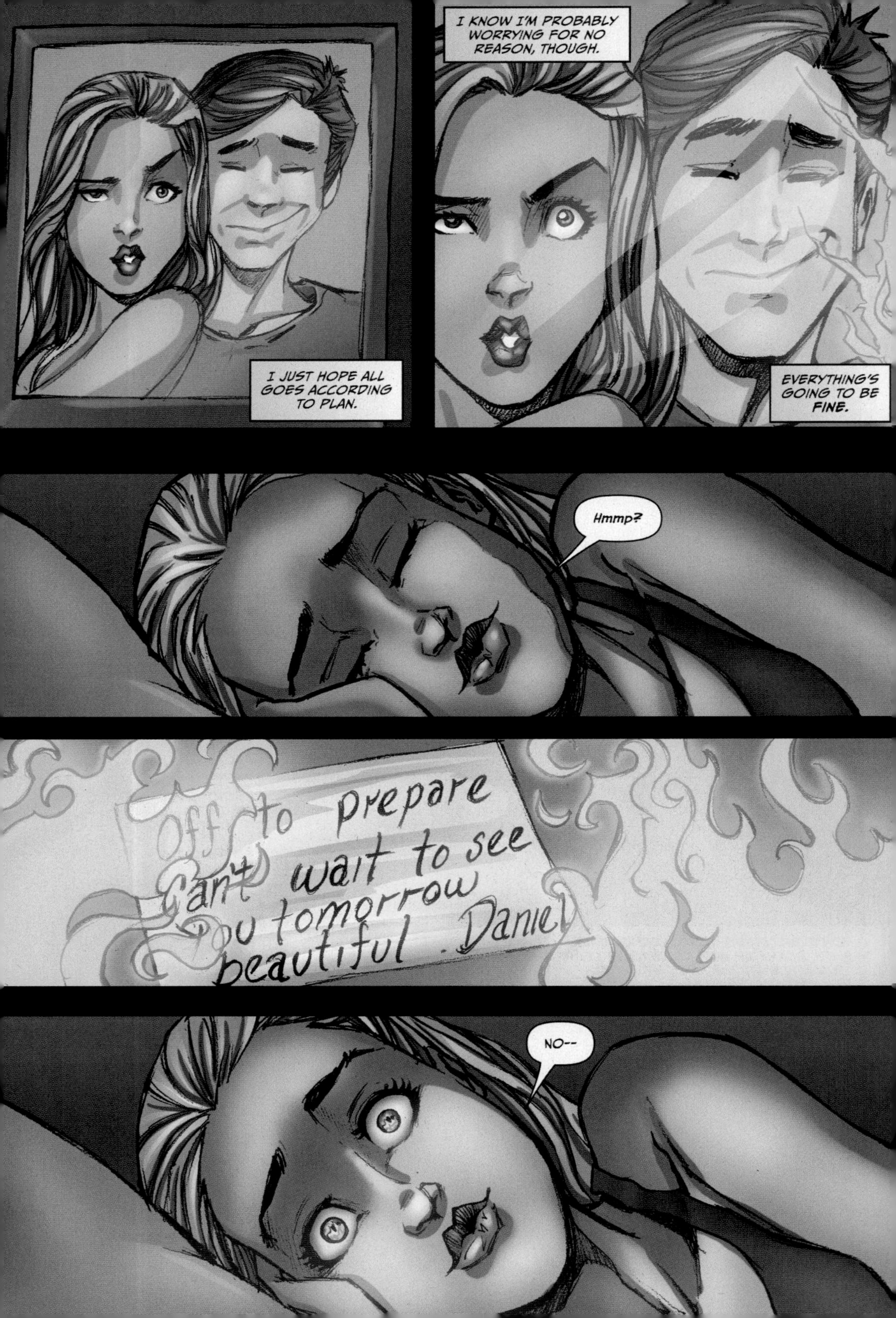
I JUST HOPE ALL GOES ACCORDING TO PLAN.
I KNOW I'M PROBABLY WORRYING FOR NO REASON, THOUGH.
EVERYTHING'S GOING TO BE FINE.
Hmmp?
Off to prepare
Can't wait to see
you tomorrow
beautiful .Daniel
NO--

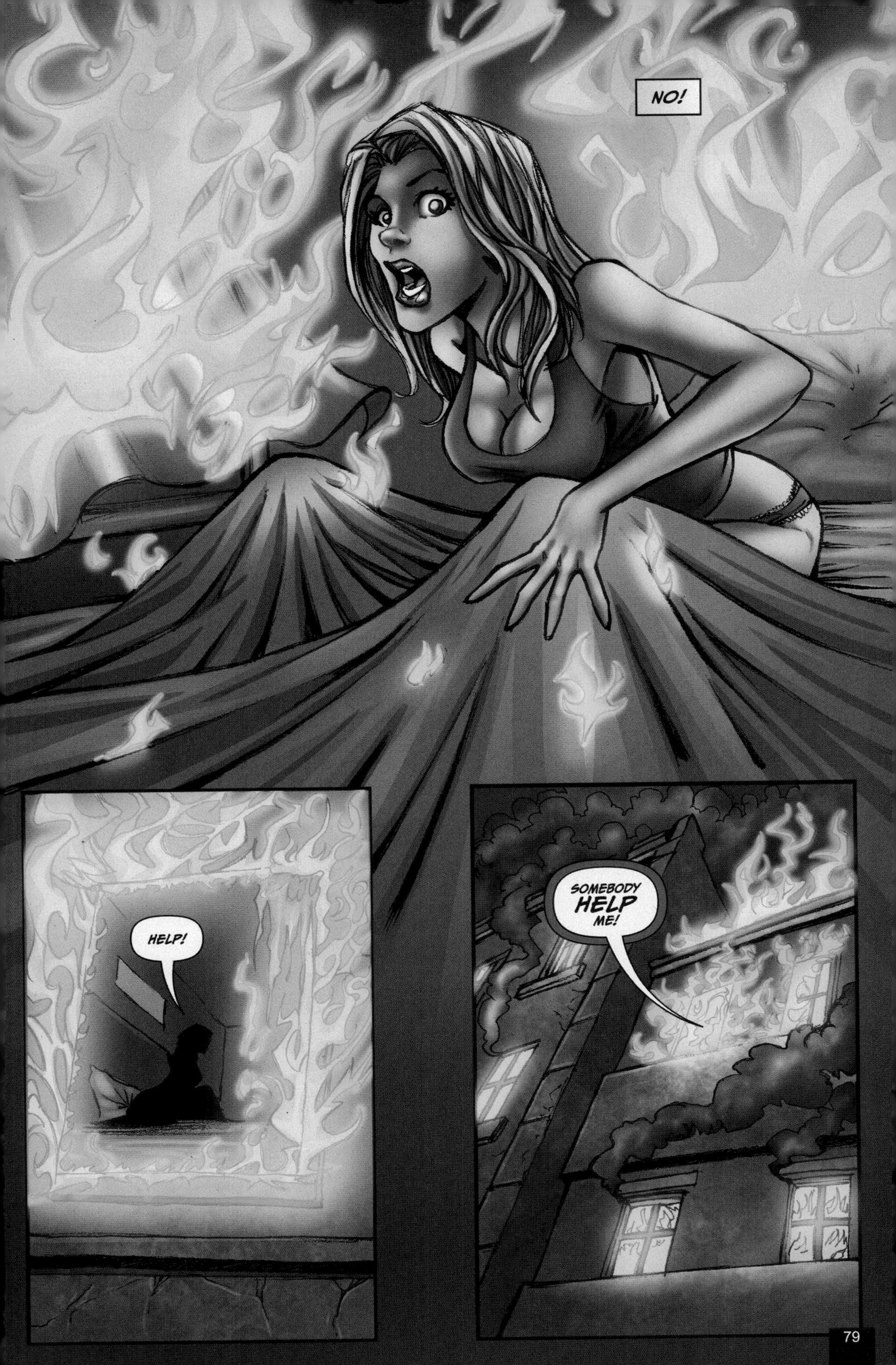
NO!
HELP!
SOMEBODY HELP ME!

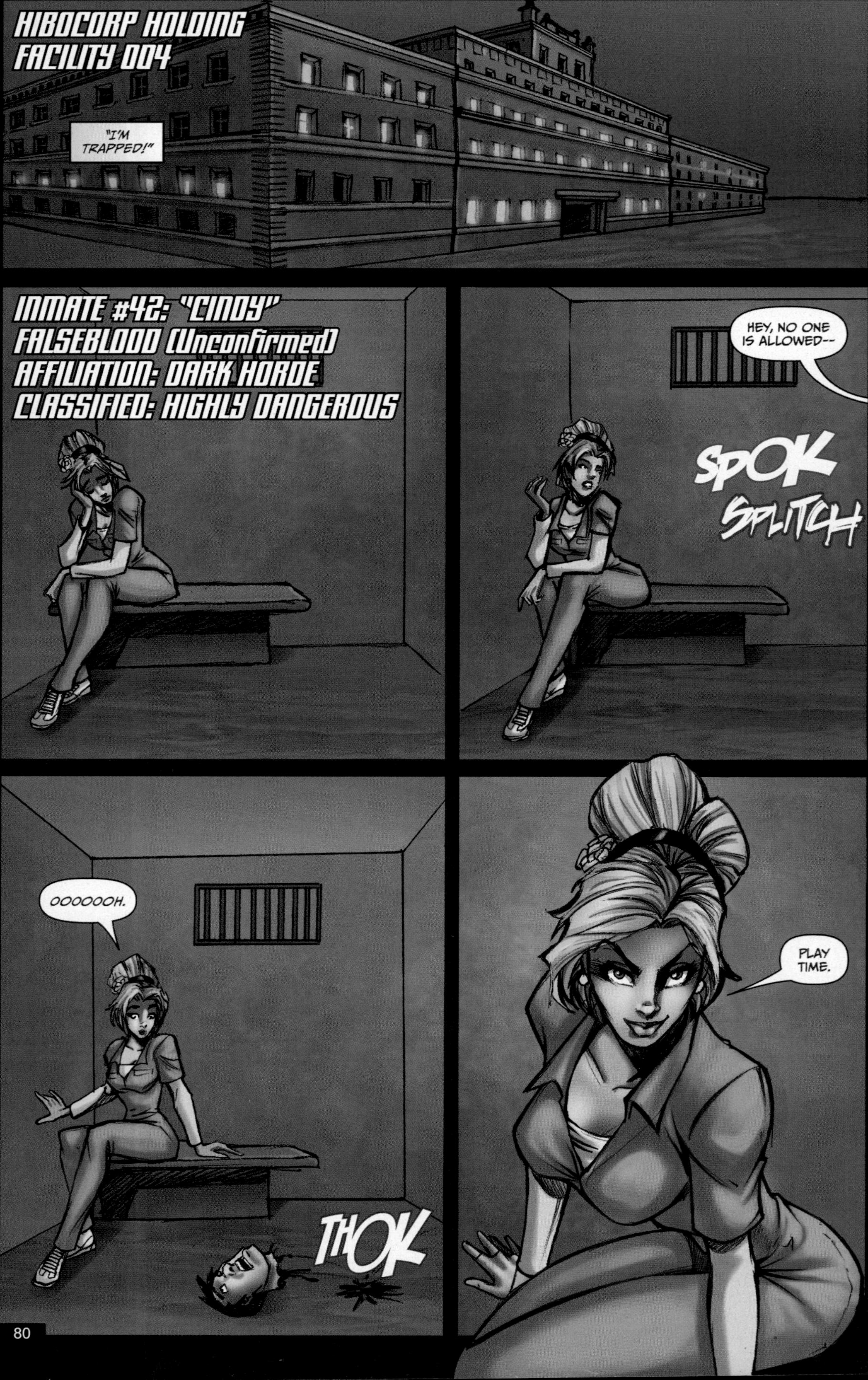
HIBOCORP HOLDING FACILITY 004
"I'M TRAPPED!"
INMATE #42: "CINDY"
FALSEBLOOD (Unconfirmed)
AFFILIATION: DARK HORDE
CLASSIFIED: HIGHLY DANGEROUS
HEY, NO ONE IS ALLOWED--
SPOK
SPLITCH
OOOOOOH.
THOK
PLAY TIME.

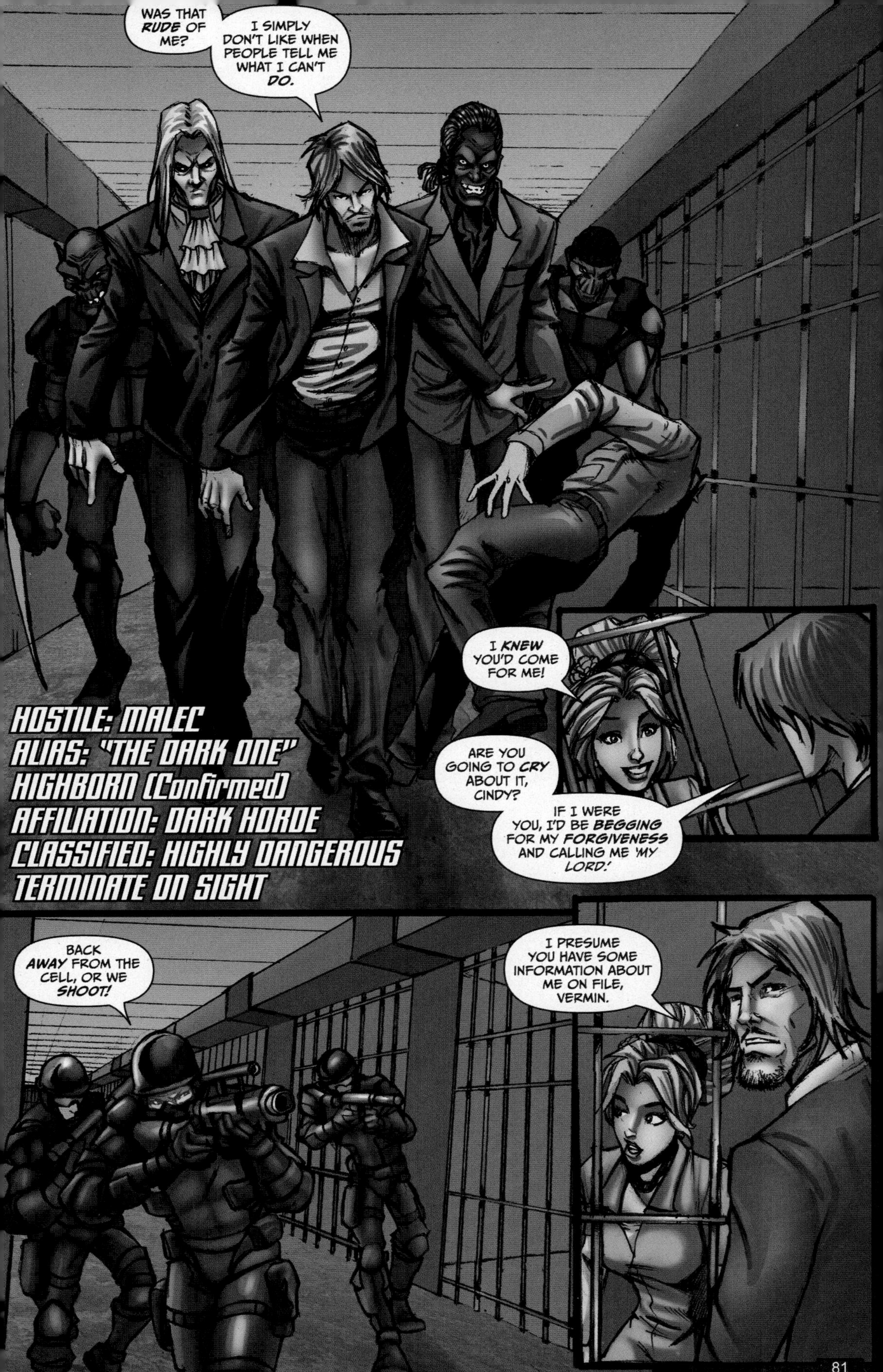
WAS THAT RUDE OF ME?
I SIMPLY DON'T LIKE WHEN PEOPLE TELL ME WHAT I CAN'T DO.
HOSTILE: MALEC
ALIAS: "THE DARK ONE"
HIGHBORN (Confirmed)
AFFILIATION: DARK HORDE
CLASSIFIED: HIGHLY DANGEROUS
TERMINATE ON SIGHT
I KNEW YOU'D COME FOR ME!
ARE YOU GOING TO CRY ABOUT IT, CINDY?
IF I WERE YOU, I'D BE BEGGING FOR MY FORGIVENESS AND CALLING ME 'MY LORD.'
BACK AWAY FROM THE CELL, OR WE SHOOT!
I PRESUME YOU HAVE SOME INFORMATION ABOUT ME ON FILE, VERMIN.

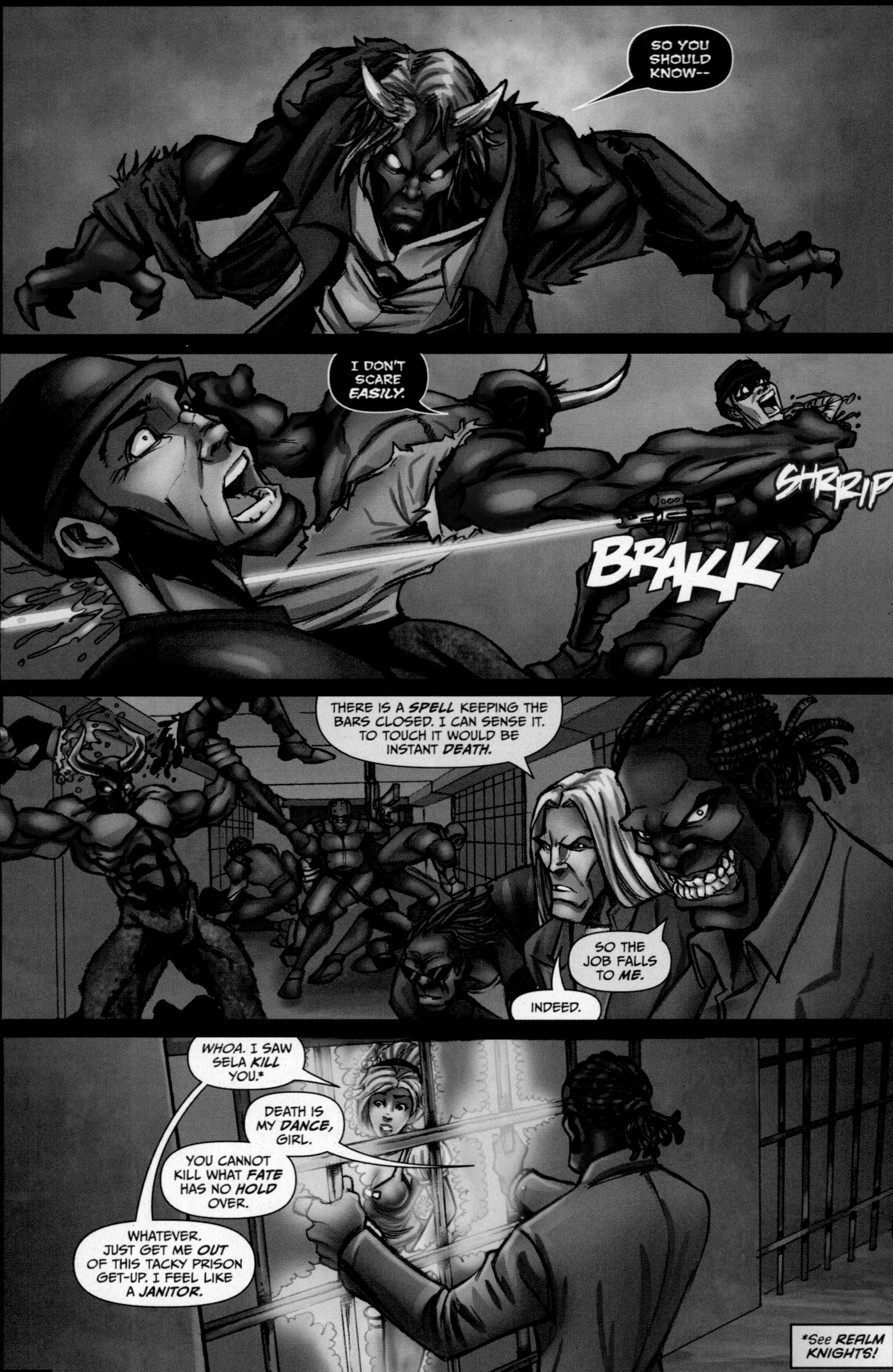

SO YOU SHOULD KNOW--
I DON'T SCARE *EASILY.*
SHRRIP
BRAKK
THERE IS A *SPELL* KEEPING THE BARS CLOSED. I CAN SENSE IT. TO TOUCH IT WOULD BE INSTANT *DEATH.*
SO THE JOB FALLS TO *ME.*
INDEED.
WHOA. I SAW SELA *KILL* YOU.*
DEATH IS MY *DANCE,* GIRL.
YOU CANNOT KILL WHAT *FATE* HAS NO *HOLD* OVER.
WHATEVER. JUST GET ME *OUT* OF THIS TACKY PRISON GET-UP. I FEEL LIKE A *JANITOR.*
*See *REALM KNIGHTS!*

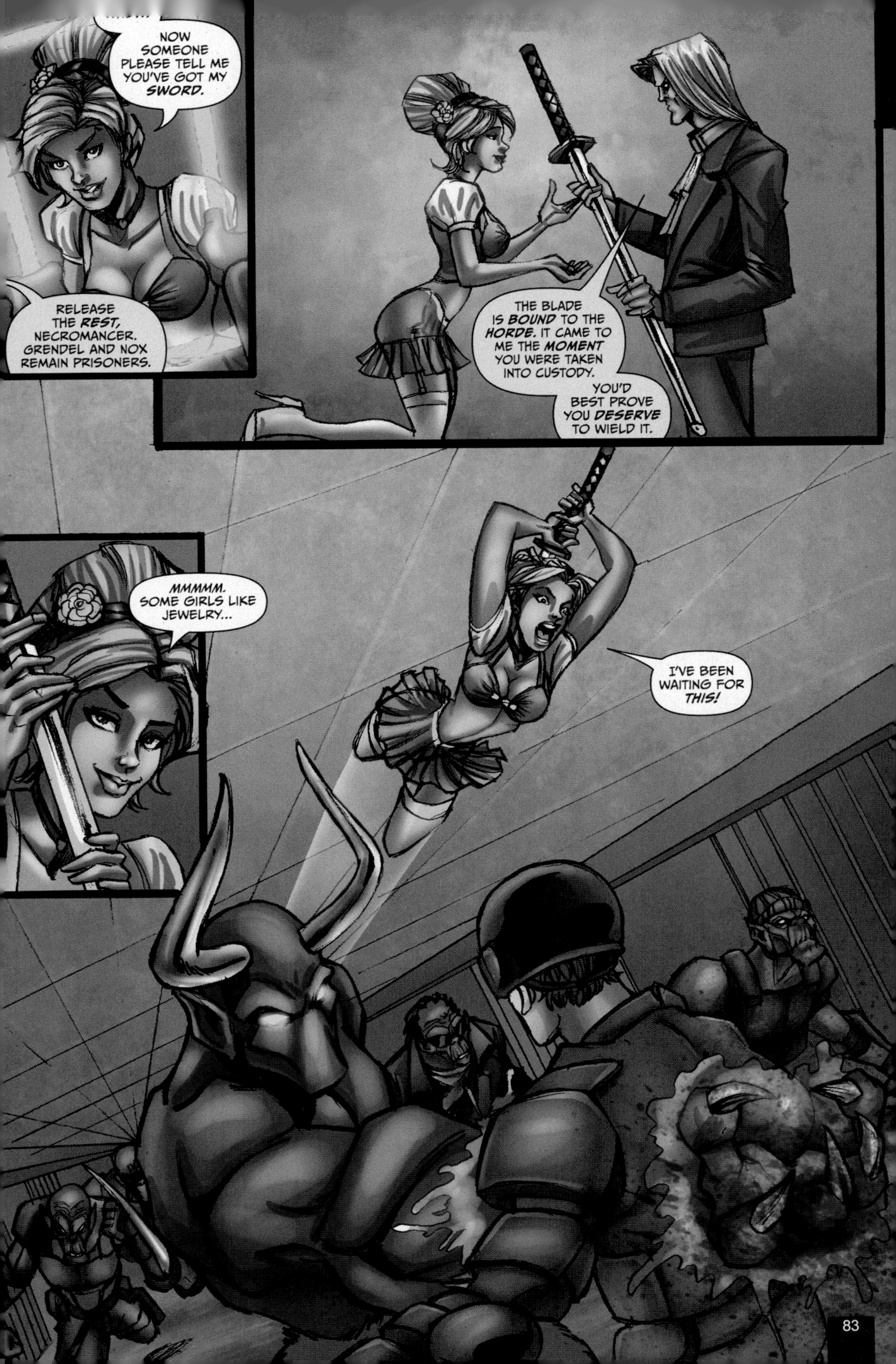
NOW SOMEONE PLEASE TELL ME YOU'VE GOT MY SWORD.
RELEASE THE REST, NECROMANCER. GRENDEL AND NOX REMAIN PRISONERS.
THE BLADE IS BOUND TO THE HORDE. IT CAME TO ME THE MOMENT YOU WERE TAKEN INTO CUSTODY.
YOU'D BEST PROVE YOU DESERVE TO WIELD IT.
MMMMM. SOME GIRLS LIKE JEWELRY...
I'VE BEEN WAITING FOR THIS!

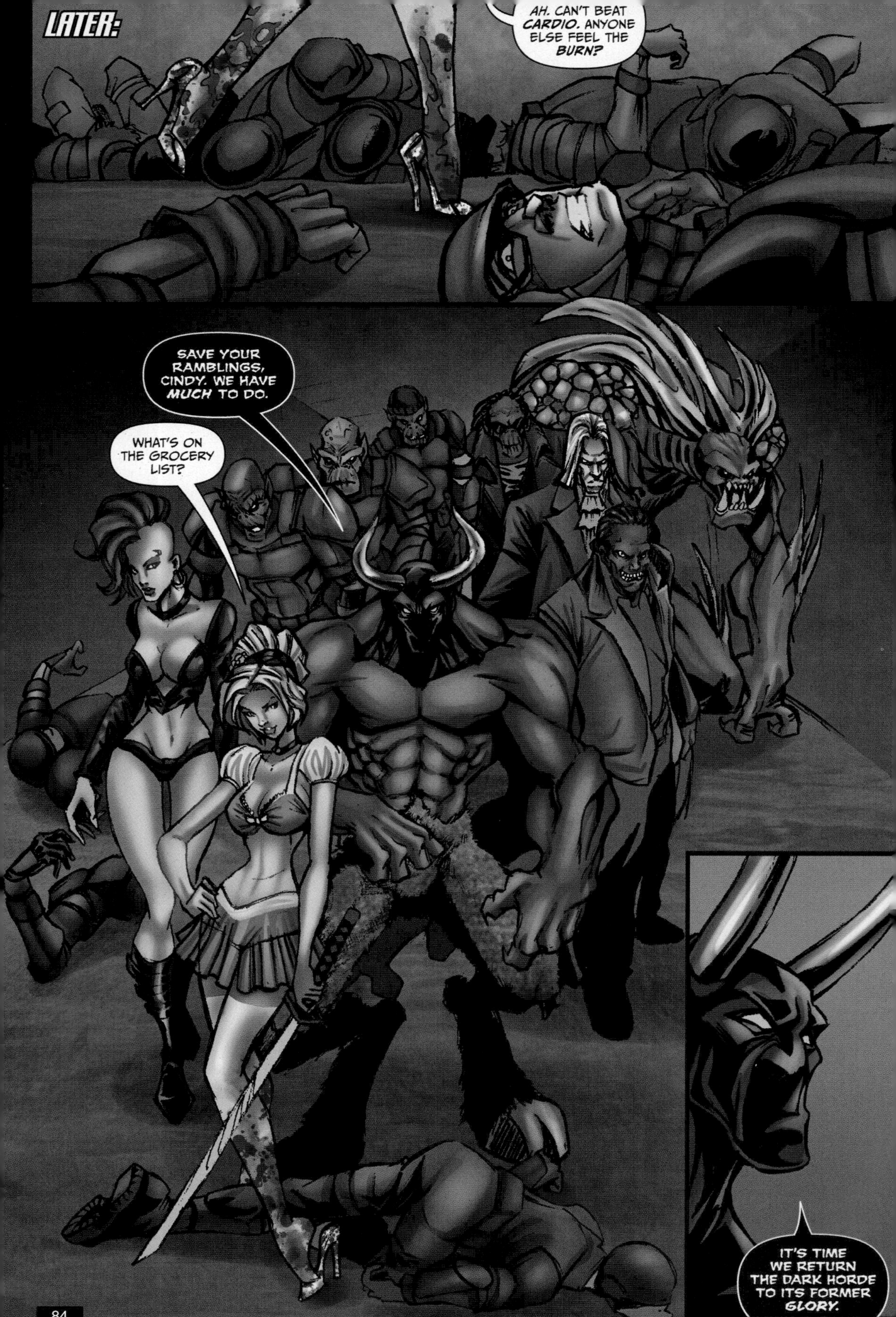
LATER:
AH. CAN'T BEAT CARDIO. ANYONE ELSE FEEL THE BURN?
SAVE YOUR RAMBLINGS, CINDY. WE HAVE MUCH TO DO.
WHAT'S ON THE GROCERY LIST?
IT'S TIME WE RETURN THE DARK HORDE TO ITS FORMER GLORY.

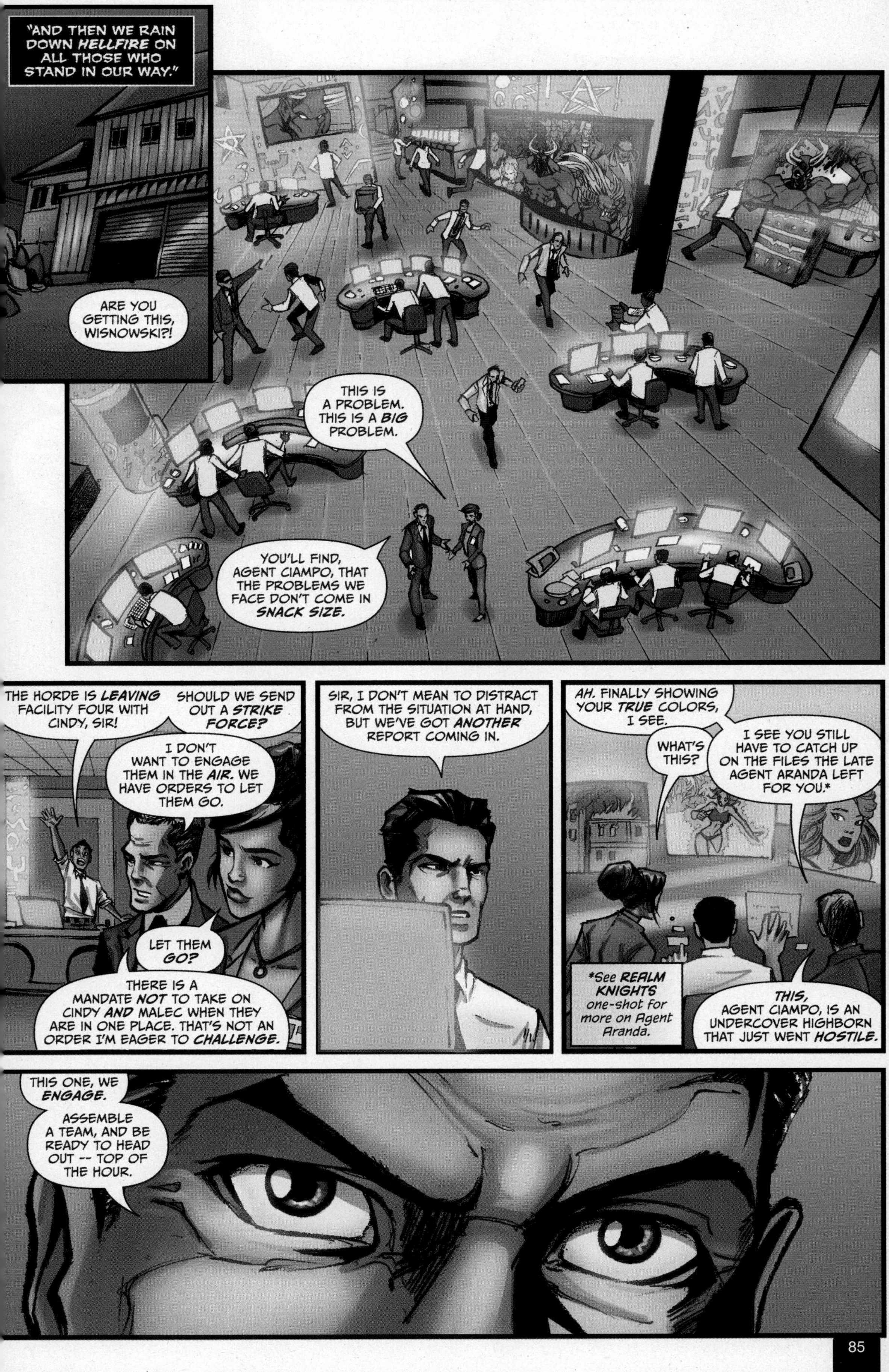
"AND THEN WE RAIN DOWN HELLFIRE ON ALL THOSE WHO STAND IN OUR WAY."
ARE YOU GETTING THIS, WISNOWSKI?!
THIS IS A PROBLEM. THIS IS A BIG PROBLEM.
YOU'LL FIND, AGENT CIAMPO, THAT THE PROBLEMS WE FACE DON'T COME IN SNACK SIZE.
THE HORDE IS LEAVING FACILITY FOUR WITH CINDY, SIR!
SHOULD WE SEND OUT A STRIKE FORCE?
I DON'T WANT TO ENGAGE THEM IN THE AIR. WE HAVE ORDERS TO LET THEM GO.
LET THEM GO?
THERE IS A MANDATE NOT TO TAKE ON CINDY AND MALEC WHEN THEY ARE IN ONE PLACE. THAT'S NOT AN ORDER I'M EAGER TO CHALLENGE.
SIR, I DON'T MEAN TO DISTRACT FROM THE SITUATION AT HAND, BUT WE'VE GOT ANOTHER REPORT COMING IN.
AH. FINALLY SHOWING YOUR TRUE COLORS, I SEE.
WHAT'S THIS?
I SEE YOU STILL HAVE TO CATCH UP ON THE FILES THE LATE AGENT ARANDA LEFT FOR YOU.*
*See REALM KNIGHTS one-shot for more on Agent Aranda.
THIS, AGENT CIAMPO, IS AN UNDERCOVER HIGHBORN THAT JUST WENT HOSTILE.
THIS ONE, WE ENGAGE.
ASSEMBLE A TEAM, AND BE READY TO HEAD OUT -- TOP OF THE HOUR.

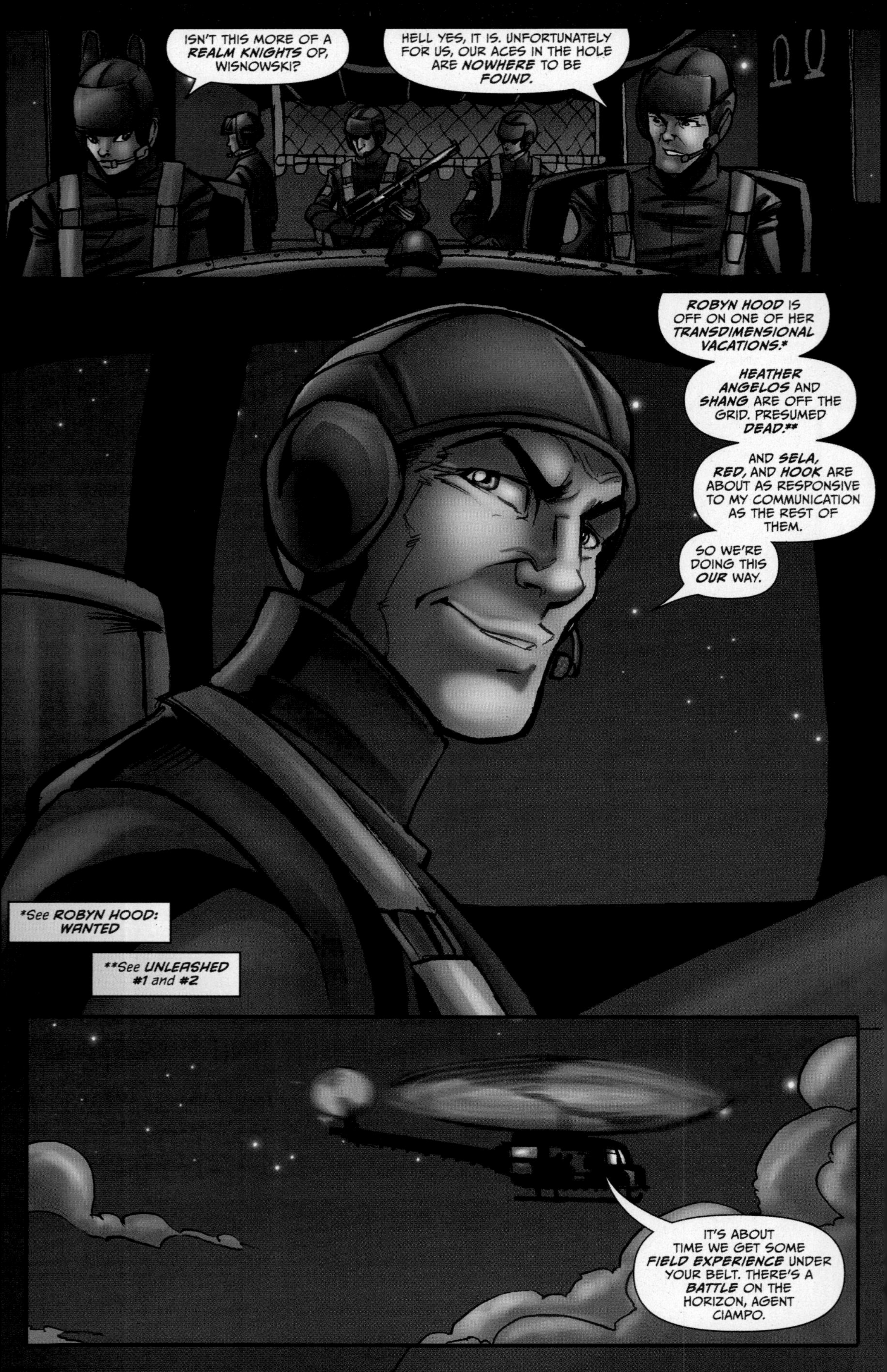

ISN'T THIS MORE OF A REALM KNIGHTS OP, WISNOWSKI?
HELL YES, IT IS. UNFORTUNATELY FOR US, OUR ACES IN THE HOLE ARE NOWHERE TO BE FOUND.
ROBYN HOOD IS OFF ON ONE OF HER TRANSDIMENSIONAL VACATIONS.*
HEATHER ANGELOS AND SHANG ARE OFF THE GRID. PRESUMED DEAD.**
AND SELA, RED, AND HOOK ARE ABOUT AS RESPONSIVE TO MY COMMUNICATION AS THE REST OF THEM.
SO WE'RE DOING THIS OUR WAY.
*See ROBYN HOOD: WANTED
**See UNLEASHED #1 and #2
IT'S ABOUT TIME WE GET SOME FIELD EXPERIENCE UNDER YOUR BELT. THERE'S A BATTLE ON THE HORIZON, AGENT CIAMPO.

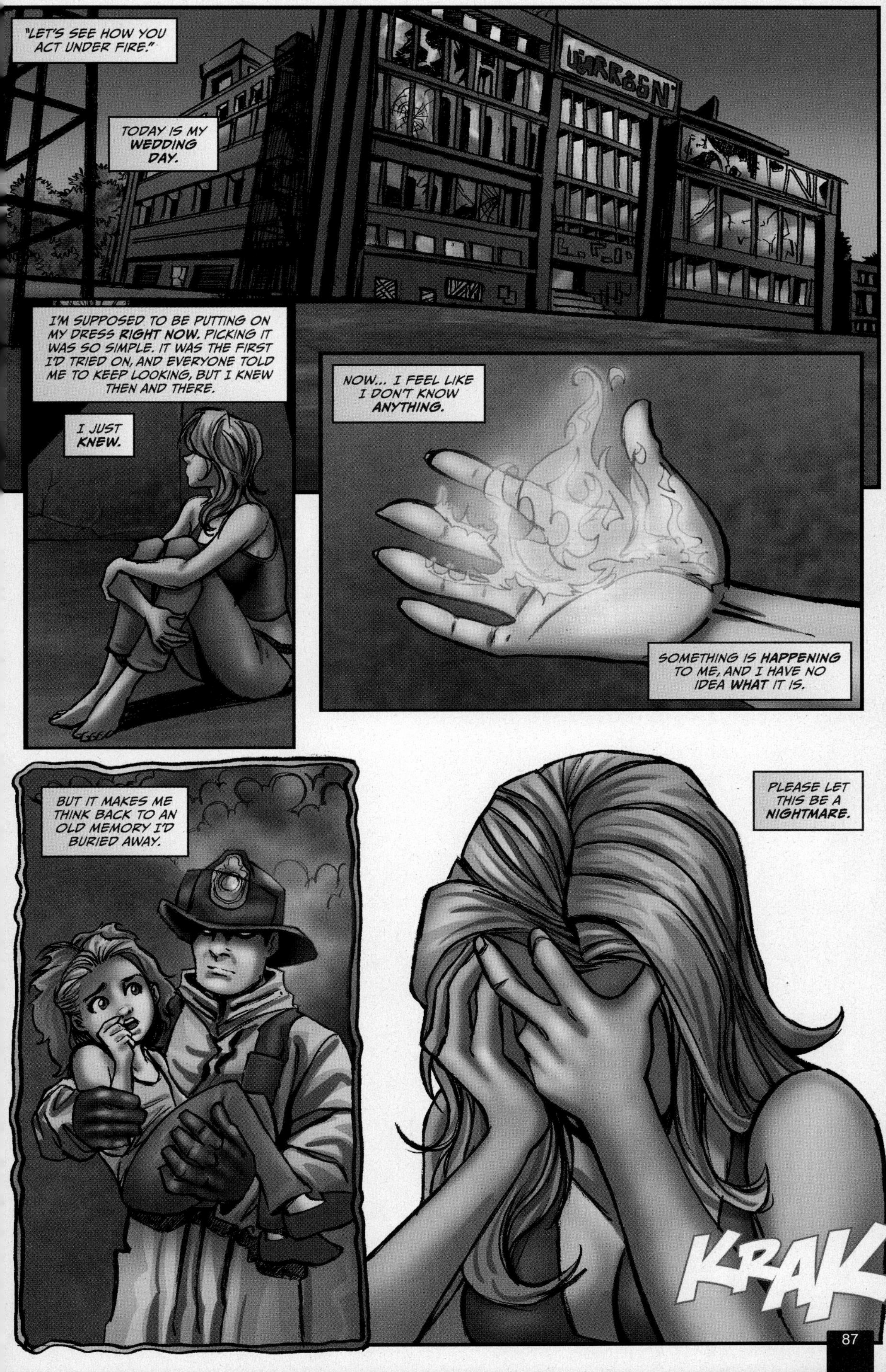

"LET'S SEE HOW YOU ACT UNDER FIRE."
TODAY IS MY WEDDING DAY.
I'M SUPPOSED TO BE PUTTING ON MY DRESS RIGHT NOW. PICKING IT WAS SO SIMPLE. IT WAS THE FIRST I'D TRIED ON, AND EVERYONE TOLD ME TO KEEP LOOKING, BUT I KNEW THEN AND THERE.
I JUST KNEW.
NOW... I FEEL LIKE I DON'T KNOW ANYTHING.
SOMETHING IS HAPPENING TO ME, AND I HAVE NO IDEA WHAT IT IS.
BUT IT MAKES ME THINK BACK TO AN OLD MEMORY I'D BURIED AWAY.
PLEASE LET THIS BE A NIGHTMARE.
KRAK

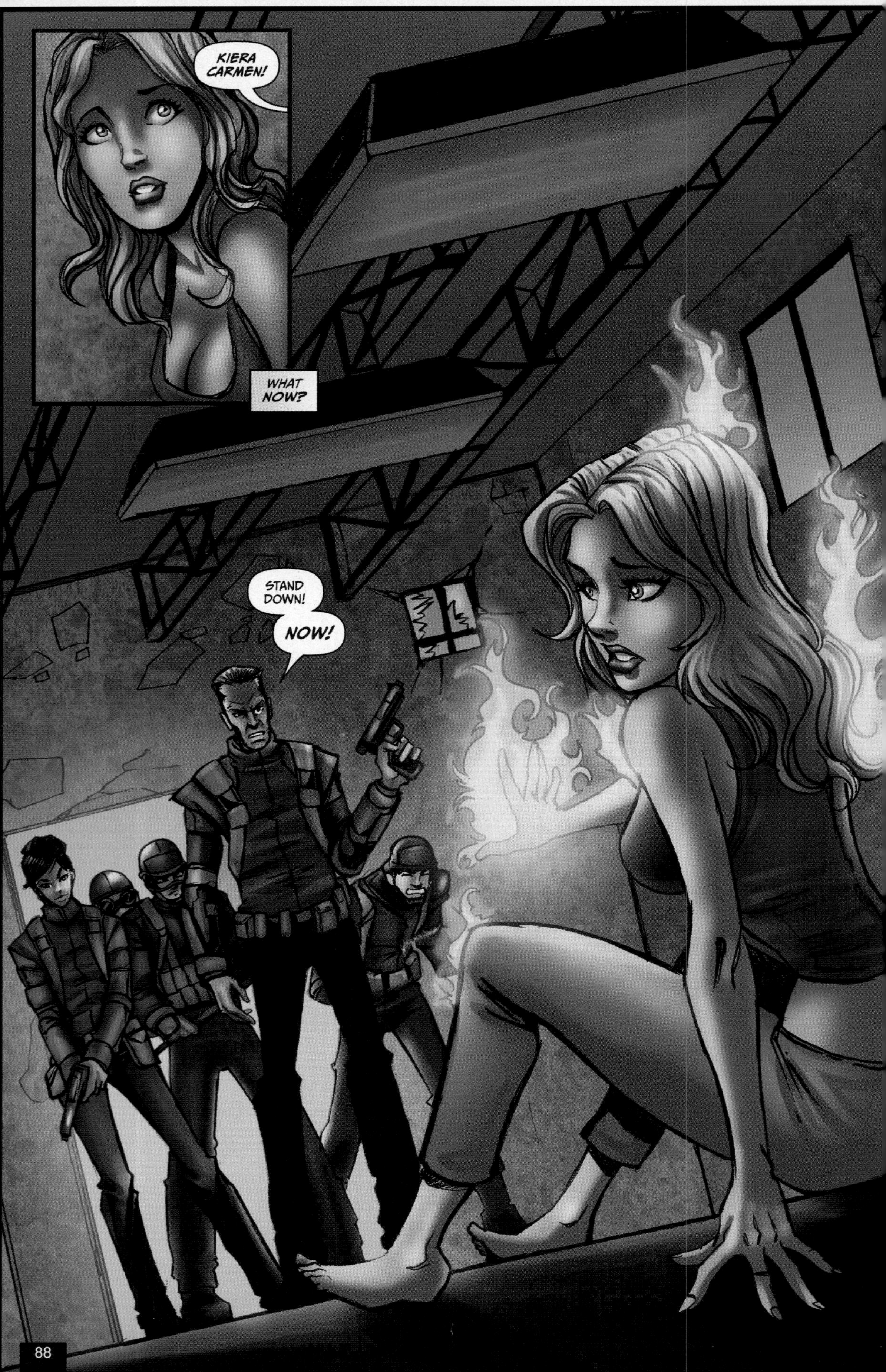
KIERA CARMEN!
WHAT NOW?
STAND DOWN!
NOW!

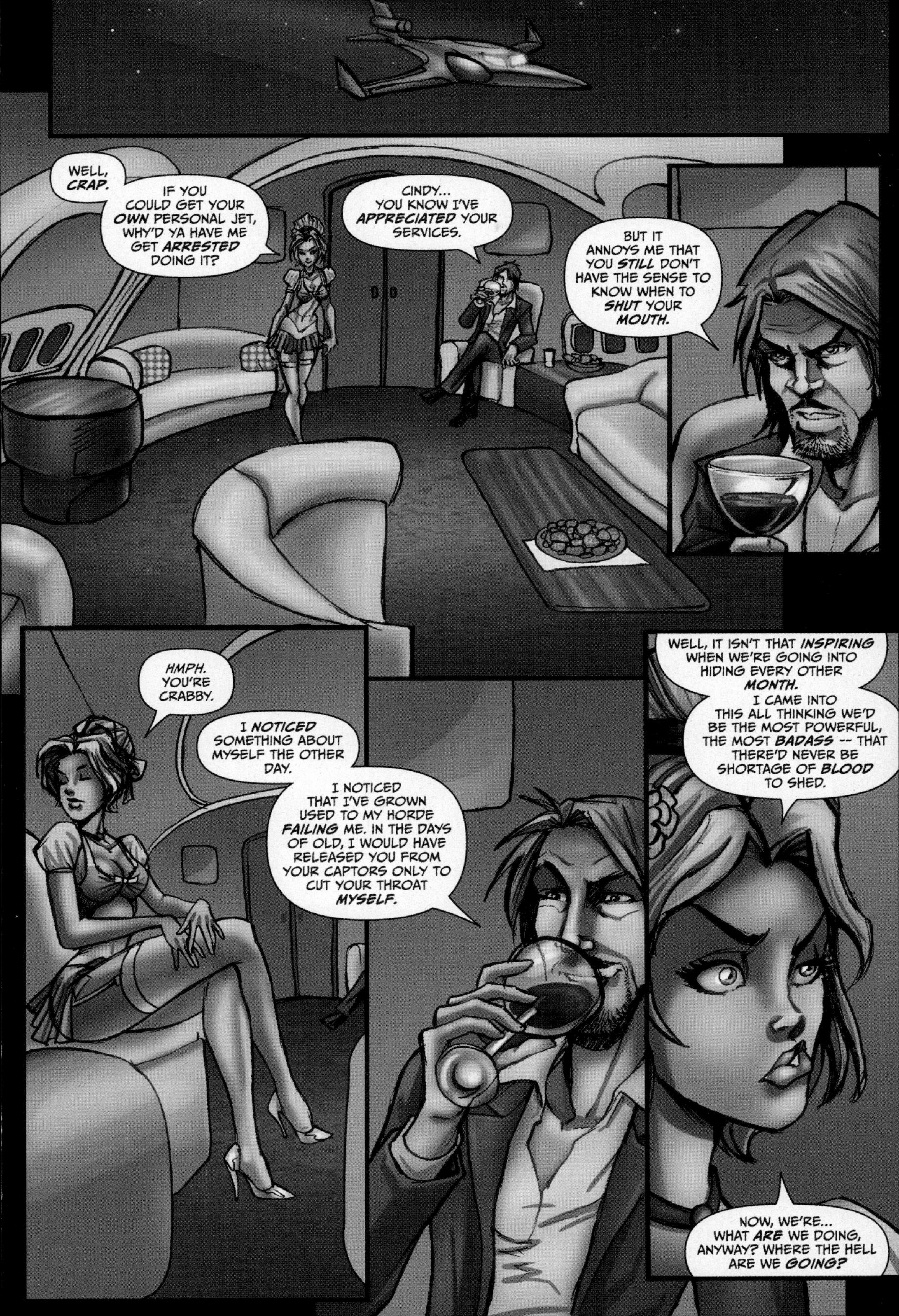
WELL, CRAP.
IF YOU COULD GET YOUR OWN PERSONAL JET, WHY'D YA HAVE ME GET ARRESTED DOING IT?
CINDY... YOU KNOW I'VE APPRECIATED YOUR SERVICES.
BUT IT ANNOYS ME THAT YOU STILL DON'T HAVE THE SENSE TO KNOW WHEN TO SHUT YOUR MOUTH.
HMPH. YOU'RE CRABBY.
I NOTICED SOMETHING ABOUT MYSELF THE OTHER DAY.
I NOTICED THAT I'VE GROWN USED TO MY HORDE FAILING ME. IN THE DAYS OF OLD, I WOULD HAVE RELEASED YOU FROM YOUR CAPTORS ONLY TO CUT YOUR THROAT MYSELF.
WELL, IT ISN'T THAT INSPIRING WHEN WE'RE GOING INTO HIDING EVERY OTHER MONTH.
I CAME INTO THIS ALL THINKING WE'D BE THE MOST POWERFUL, THE MOST BADASS -- THAT THERE'D NEVER BE SHORTAGE OF BLOOD TO SHED.
NOW, WE'RE... WHAT ARE WE DOING, ANYWAY? WHERE THE HELL ARE WE GOING?

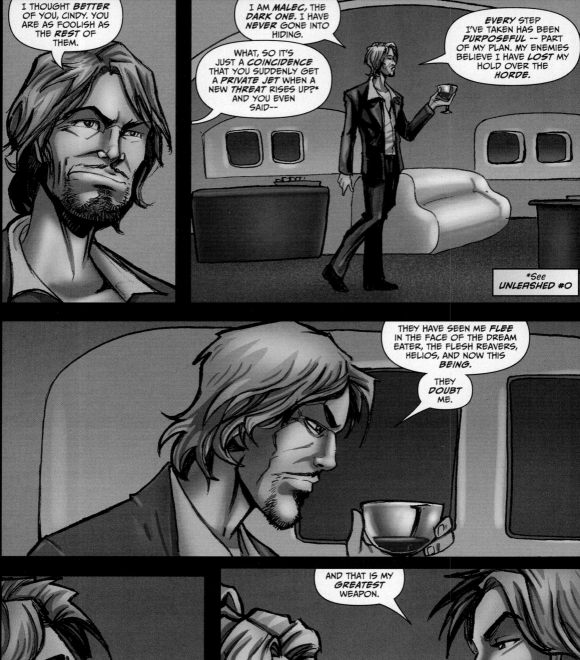

I THOUGHT *BETTER* OF YOU, CINDY. YOU ARE AS FOOLISH AS THE *REST* OF THEM.

I AM *MALEC*, THE *DARK ONE*. I HAVE *NEVER* GONE INTO HIDING.

WHAT, SO IT'S JUST A *COINCIDENCE* THAT YOU SUDDENLY GET A *PRIVATE JET* WHEN A NEW *THREAT* RISES UP?* AND YOU EVEN SAID--

EVERY STEP I'VE TAKEN HAS BEEN *PURPOSEFUL* -- PART OF MY PLAN. MY ENEMIES BELIEVE I HAVE *LOST* MY HOLD OVER THE *HORDE*.

*See UNLEASHED #0

THEY HAVE SEEN ME *FLEE* IN THE FACE OF THE DREAM EATER, THE FLESH REAVERS, HELIOS, AND NOW THIS *BEING*.

THEY *DOUBT* ME.

AND THAT IS MY *GREATEST* WEAPON.

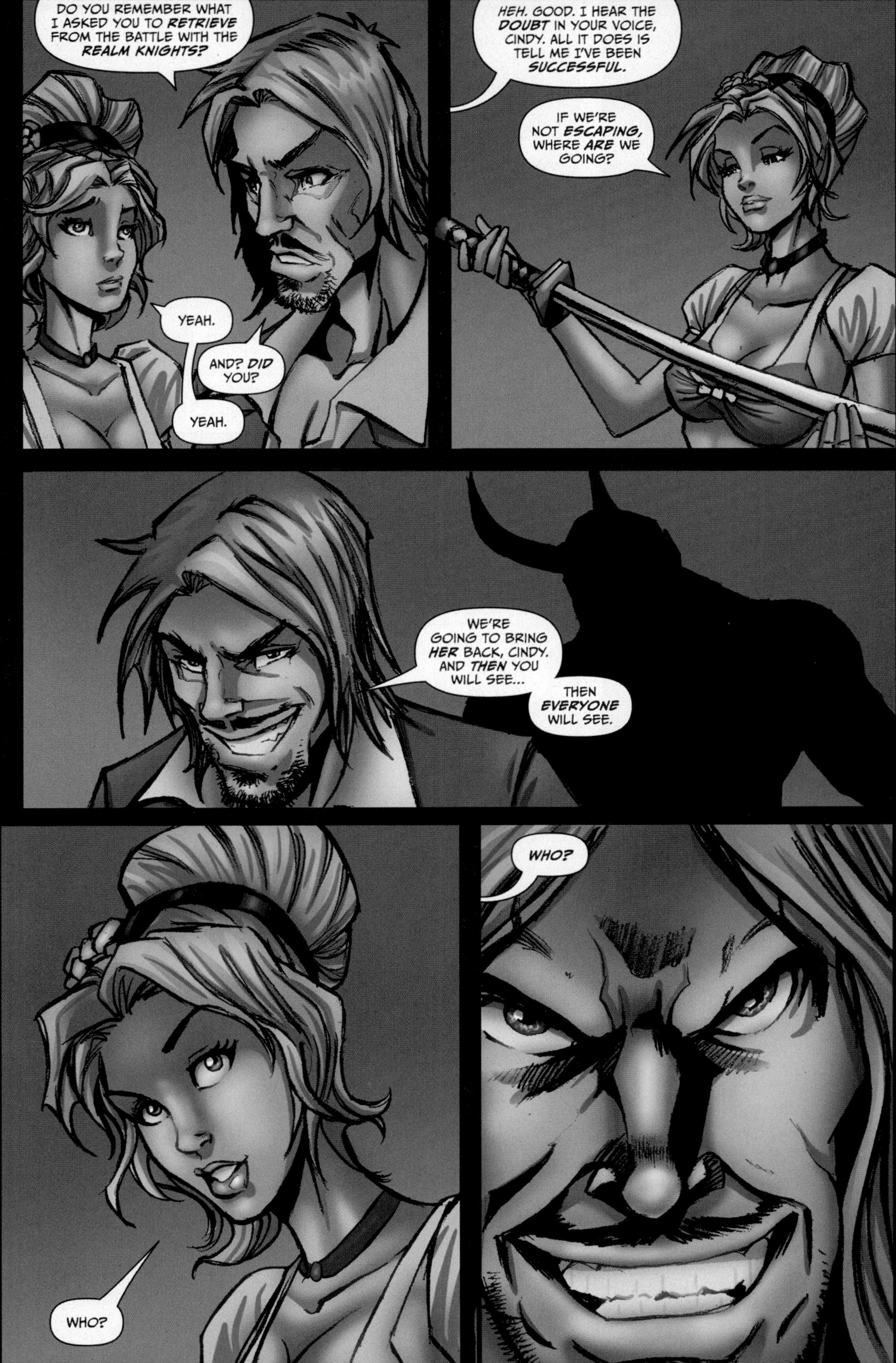
DO YOU REMEMBER WHAT I ASKED YOU TO *RETRIEVE* FROM THE BATTLE WITH THE *REALM KNIGHTS?*
YEAH.
AND? *DID* YOU?
YEAH.
HEH. GOOD. I HEAR THE *DOUBT* IN YOUR VOICE, CINDY. ALL IT DOES IS TELL ME I'VE BEEN *SUCCESSFUL.*
IF WE'RE NOT *ESCAPING,* WHERE *ARE* WE GOING?
WE'RE GOING TO BRING *HER* BACK, CINDY. AND *THEN* YOU WILL SEE...
THEN *EVERYONE* WILL SEE.
WHO?
WHO?

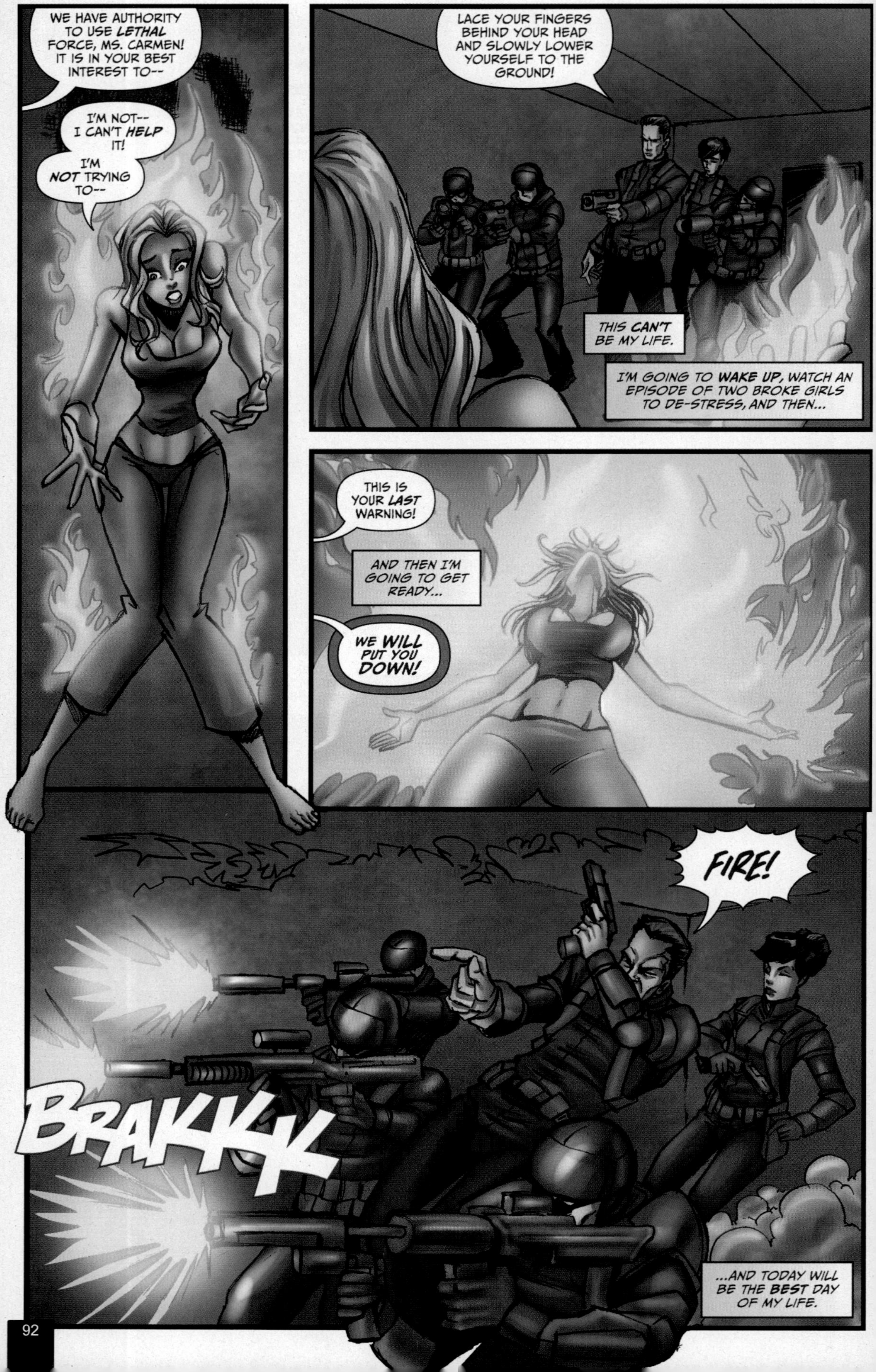
WE HAVE AUTHORITY TO USE LETHAL FORCE, MS. CARMEN! IT IS IN YOUR BEST INTEREST TO--
I'M NOT-- I CAN'T HELP IT!
I'M NOT TRYING TO--
LACE YOUR FINGERS BEHIND YOUR HEAD AND SLOWLY LOWER YOURSELF TO THE GROUND!
THIS CAN'T BE MY LIFE.
I'M GOING TO WAKE UP, WATCH AN EPISODE OF TWO BROKE GIRLS TO DE-STRESS, AND THEN...
THIS IS YOUR LAST WARNING!
AND THEN I'M GOING TO GET READY...
WE WILL PUT YOU DOWN!
FIRE!
BRAKKK
...AND TODAY WILL BE THE BEST DAY OF MY LIFE.

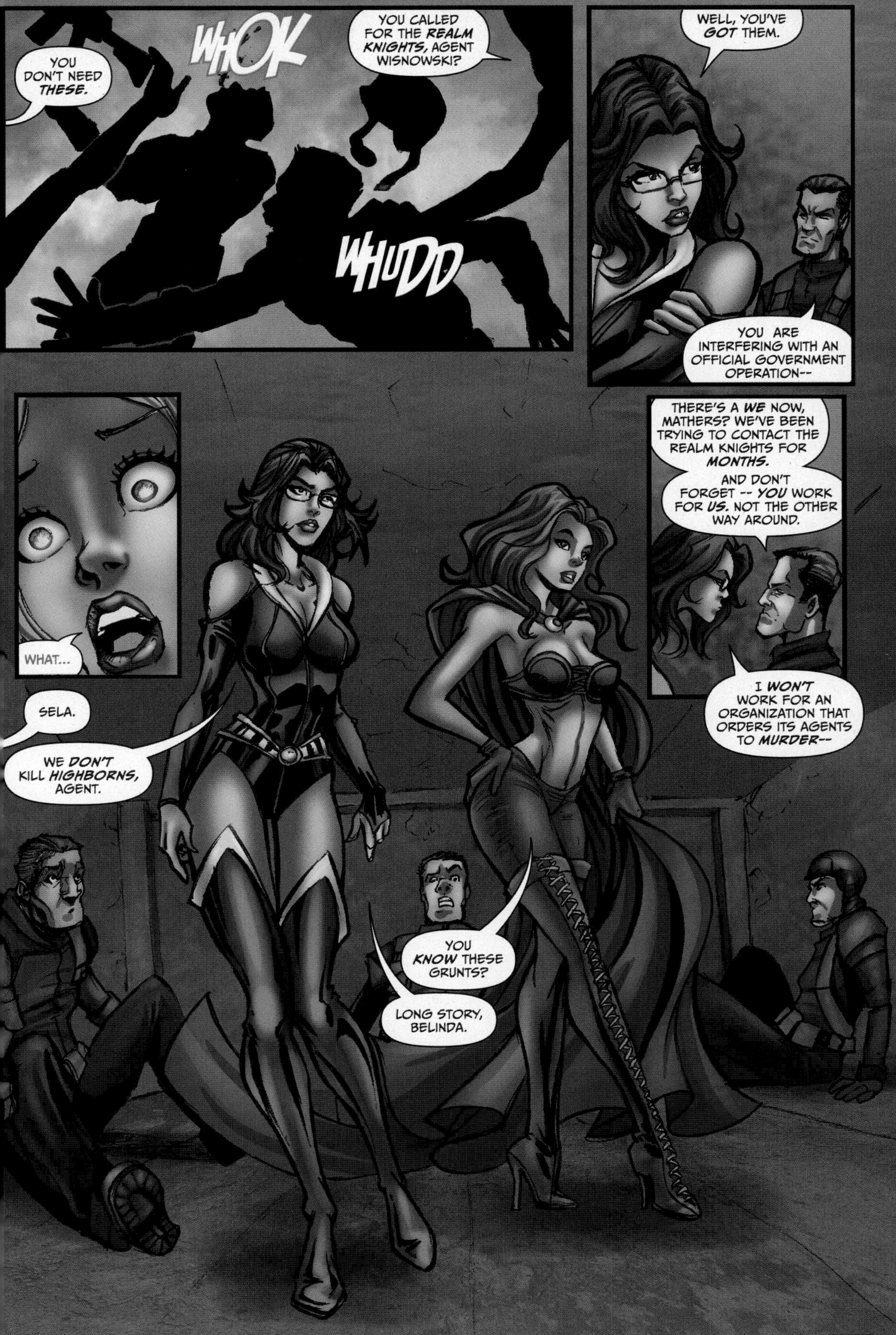

YOU DON'T NEED THESE.
WHOK
YOU CALLED FOR THE REALM KNIGHTS, AGENT WISNOWSKI?
WHUDD
WELL, YOU'VE GOT THEM.
YOU ARE INTERFERING WITH AN OFFICIAL GOVERNMENT OPERATION--
WHAT...
SELA.
WE DON'T KILL HIGHBORNS, AGENT.
THERE'S A WE NOW, MATHERS? WE'VE BEEN TRYING TO CONTACT THE REALM KNIGHTS FOR MONTHS.
AND DON'T FORGET -- YOU WORK FOR US. NOT THE OTHER WAY AROUND.
I WON'T WORK FOR AN ORGANIZATION THAT ORDERS ITS AGENTS TO MURDER--
YOU KNOW THESE GRUNTS?
LONG STORY, BELINDA.

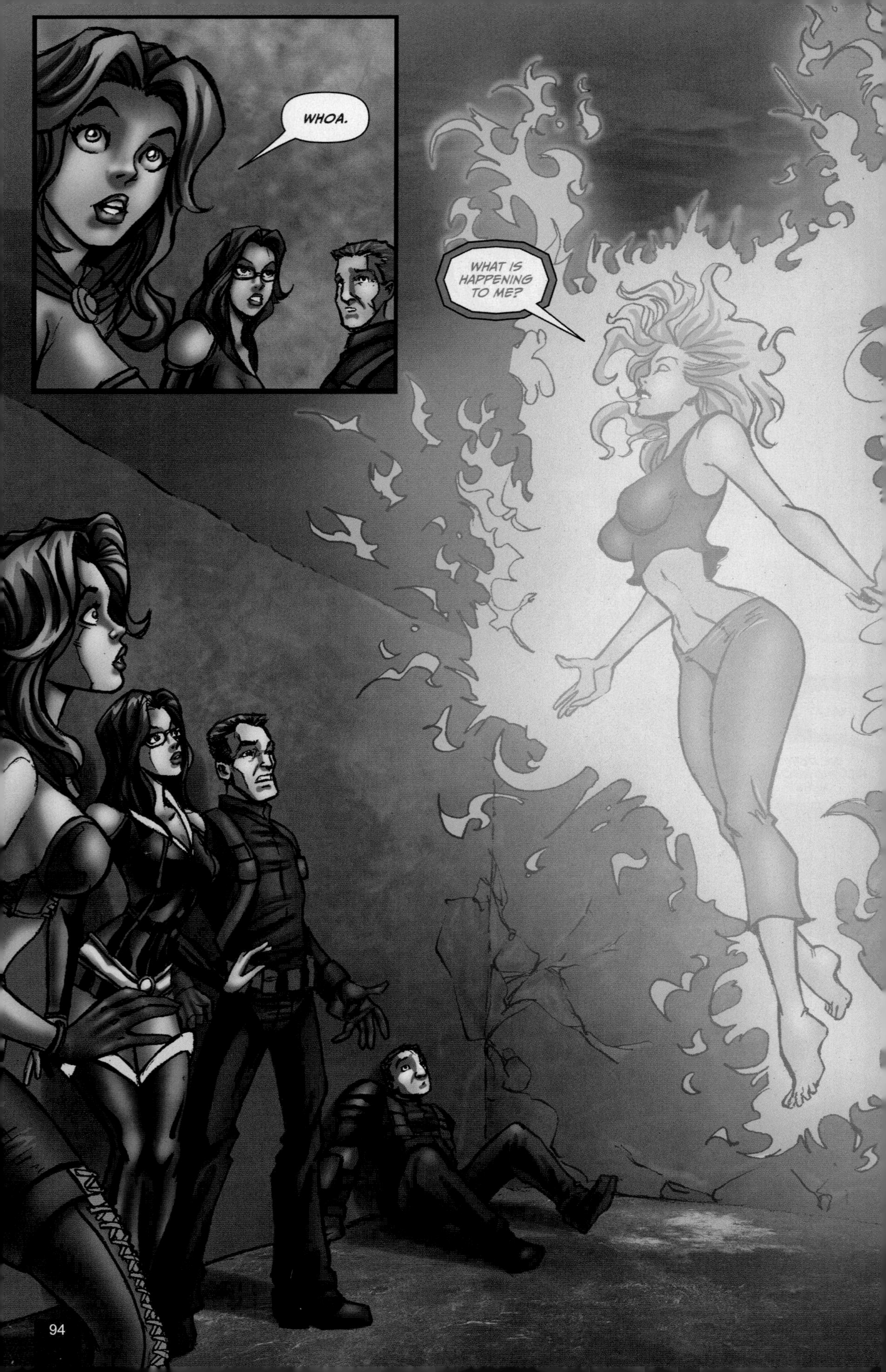
WHOA.
WHAT IS HAPPENING TO ME?

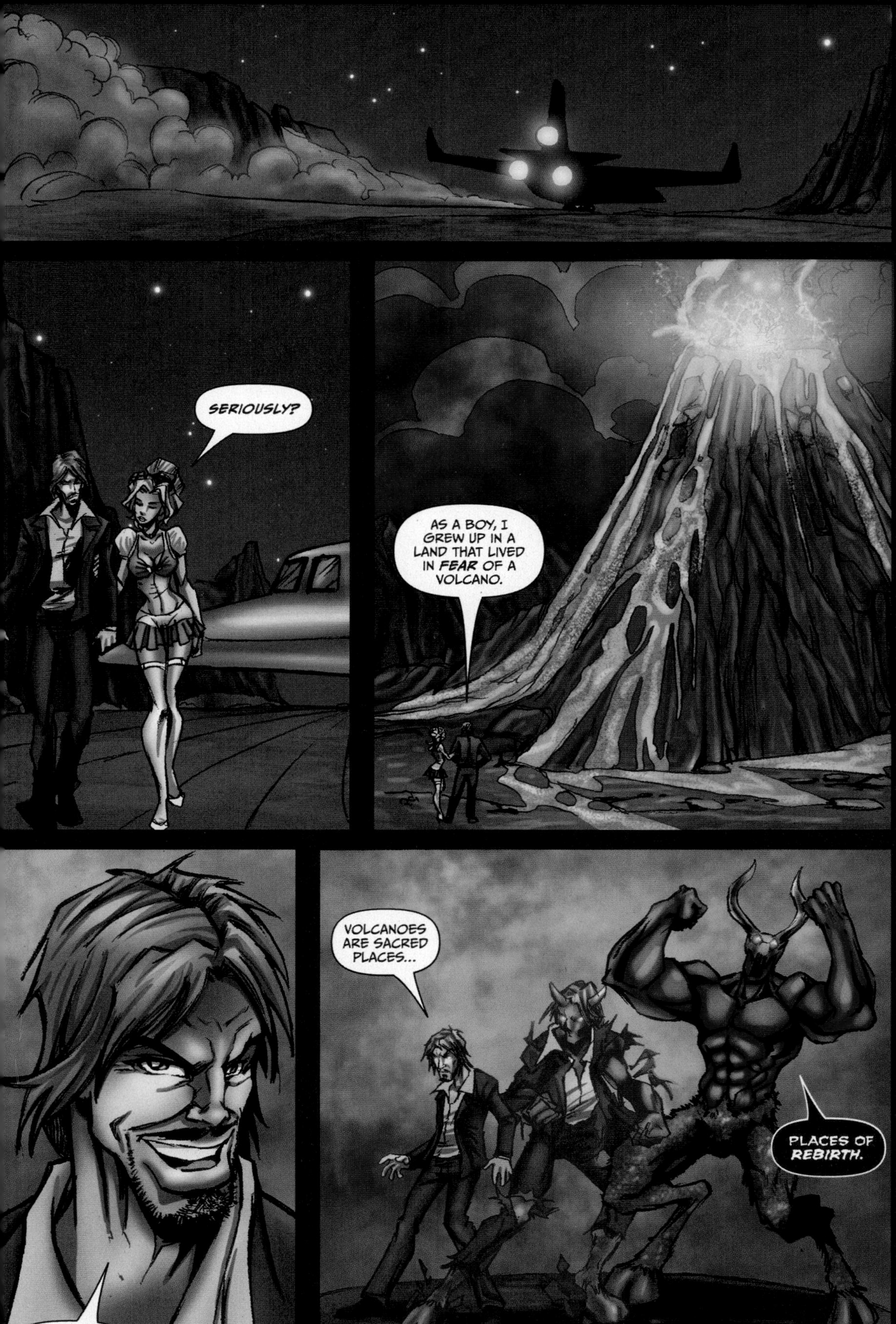
SERIOUSLY?
AS A BOY, I GREW UP IN A LAND THAT LIVED IN FEAR OF A VOLCANO.
BUT THE TRUTH IS QUITE DIFFERENT.
VOLCANOES ARE SACRED PLACES...
PLACES OF REBIRTH.

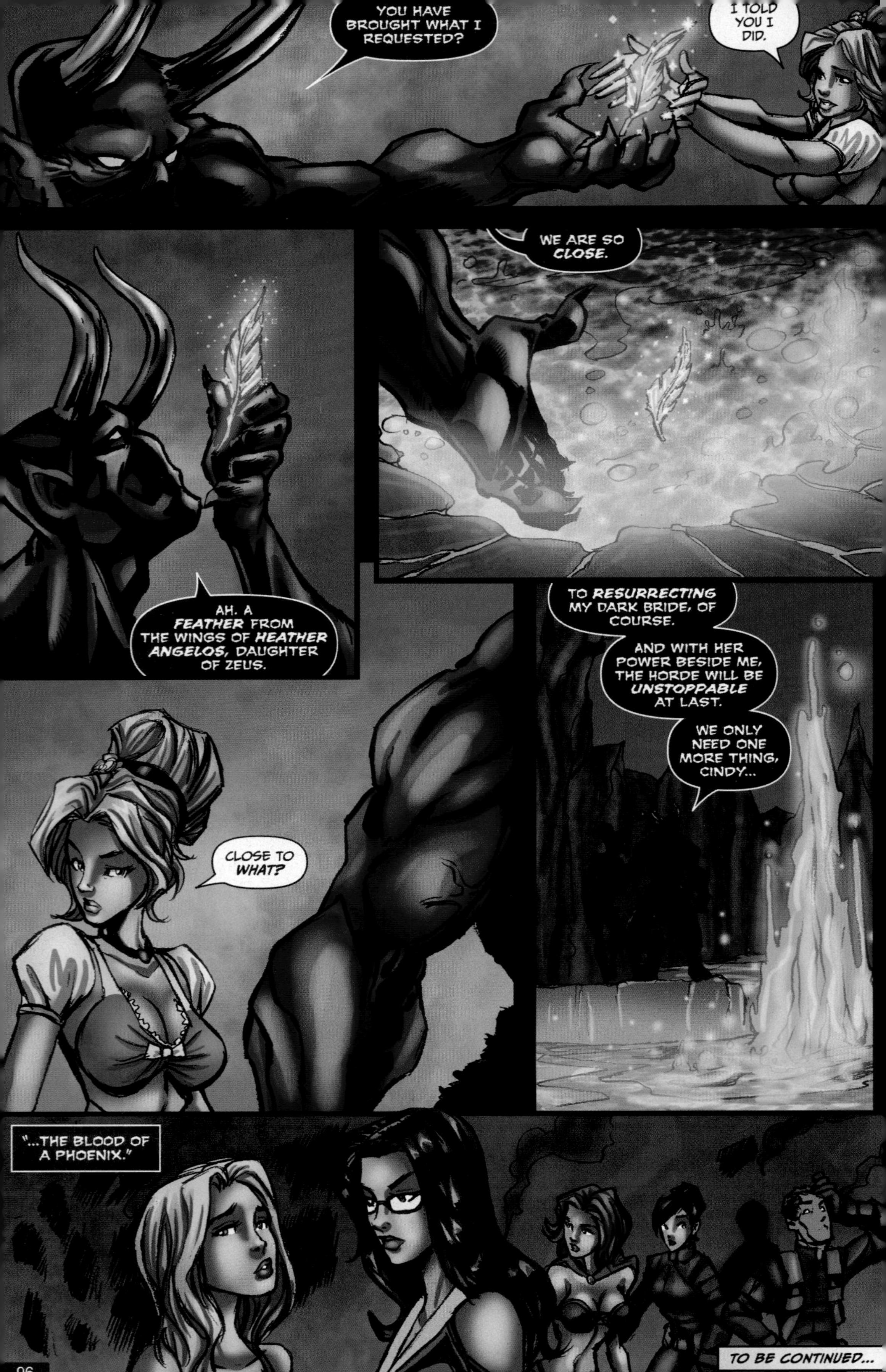
YOU HAVE BROUGHT WHAT I REQUESTED?
I TOLD YOU I DID.
AH. A FEATHER FROM THE WINGS OF HEATHER ANGELOS, DAUGHTER OF ZEUS.
WE ARE SO CLOSE.
CLOSE TO WHAT?
TO RESURRECTING MY DARK BRIDE, OF COURSE.
AND WITH HER POWER BESIDE ME, THE HORDE WILL BE UNSTOPPABLE AT LAST.
WE ONLY NEED ONE MORE THING, CINDY...
"...THE BLOOD OF A PHOENIX."
TO BE CONTINUED...

Grimm Fairy Tales

Volume 14

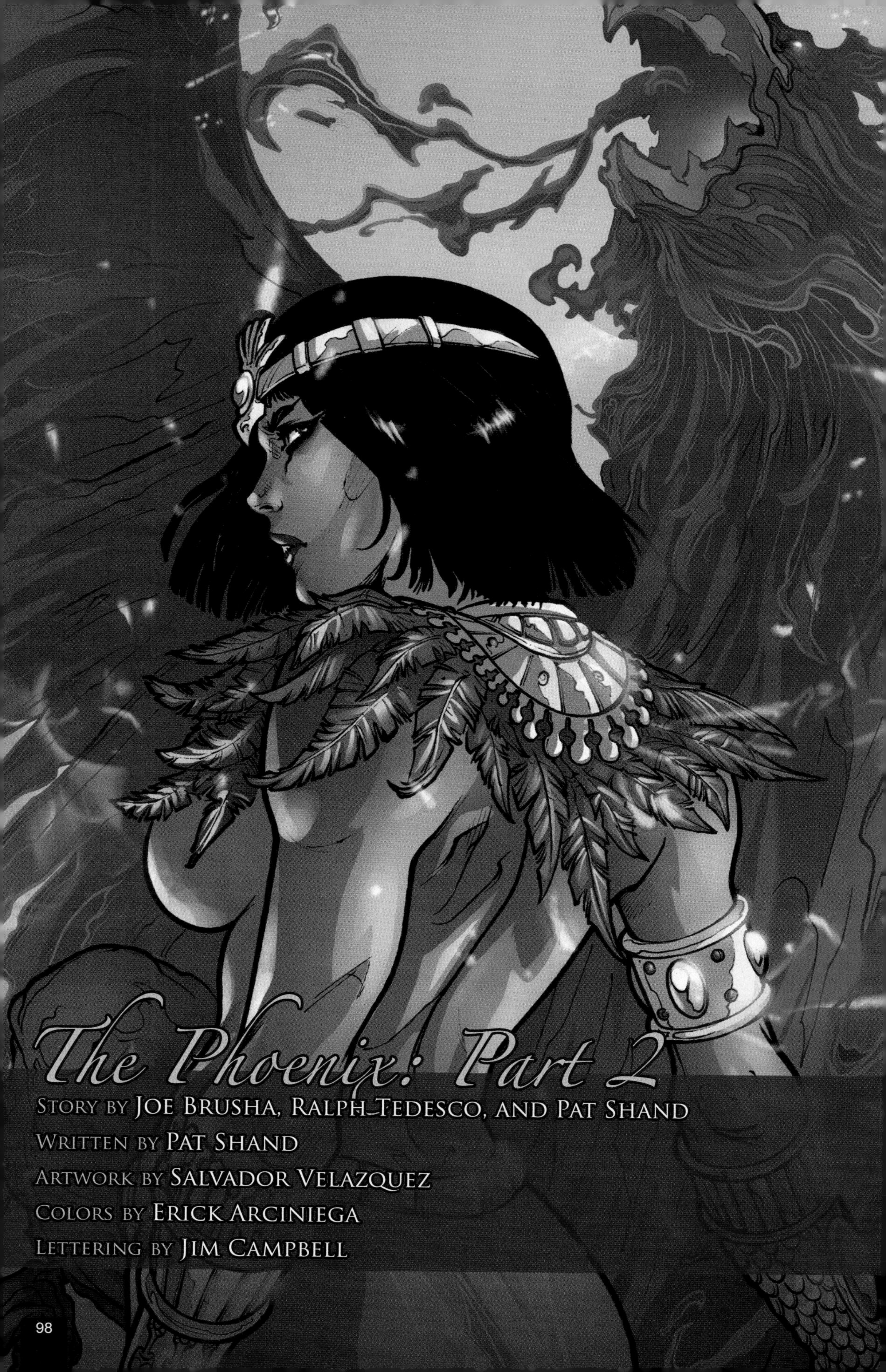

The Phoenix: Part 2

Story by Joe Brusha, Ralph Tedesco, and Pat Shand
Written by Pat Shand
Artwork by Salvador Velazquez
Colors by Erick Arciniega
Lettering by Jim Campbell

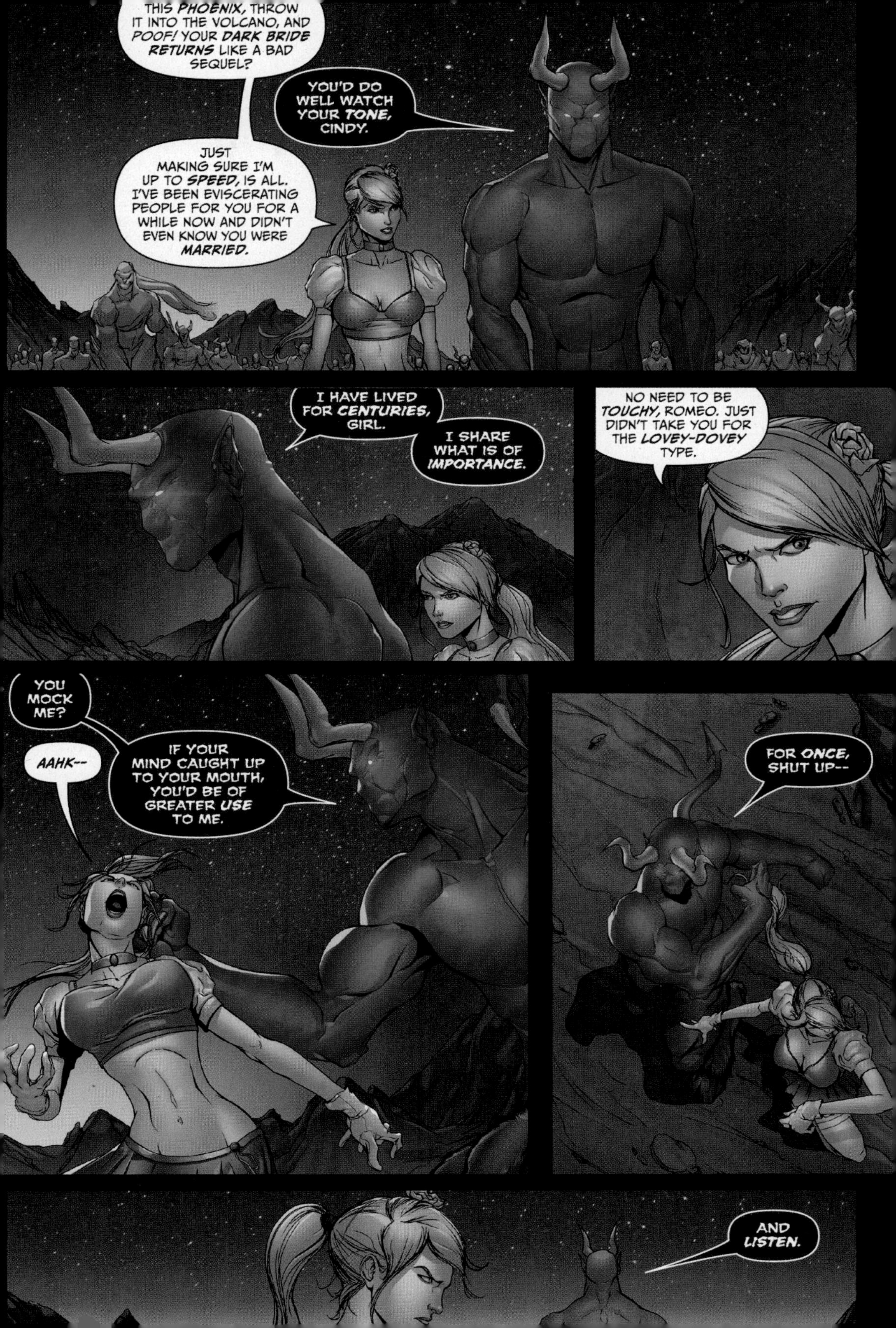
THIS PHOENIX, THROW IT INTO THE VOLCANO, AND POOF! YOUR DARK BRIDE RETURNS LIKE A BAD SEQUEL?
YOU'D DO WELL WATCH YOUR TONE, CINDY.
JUST MAKING SURE I'M UP TO SPEED, IS ALL. I'VE BEEN EVISCERATING PEOPLE FOR YOU FOR A WHILE NOW AND DIDN'T EVEN KNOW YOU WERE MARRIED.
I HAVE LIVED FOR CENTURIES, GIRL.
I SHARE WHAT IS OF IMPORTANCE.
NO NEED TO BE TOUCHY, ROMEO. JUST DIDN'T TAKE YOU FOR THE LOVEY-DOVEY TYPE.
YOU MOCK ME?
AAHK--
IF YOUR MIND CAUGHT UP TO YOUR MOUTH, YOU'D BE OF GREATER USE TO ME.
FOR ONCE, SHUT UP--
AND LISTEN.

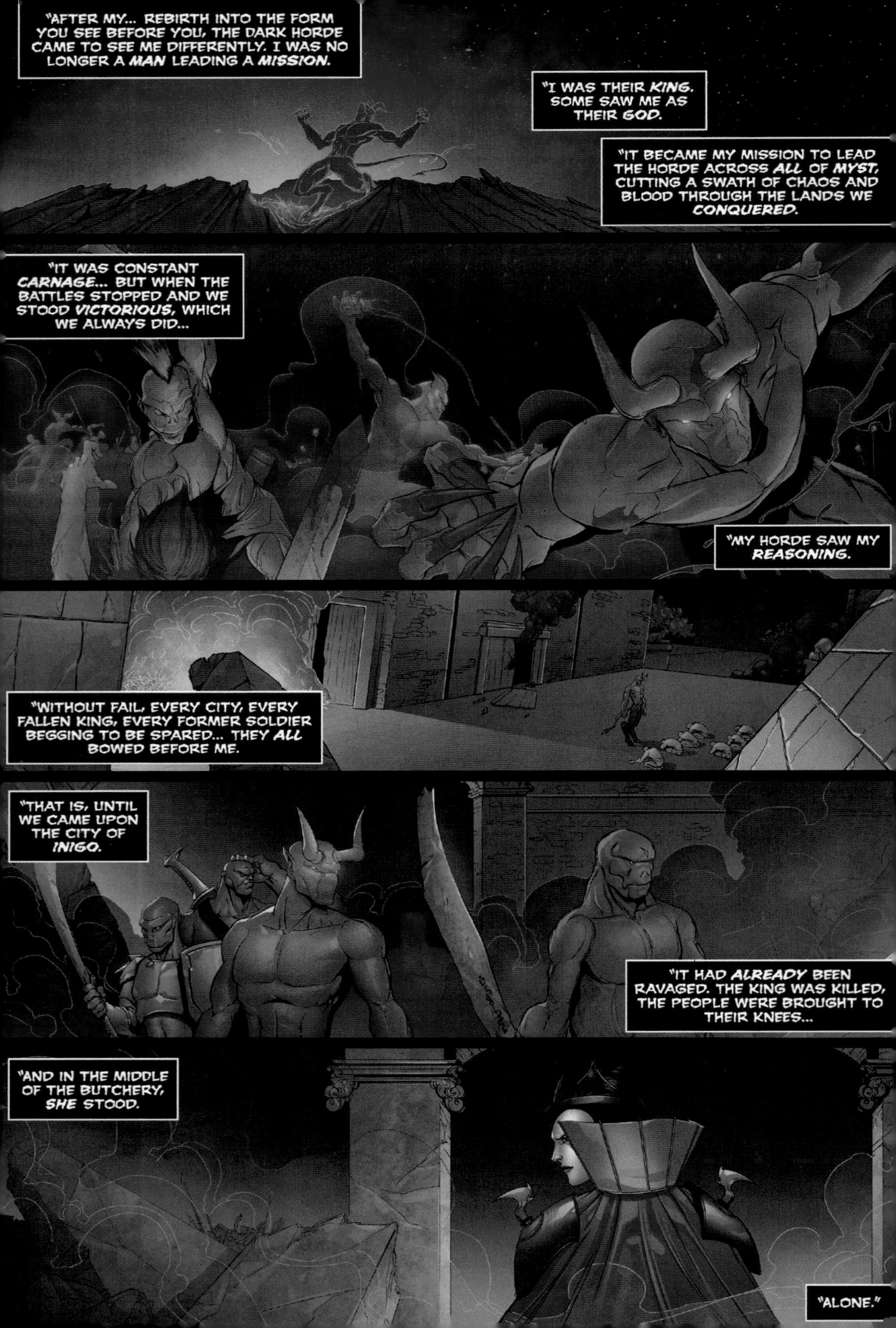
"AFTER MY... REBIRTH INTO THE FORM YOU SEE BEFORE YOU, THE DARK HORDE CAME TO SEE ME DIFFERENTLY. I WAS NO LONGER A *MAN* LEADING A *MISSION*.
"I WAS THEIR *KING*. SOME SAW ME AS THEIR *GOD*.
"IT BECAME MY MISSION TO LEAD THE HORDE ACROSS *ALL* OF *MYST*, CUTTING A SWATH OF CHAOS AND BLOOD THROUGH THE LANDS WE *CONQUERED*.
"IT WAS CONSTANT *CARNAGE*... BUT WHEN THE BATTLES STOPPED AND WE STOOD *VICTORIOUS*, WHICH WE ALWAYS DID...
"MY HORDE SAW MY *REASONING*.
"WITHOUT FAIL, EVERY CITY, EVERY FALLEN KING, EVERY FORMER SOLDIER BEGGING TO BE SPARED... THEY *ALL* BOWED BEFORE ME.
"THAT IS, UNTIL WE CAME UPON THE CITY OF *INIGO*.
"IT HAD *ALREADY* BEEN RAVAGED. THE KING WAS KILLED, THE PEOPLE WERE BROUGHT TO THEIR KNEES...
"AND IN THE MIDDLE OF THE BUTCHERY, *SHE* STOOD.
"ALONE."

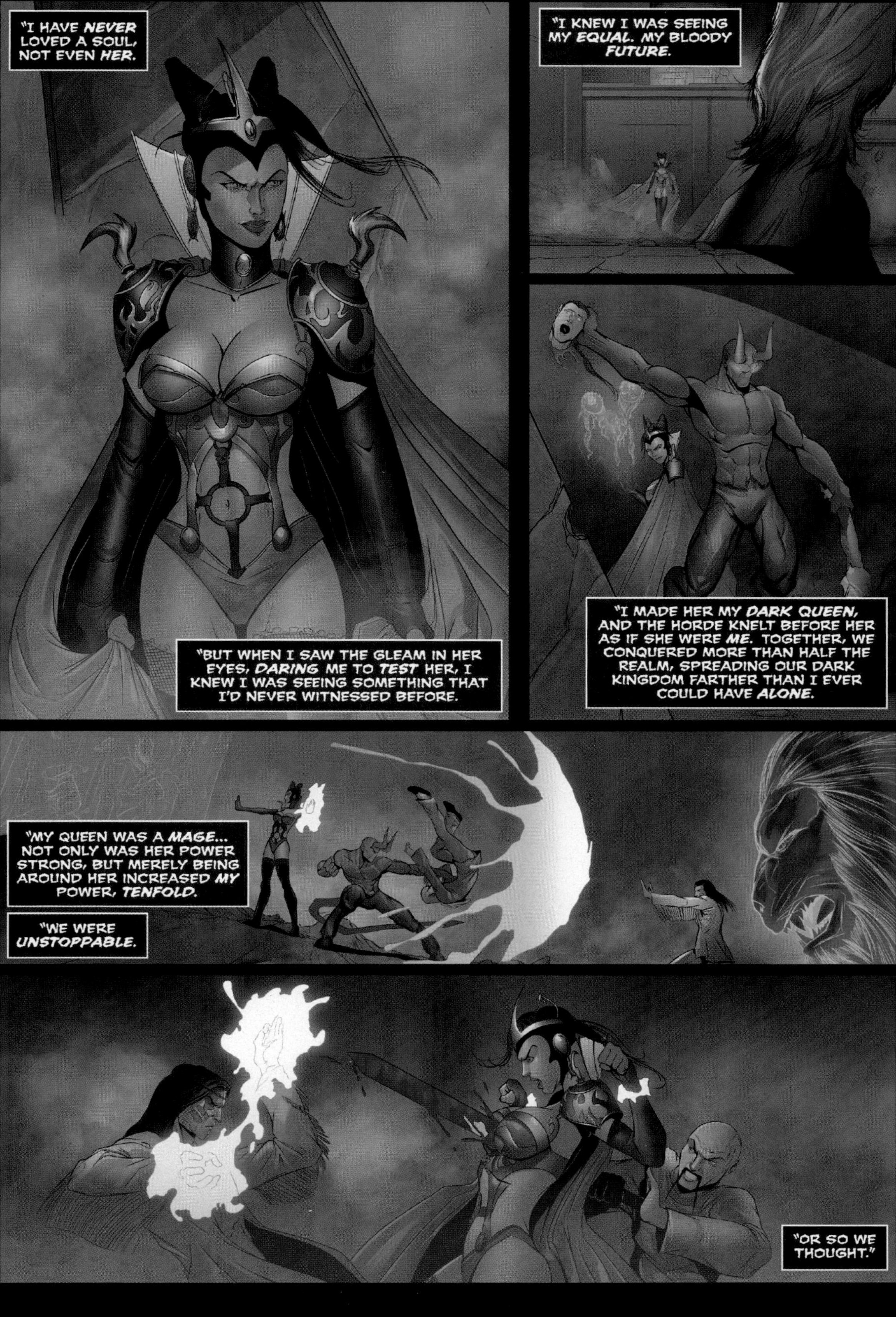
"I HAVE NEVER LOVED A SOUL, NOT EVEN HER.
"BUT WHEN I SAW THE GLEAM IN HER EYES, DARING ME TO TEST HER, I KNEW I WAS SEEING SOMETHING THAT I'D NEVER WITNESSED BEFORE.
"I KNEW I WAS SEEING MY EQUAL. MY BLOODY FUTURE.
"I MADE HER MY DARK QUEEN, AND THE HORDE KNELT BEFORE HER AS IF SHE WERE ME. TOGETHER, WE CONQUERED MORE THAN HALF THE REALM, SPREADING OUR DARK KINGDOM FARTHER THAN I EVER COULD HAVE ALONE.
"MY QUEEN WAS A MAGE... NOT ONLY WAS HER POWER STRONG, BUT MERELY BEING AROUND HER INCREASED MY POWER, TENFOLD.
"WE WERE UNSTOPPABLE.
"OR SO WE THOUGHT."

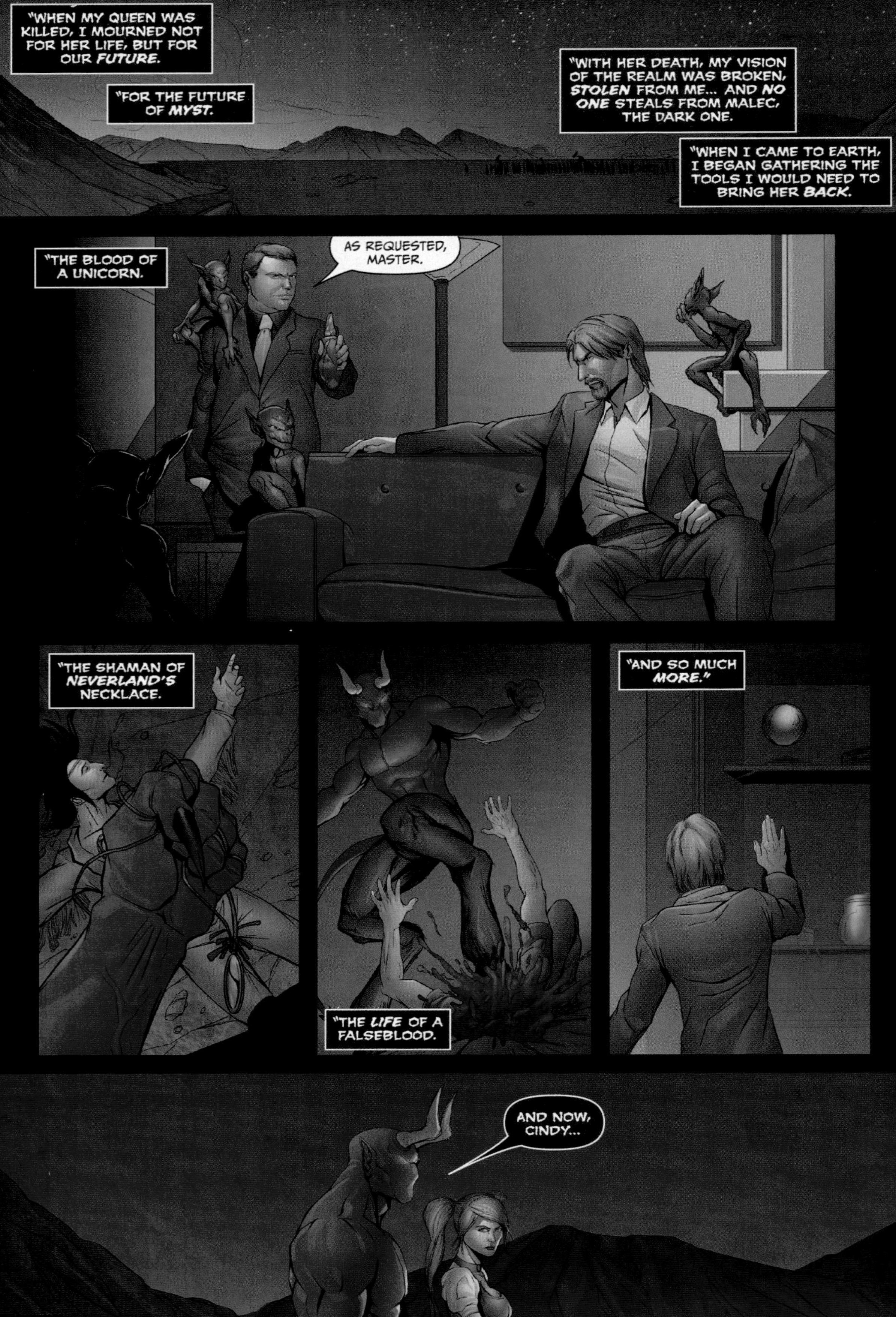
"WHEN MY QUEEN WAS KILLED, I MOURNED NOT FOR HER LIFE, BUT FOR OUR FUTURE.
"FOR THE FUTURE OF MYST.
"WITH HER DEATH, MY VISION OF THE REALM WAS BROKEN, STOLEN FROM ME... AND NO ONE STEALS FROM MALEC, THE DARK ONE.
"WHEN I CAME TO EARTH, I BEGAN GATHERING THE TOOLS I WOULD NEED TO BRING HER BACK.
"THE BLOOD OF A UNICORN.
AS REQUESTED, MASTER.
"THE SHAMAN OF NEVERLAND'S NECKLACE.
"THE LIFE OF A FALSEBLOOD.
"AND SO MUCH MORE."
AND NOW, CINDY...

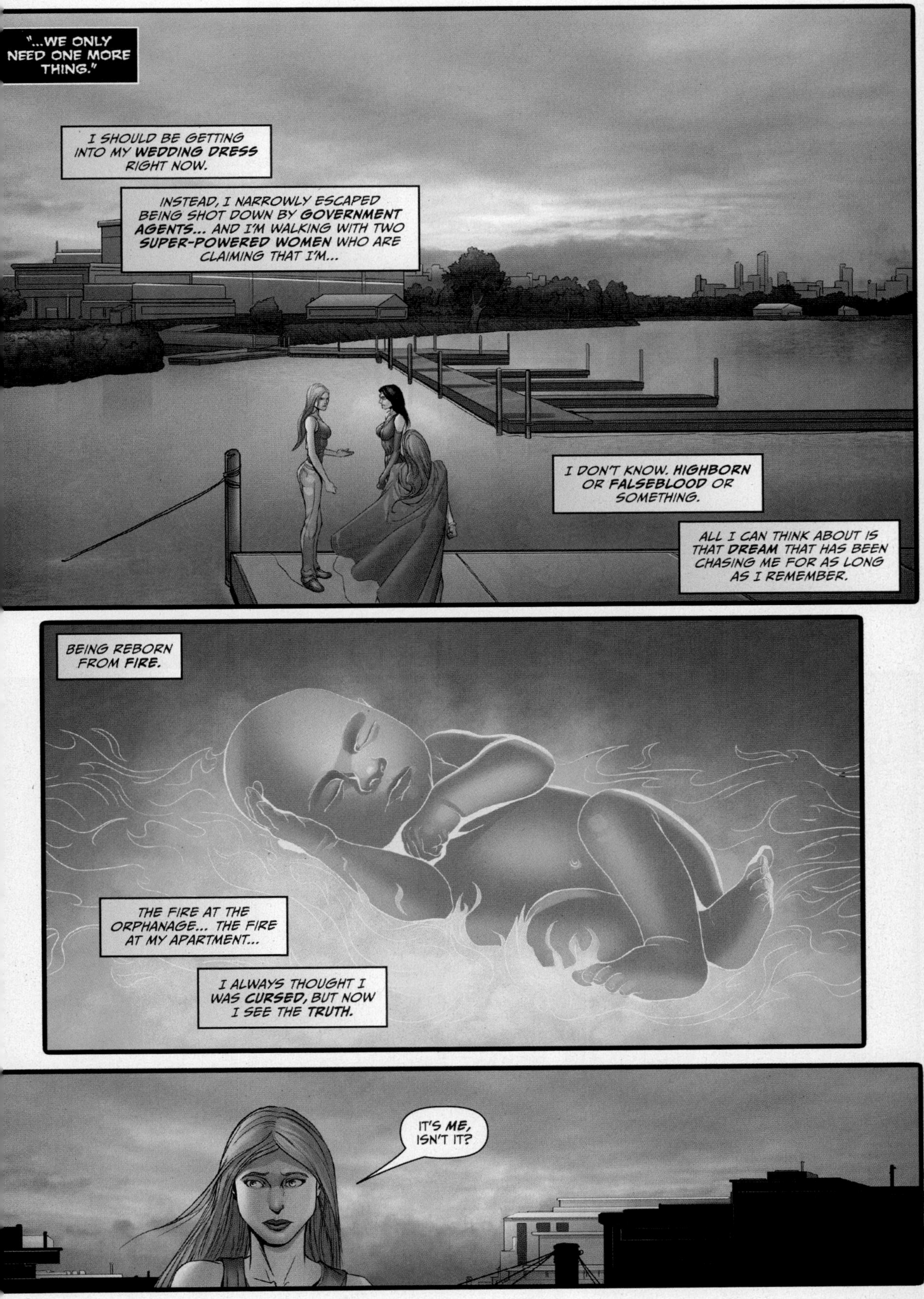
"...WE ONLY NEED ONE MORE THING."
I SHOULD BE GETTING INTO MY WEDDING DRESS RIGHT NOW.
INSTEAD, I NARROWLY ESCAPED BEING SHOT DOWN BY GOVERNMENT AGENTS... AND I'M WALKING WITH TWO SUPER-POWERED WOMEN WHO ARE CLAIMING THAT I'M...
I DON'T KNOW. HIGHBORN OR FALSEBLOOD OR SOMETHING.
ALL I CAN THINK ABOUT IS THAT DREAM THAT HAS BEEN CHASING ME FOR AS LONG AS I REMEMBER.
BEING REBORN FROM FIRE.
THE FIRE AT THE ORPHANAGE... THE FIRE AT MY APARTMENT...
I ALWAYS THOUGHT I WAS CURSED, BUT NOW I SEE THE TRUTH.
IT'S ME, ISN'T IT?

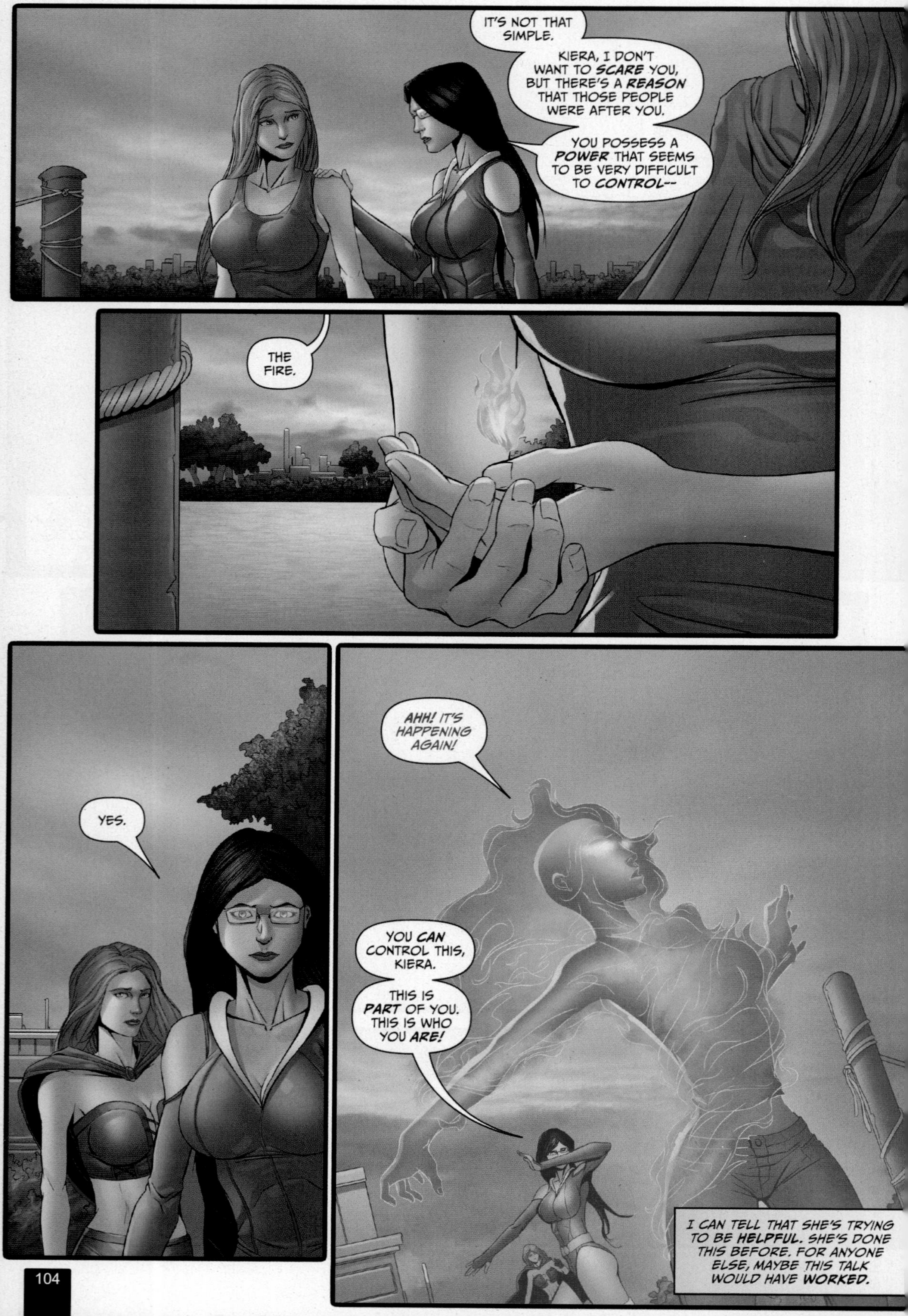
IT'S NOT THAT SIMPLE.
KIERA, I DON'T WANT TO SCARE YOU, BUT THERE'S A REASON THAT THOSE PEOPLE WERE AFTER YOU.
YOU POSSESS A POWER THAT SEEMS TO BE VERY DIFFICULT TO CONTROL--
THE FIRE.
YES.
AHH! IT'S HAPPENING AGAIN!
YOU CAN CONTROL THIS, KIERA.
THIS IS PART OF YOU. THIS IS WHO YOU ARE!
I CAN TELL THAT SHE'S TRYING TO BE HELPFUL. SHE'S DONE THIS BEFORE. FOR ANYONE ELSE, MAYBE THIS TALK WOULD HAVE WORKED.

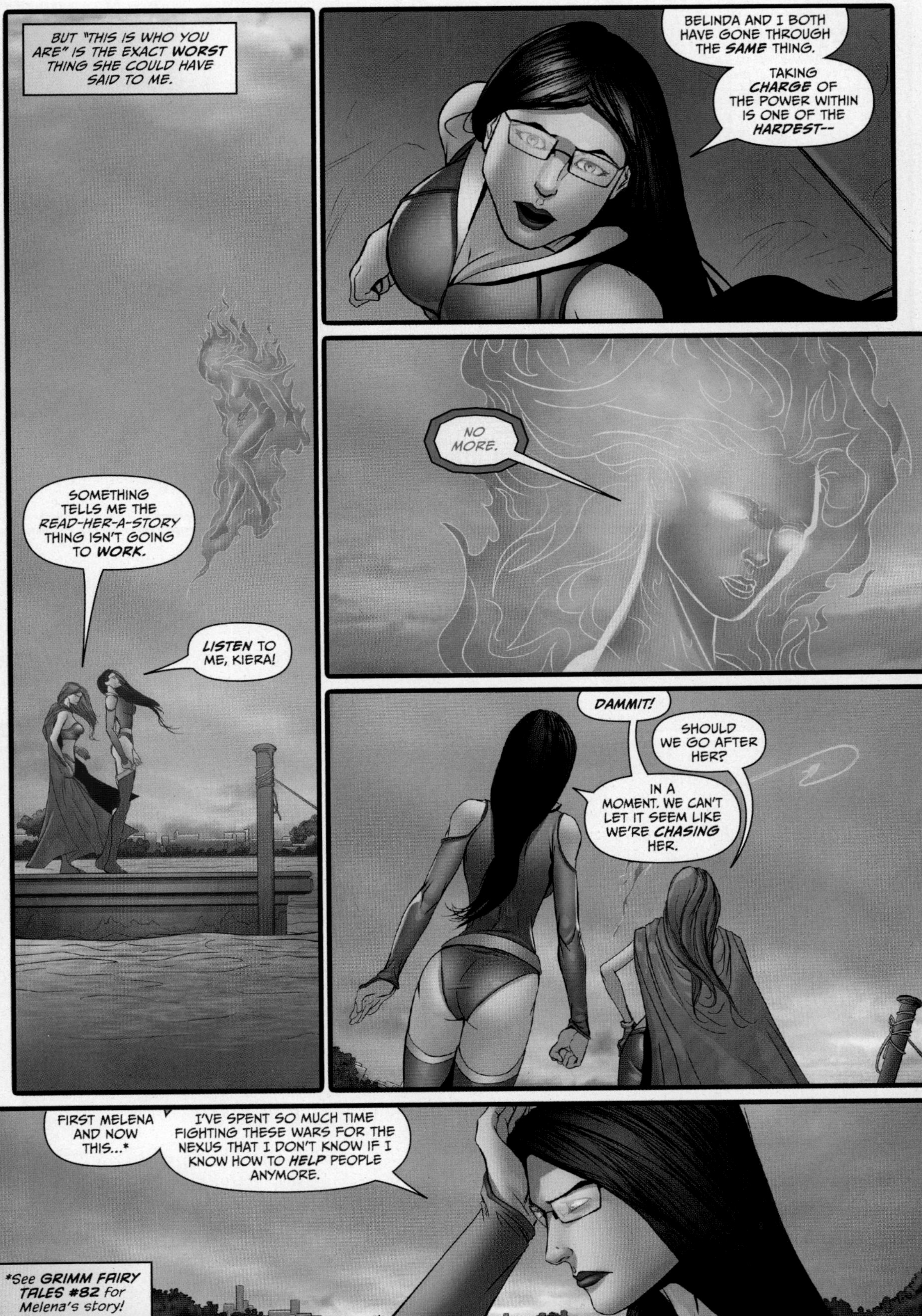

BUT "THIS IS WHO YOU ARE" IS THE EXACT WORST THING SHE COULD HAVE SAID TO ME.
BELINDA AND I BOTH HAVE GONE THROUGH THE SAME THING.
TAKING CHARGE OF THE POWER WITHIN IS ONE OF THE HARDEST--
NO MORE.
SOMETHING TELLS ME THE READ-HER-A-STORY THING ISN'T GOING TO WORK.
LISTEN TO ME, KIERA!
DAMMIT!
SHOULD WE GO AFTER HER?
IN A MOMENT. WE CAN'T LET IT SEEM LIKE WE'RE CHASING HER.
FIRST MELENA AND NOW THIS...*
I'VE SPENT SO MUCH TIME FIGHTING THESE WARS FOR THE NEXUS THAT I DON'T KNOW IF I KNOW HOW TO HELP PEOPLE ANYMORE.
*See GRIMM FAIRY TALES #82 for Melena's story!

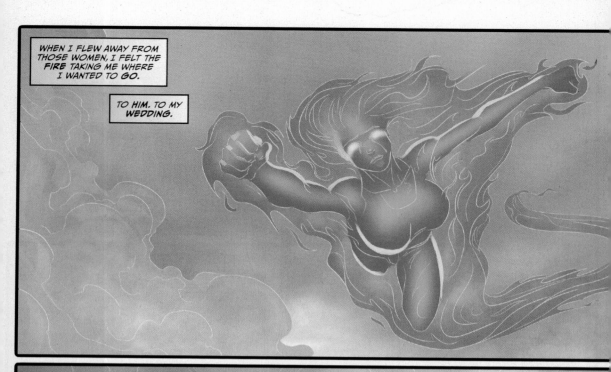

WHEN I FLEW AWAY FROM THOSE WOMEN, I FELT THE *FIRE* TAKING ME WHERE I WANTED TO GO.

TO HIM. TO MY WEDDING.

BUT WHAT WOULD HE SAY IF HE SAW ME LIKE *THIS?*

I BET HE'D BE AS *SCARED* OF ME AS I AM.

AND THAT... THAT WOULD *BREAK* ME.

HUH... AHUH... AHUH...

HEY... ARE YOU *OKAY?*

WHO ARE *YOU?*

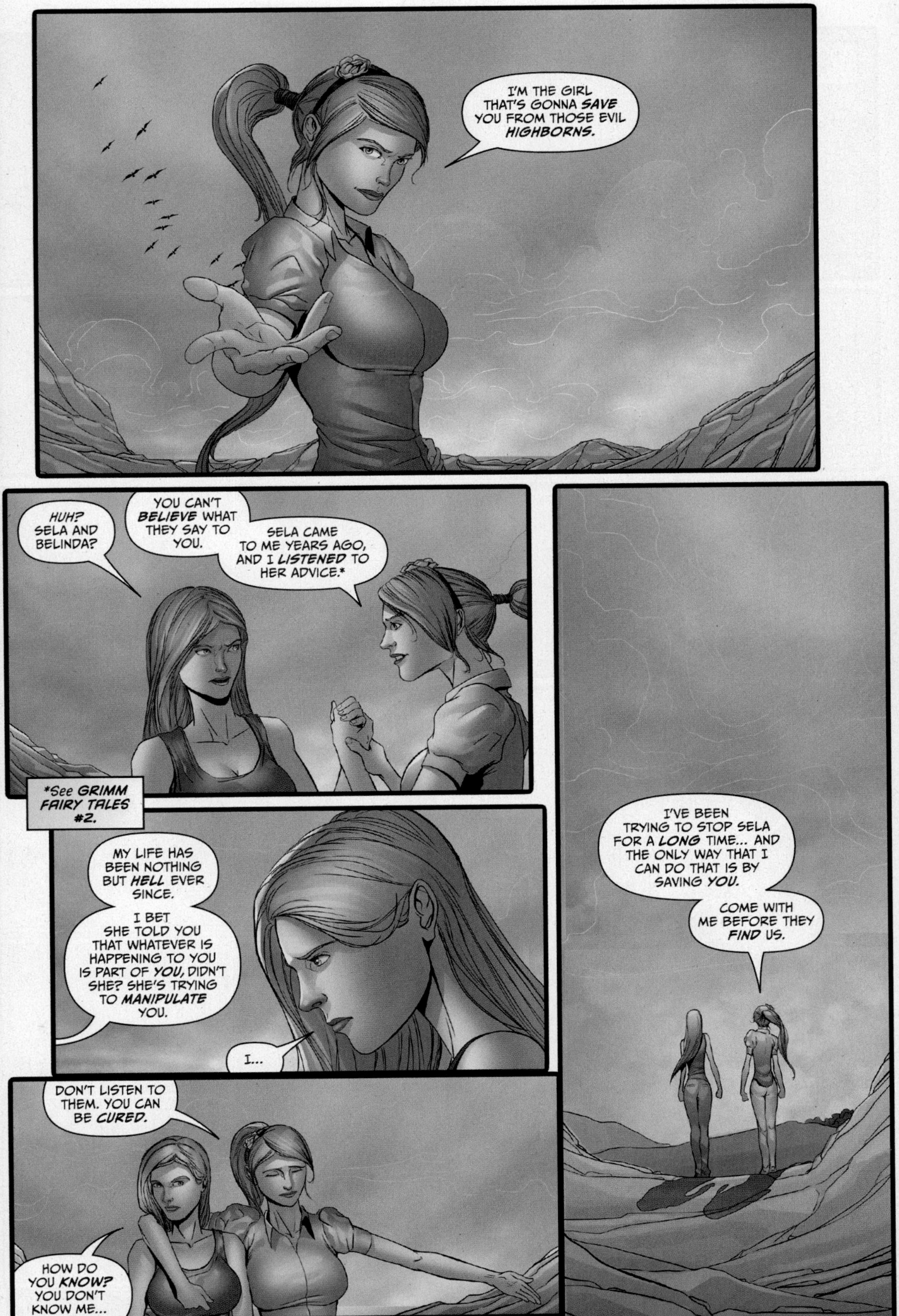
I'M THE GIRL THAT'S GONNA SAVE YOU FROM THOSE EVIL HIGHBORNS.
HUH? SELA AND BELINDA?
YOU CAN'T BELIEVE WHAT THEY SAY TO YOU.
SELA CAME TO ME YEARS AGO, AND I LISTENED TO HER ADVICE.*
*See GRIMM FAIRY TALES #2.
MY LIFE HAS BEEN NOTHING BUT HELL EVER SINCE.
I BET SHE TOLD YOU THAT WHATEVER IS HAPPENING TO YOU IS PART OF YOU, DIDN'T SHE? SHE'S TRYING TO MANIPULATE YOU.
I...
DON'T LISTEN TO THEM. YOU CAN BE CURED.
HOW DO YOU KNOW? YOU DON'T KNOW ME...
I'VE BEEN TRYING TO STOP SELA FOR A LONG TIME... AND THE ONLY WAY THAT I CAN DO THAT IS BY SAVING YOU.
COME WITH ME BEFORE THEY FIND US.

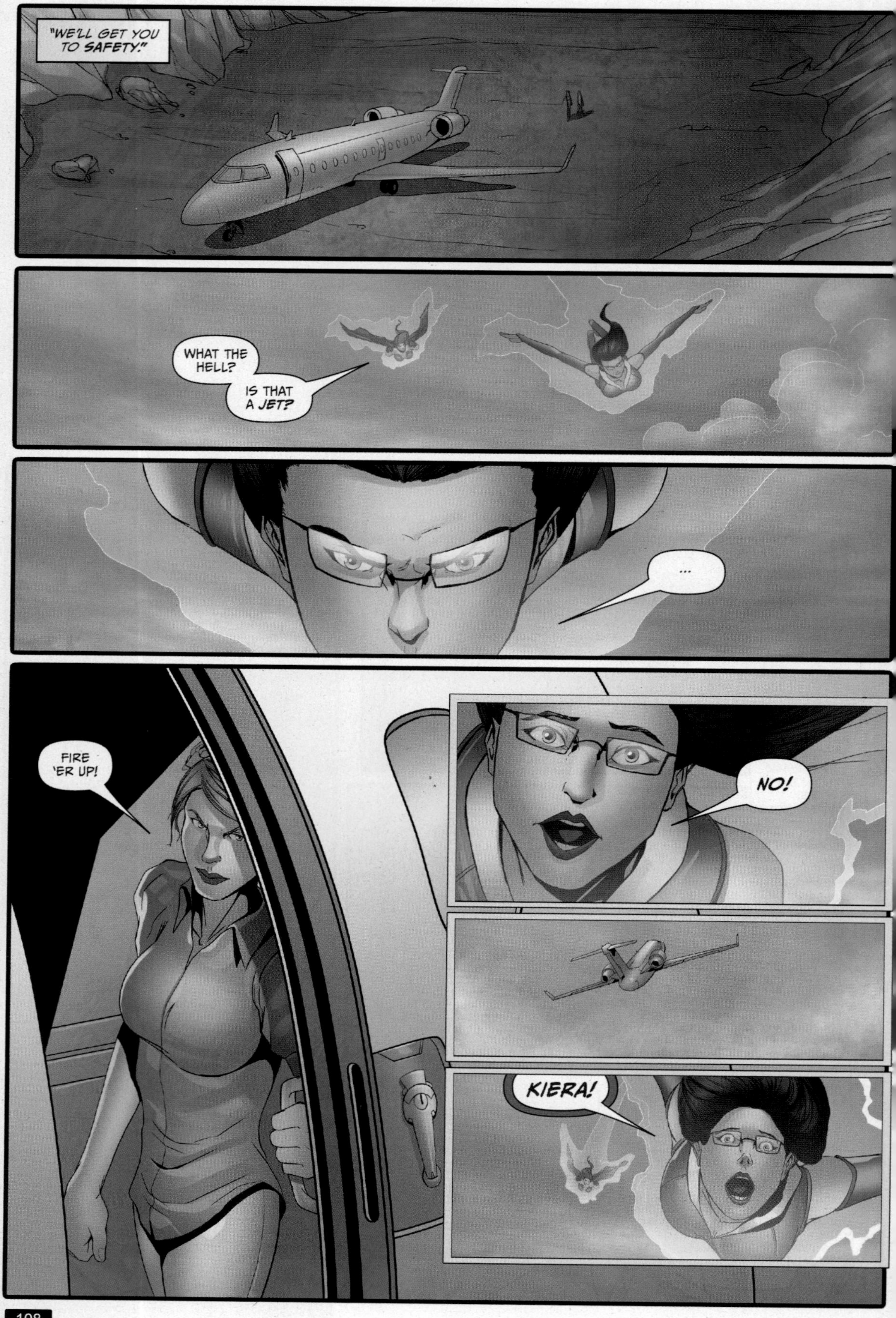
"WE'LL GET YOU TO SAFETY."
WHAT THE HELL?
IS THAT A JET?
...
FIRE 'ER UP!
NO!
KIERA!

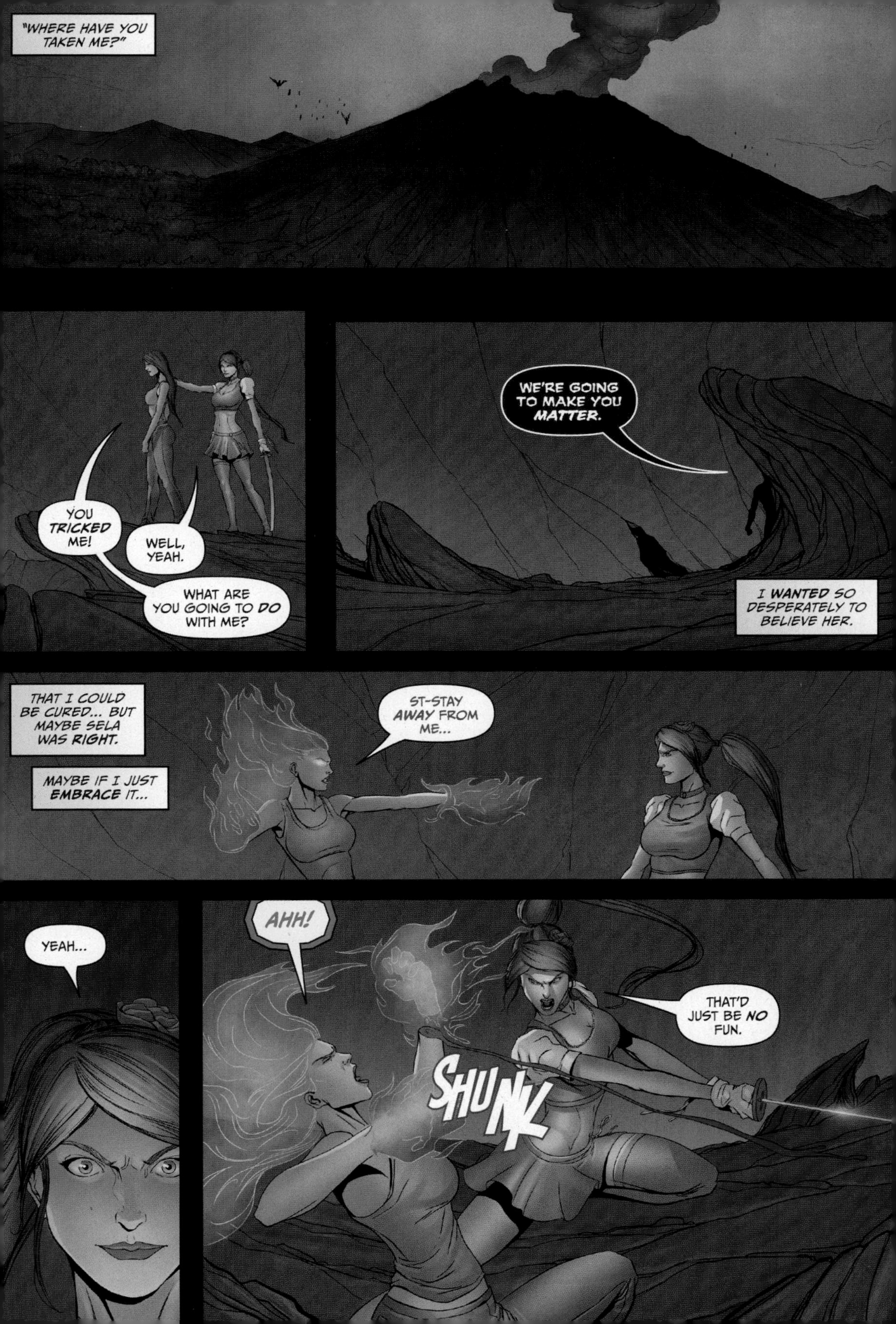
"WHERE HAVE YOU TAKEN ME?"
YOU *TRICKED* ME!
WELL, YEAH.
WHAT ARE YOU GOING TO *DO* WITH ME?
WE'RE GOING TO MAKE YOU *MATTER.*
I WANTED SO DESPERATELY TO BELIEVE HER.
THAT I COULD BE CURED... BUT MAYBE SELA WAS RIGHT.
MAYBE IF I JUST EMBRACE IT...
ST-STAY *AWAY* FROM ME...
YEAH...
AHH!
SHUNK
THAT'D JUST BE *NO* FUN.

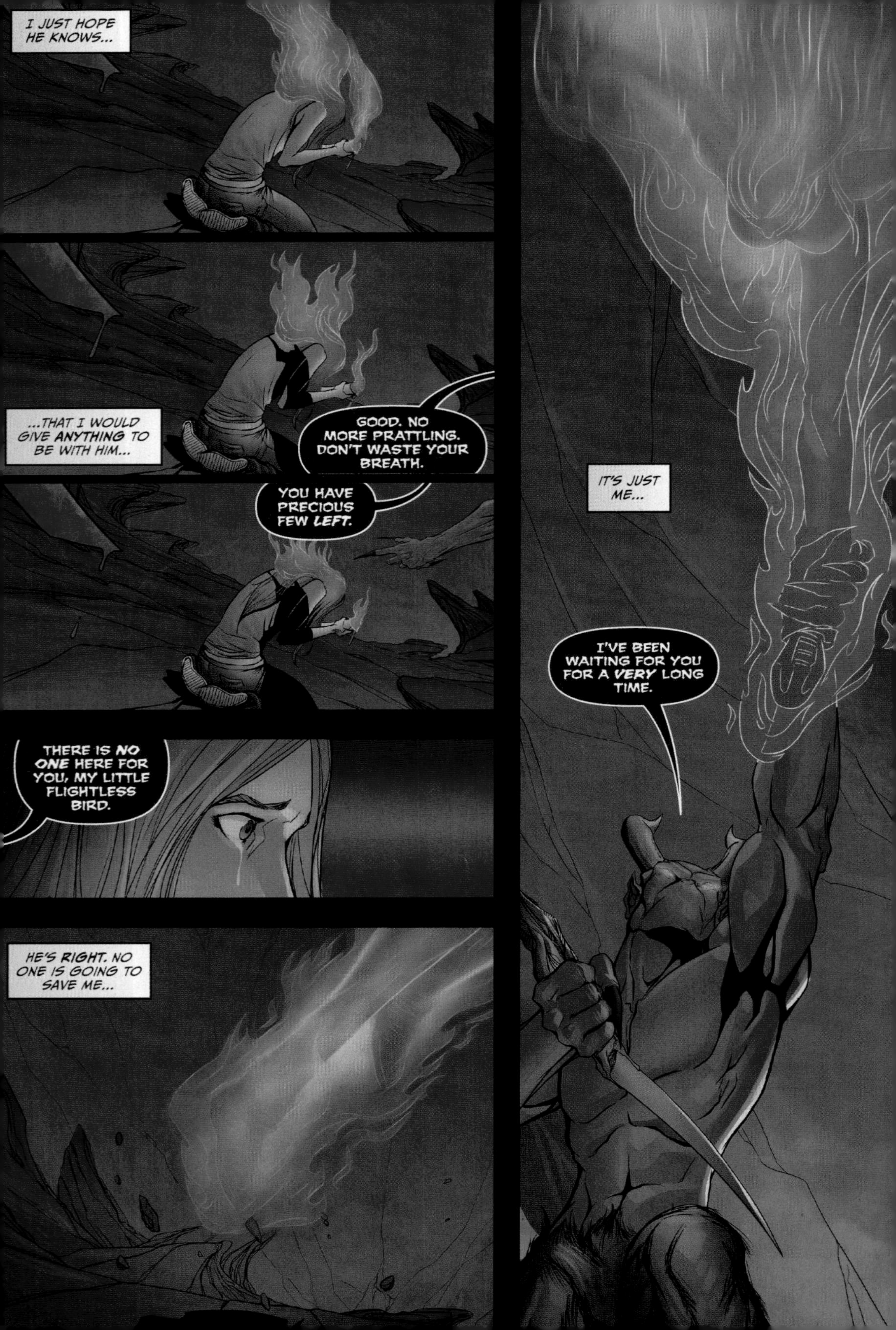
I JUST HOPE HE KNOWS...
...THAT I WOULD GIVE ANYTHING TO BE WITH HIM...
GOOD. NO MORE PRATTLING. DON'T WASTE YOUR BREATH.
YOU HAVE PRECIOUS FEW LEFT.
THERE IS NO ONE HERE FOR YOU, MY LITTLE FLIGHTLESS BIRD.
HE'S RIGHT. NO ONE IS GOING TO SAVE ME...
IT'S JUST ME...
I'VE BEEN WAITING FOR YOU FOR A VERY LONG TIME.

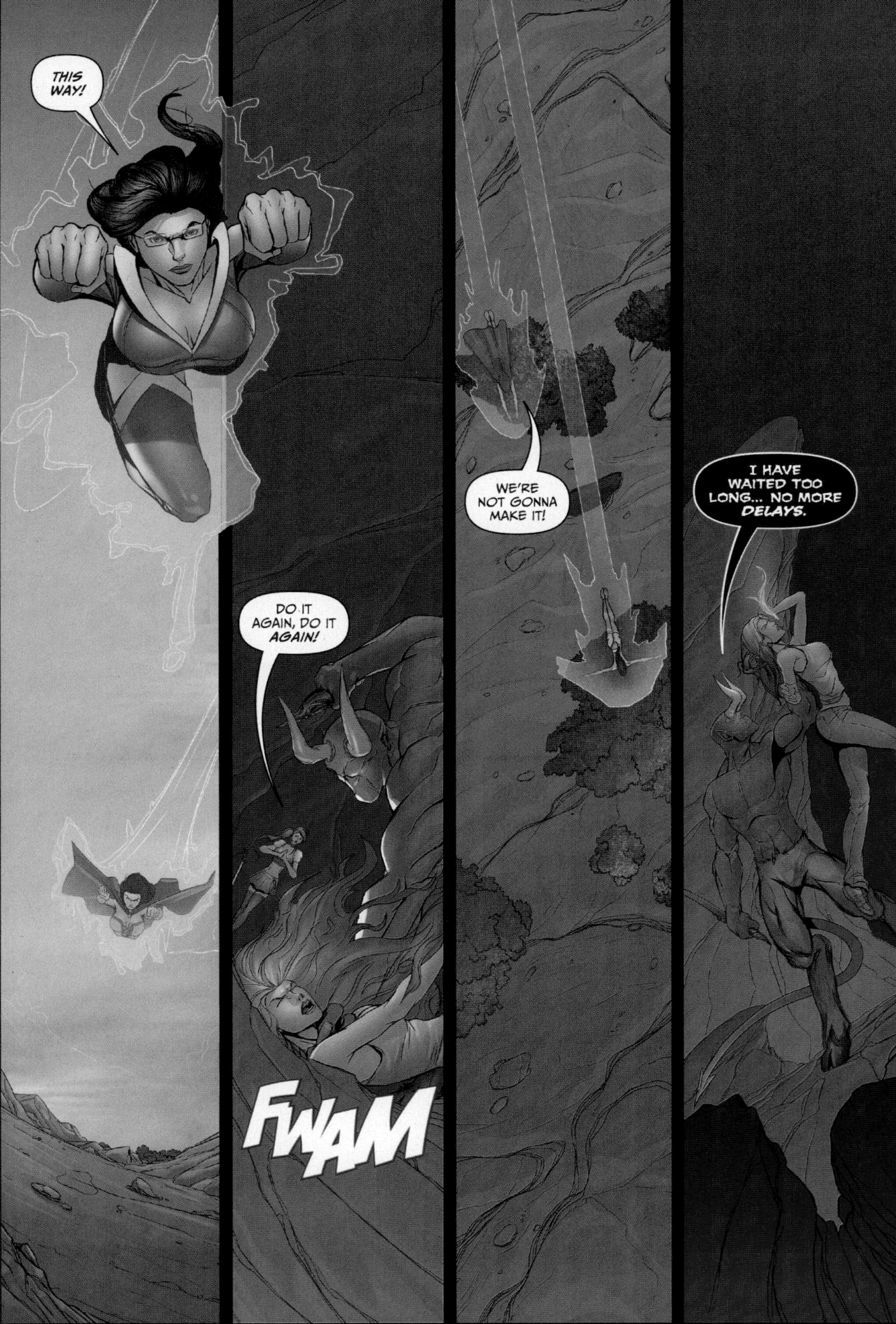
THIS WAY!
DO IT AGAIN, DO IT AGAIN!
FWAM
WE'RE NOT GONNA MAKE IT!
I HAVE WAITED TOO LONG... NO MORE DELAYS.

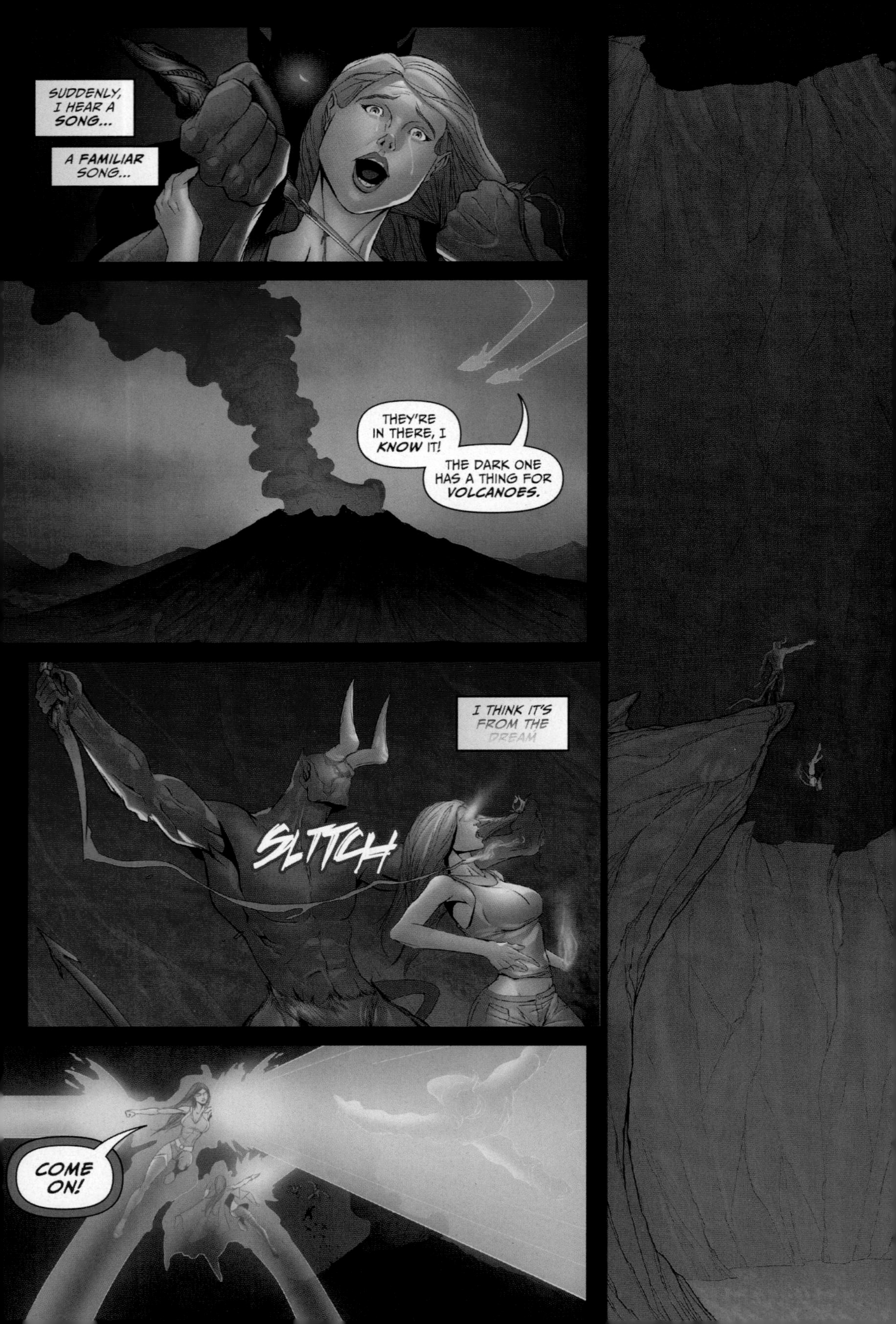
SUDDENLY, I HEAR A SONG...
A FAMILIAR SONG...
THEY'RE IN THERE, I KNOW IT!
THE DARK ONE HAS A THING FOR VOLCANOES.
I THINK IT'S FROM THE DREAM
SLITCH
COME ON!

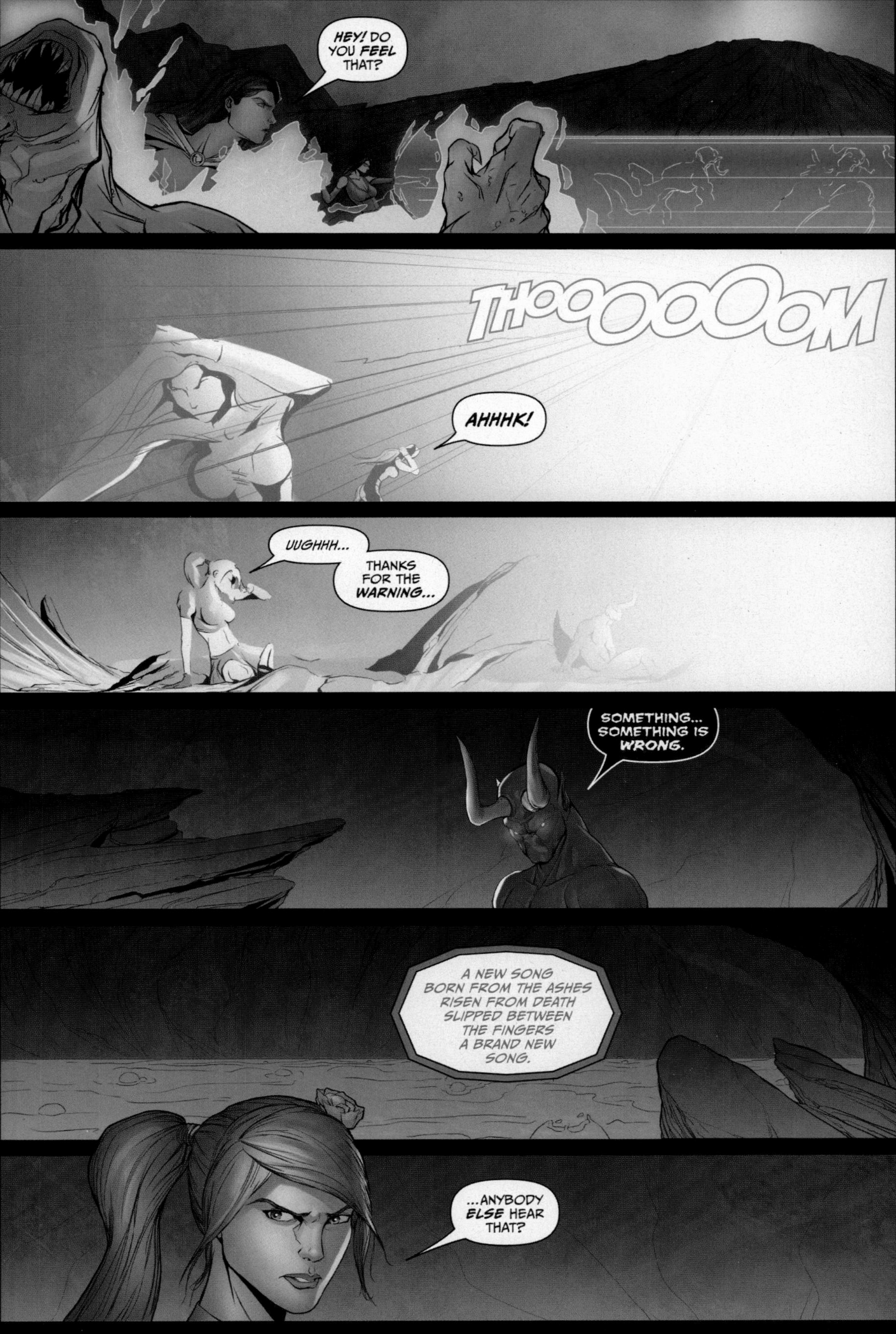

HEY! DO YOU FEEL THAT?
THOOOOOOOM
AHHHK!
UUGHHH...
THANKS FOR THE WARNING...
SOMETHING... SOMETHING IS WRONG.
A NEW SONG BORN FROM THE ASHES RISEN FROM DEATH SLIPPED BETWEEN THE FINGERS A BRAND NEW SONG.
...ANYBODY ELSE HEAR THAT?

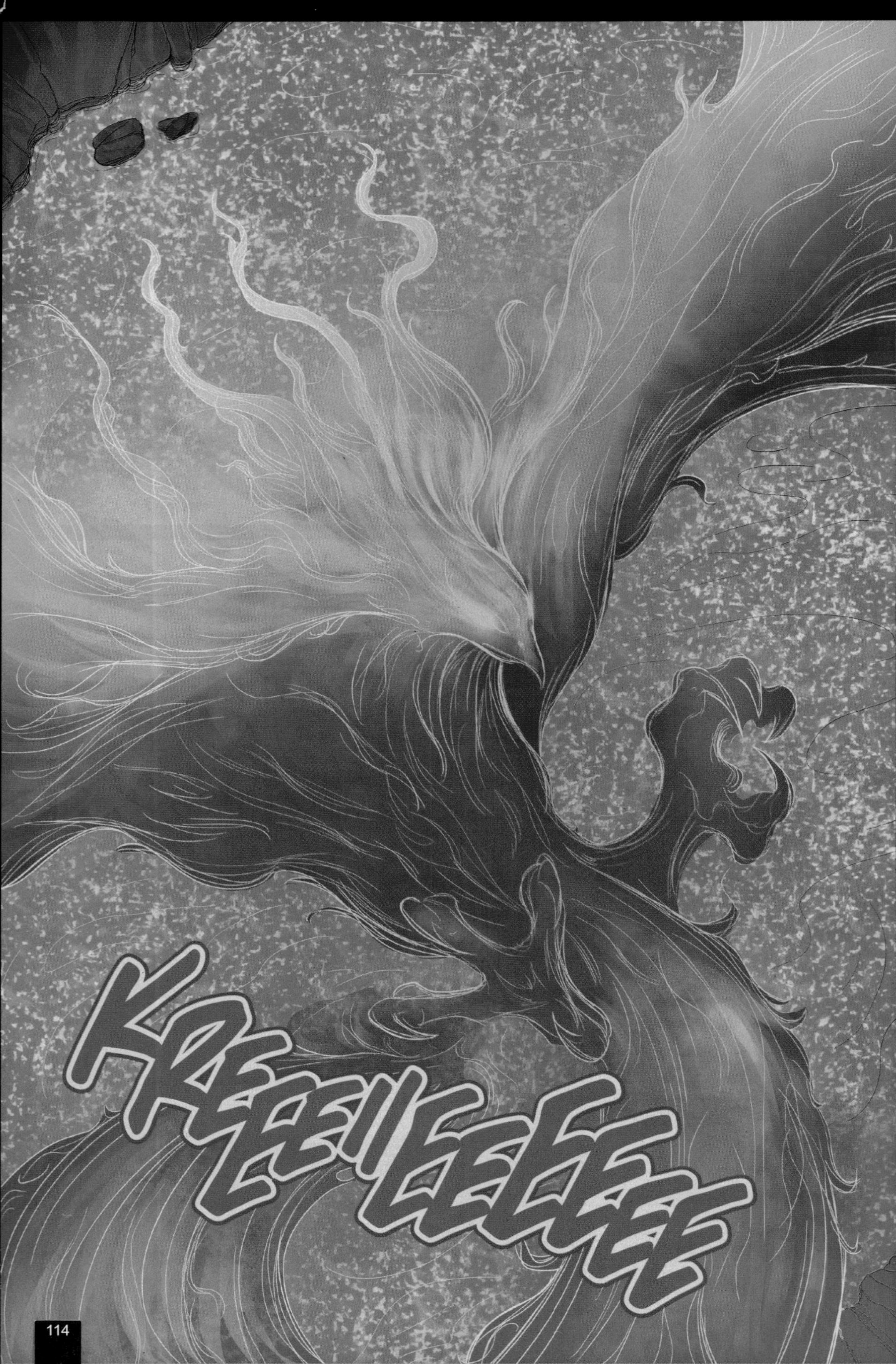
KREEEEEEEEEE

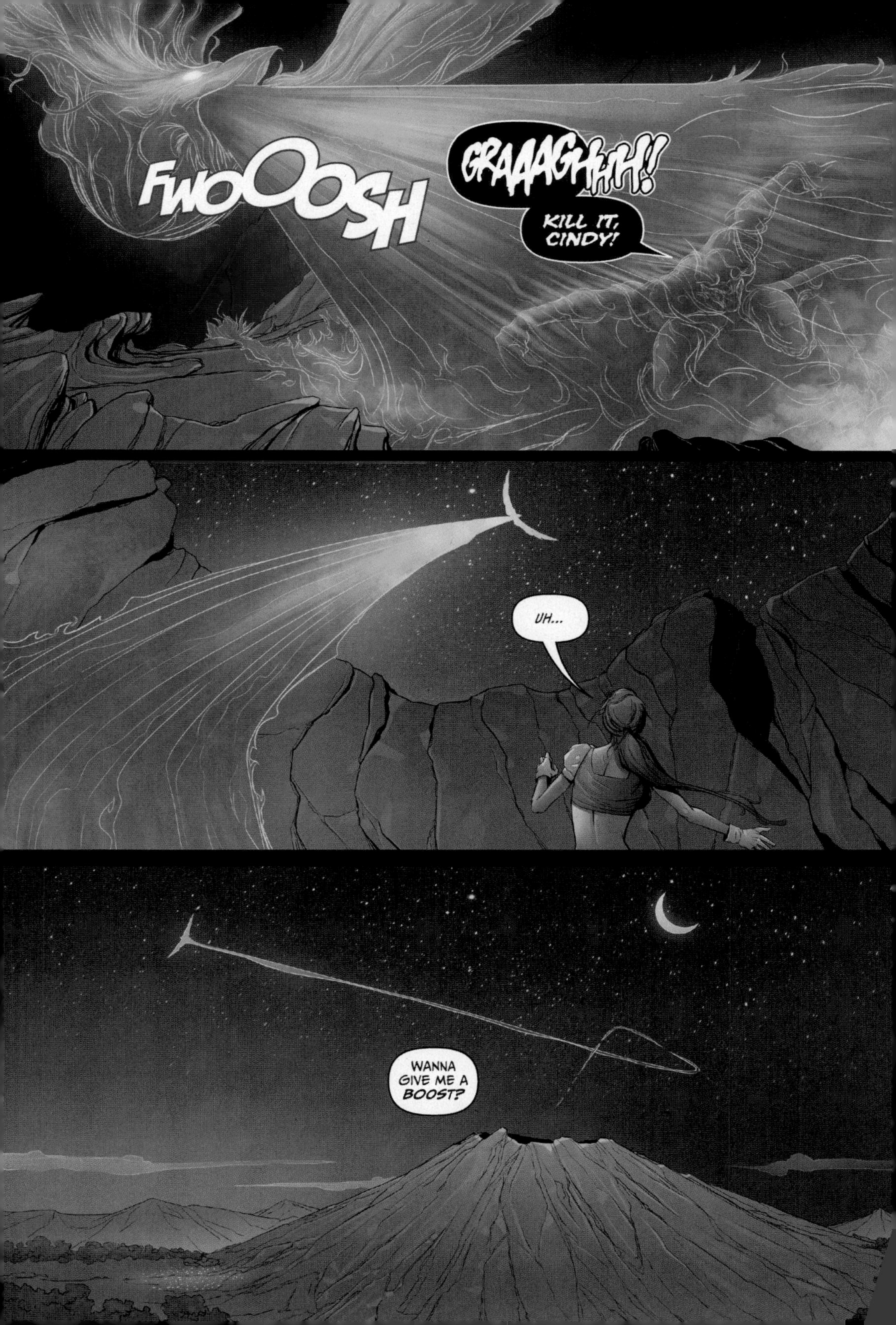
FWOOOOSH
GRAAAGHHHH!
KILL IT, CINDY!
UH...
WANNA GIVE ME A BOOST?

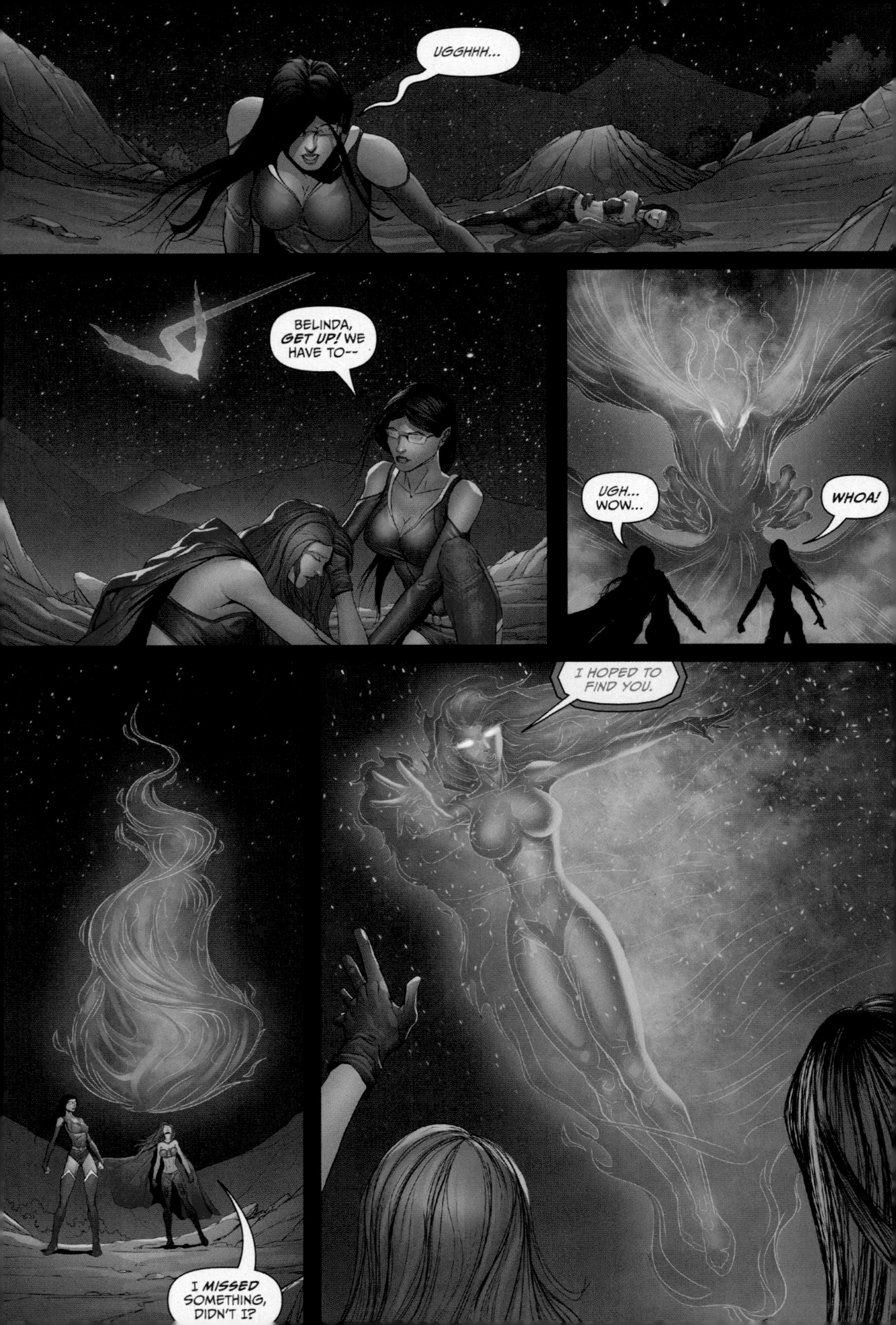
UGGHHH...
BELINDA, GET UP! WE HAVE TO--
UGH... WOW...
WHOA!
I MISSED SOMETHING, DIDN'T I?
I HOPED TO FIND YOU.

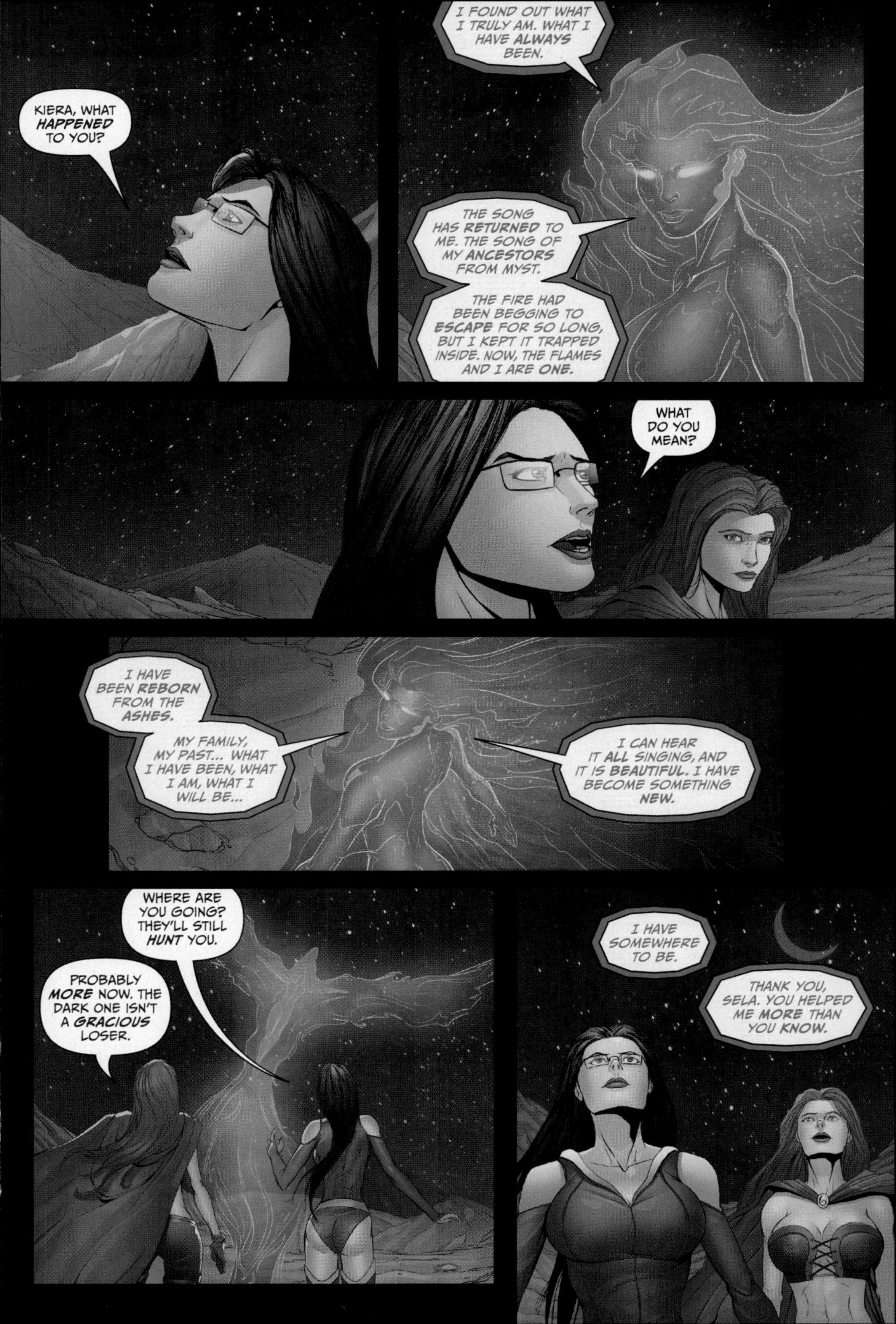
KIERA, WHAT HAPPENED TO YOU?
I FOUND OUT WHAT I TRULY AM. WHAT I HAVE ALWAYS BEEN.
THE SONG HAS RETURNED TO ME. THE SONG OF MY ANCESTORS FROM MYST.
THE FIRE HAD BEEN BEGGING TO ESCAPE FOR SO LONG, BUT I KEPT IT TRAPPED INSIDE. NOW, THE FLAMES AND I ARE ONE.
WHAT DO YOU MEAN?
I HAVE BEEN REBORN FROM THE ASHES.
MY FAMILY, MY PAST... WHAT I HAVE BEEN, WHAT I AM, WHAT I WILL BE...
I CAN HEAR IT ALL SINGING, AND IT IS BEAUTIFUL. I HAVE BECOME SOMETHING NEW.
WHERE ARE YOU GOING? THEY'LL STILL HUNT YOU.
PROBABLY MORE NOW. THE DARK ONE ISN'T A GRACIOUS LOSER.
I HAVE SOMEWHERE TO BE.
THANK YOU, SELA. YOU HELPED ME MORE THAN YOU KNOW.

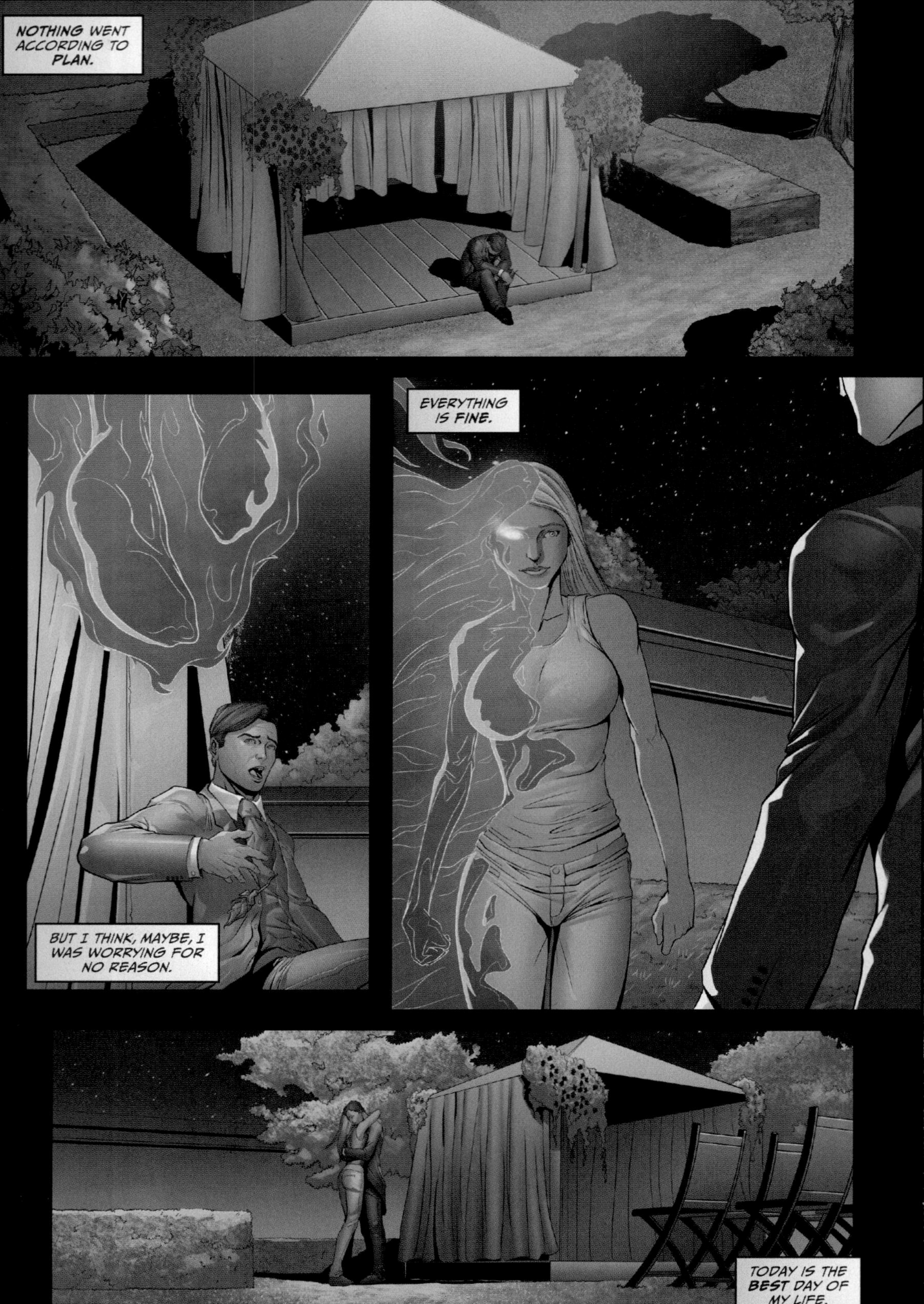
NOTHING WENT ACCORDING TO PLAN.
BUT I THINK, MAYBE, I WAS WORRYING FOR NO REASON.
EVERYTHING IS FINE.
TODAY IS THE BEST DAY OF MY LIFE.

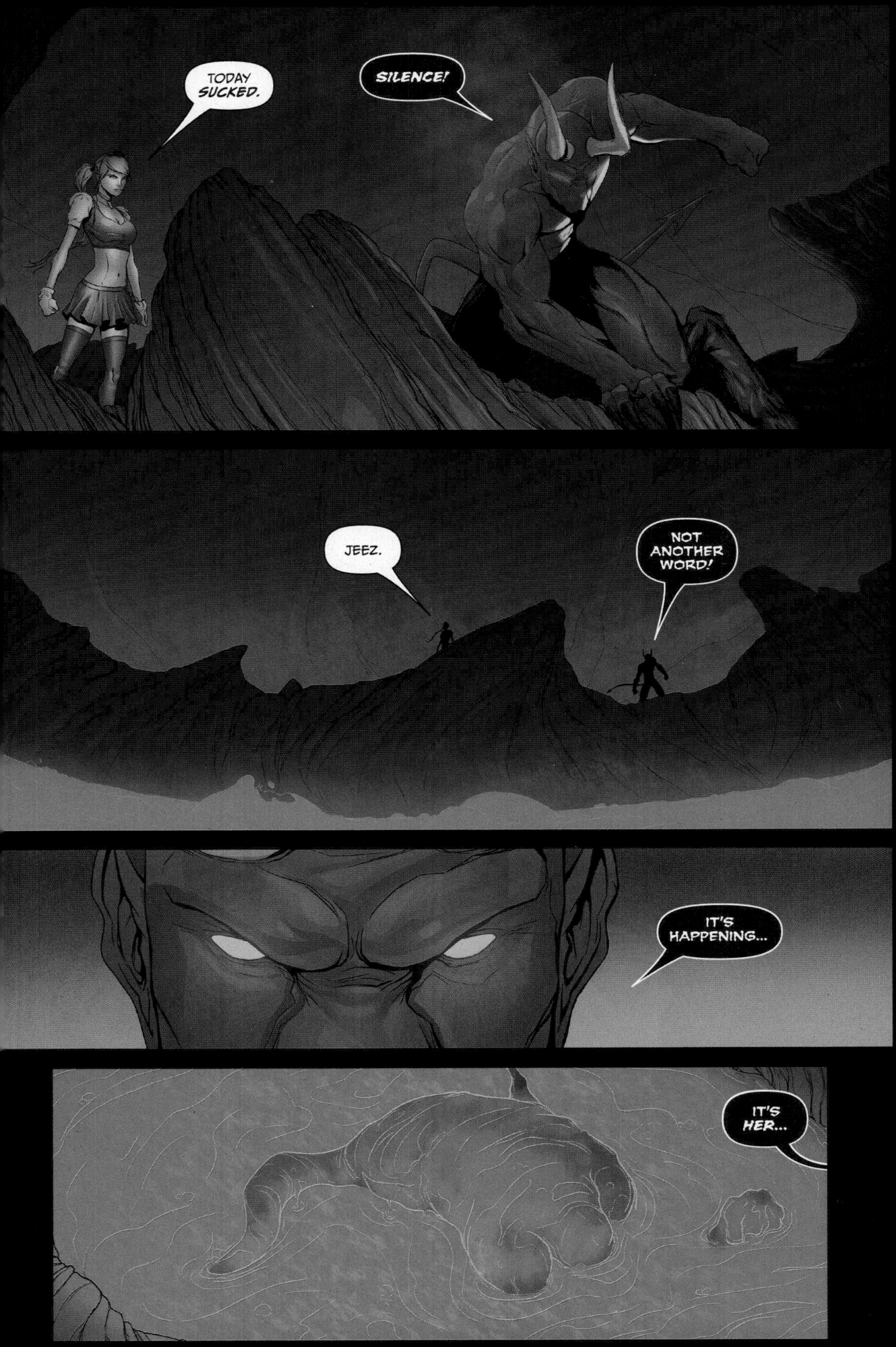
TODAY SUCKED.
SILENCE!
JEEZ.
NOT ANOTHER WORD!
IT'S HAPPENING...
IT'S HER...

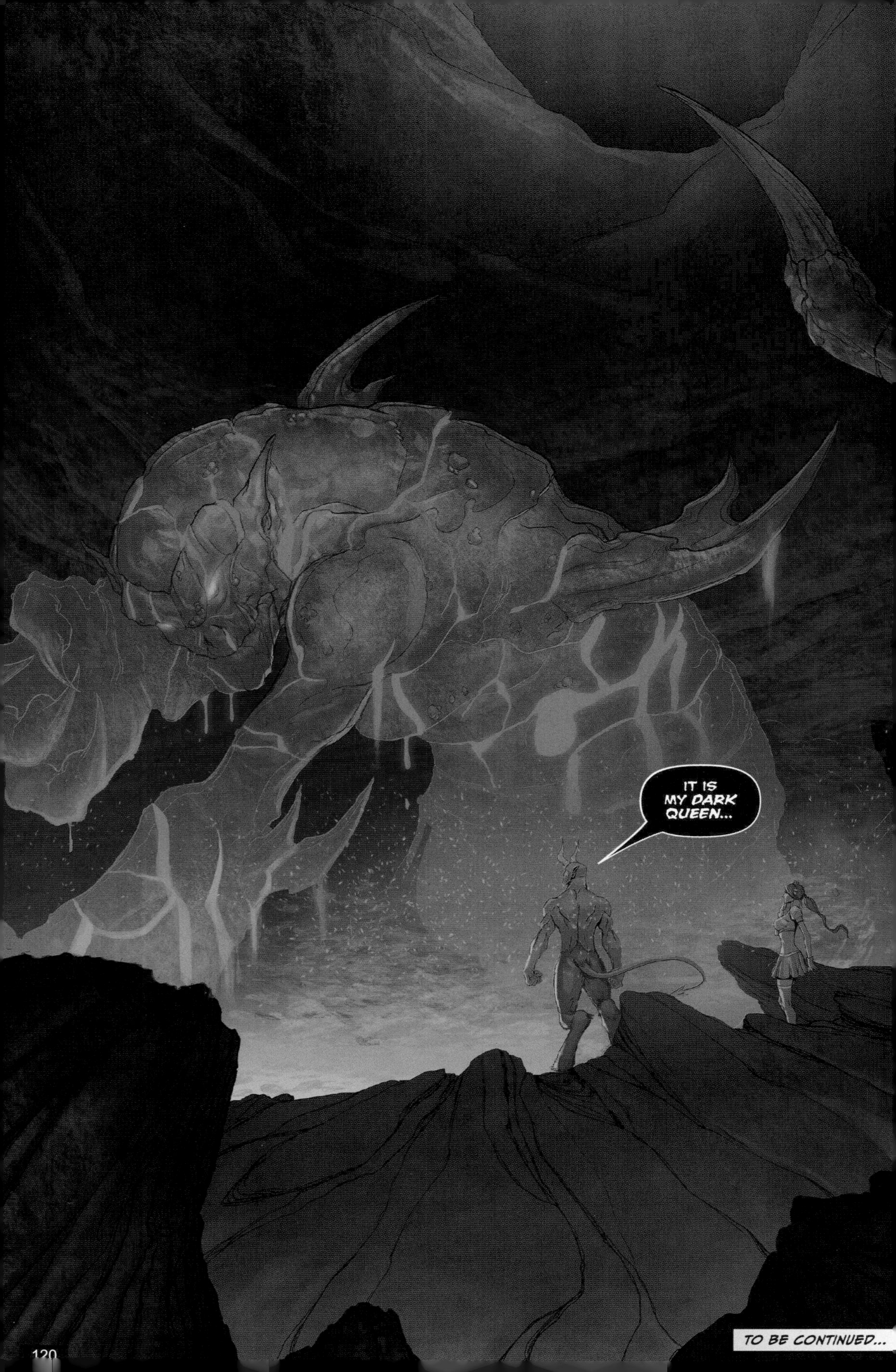
IT IS MY DARK QUEEN...
TO BE CONTINUED...

Grimm Fairy Tales

Volume 14

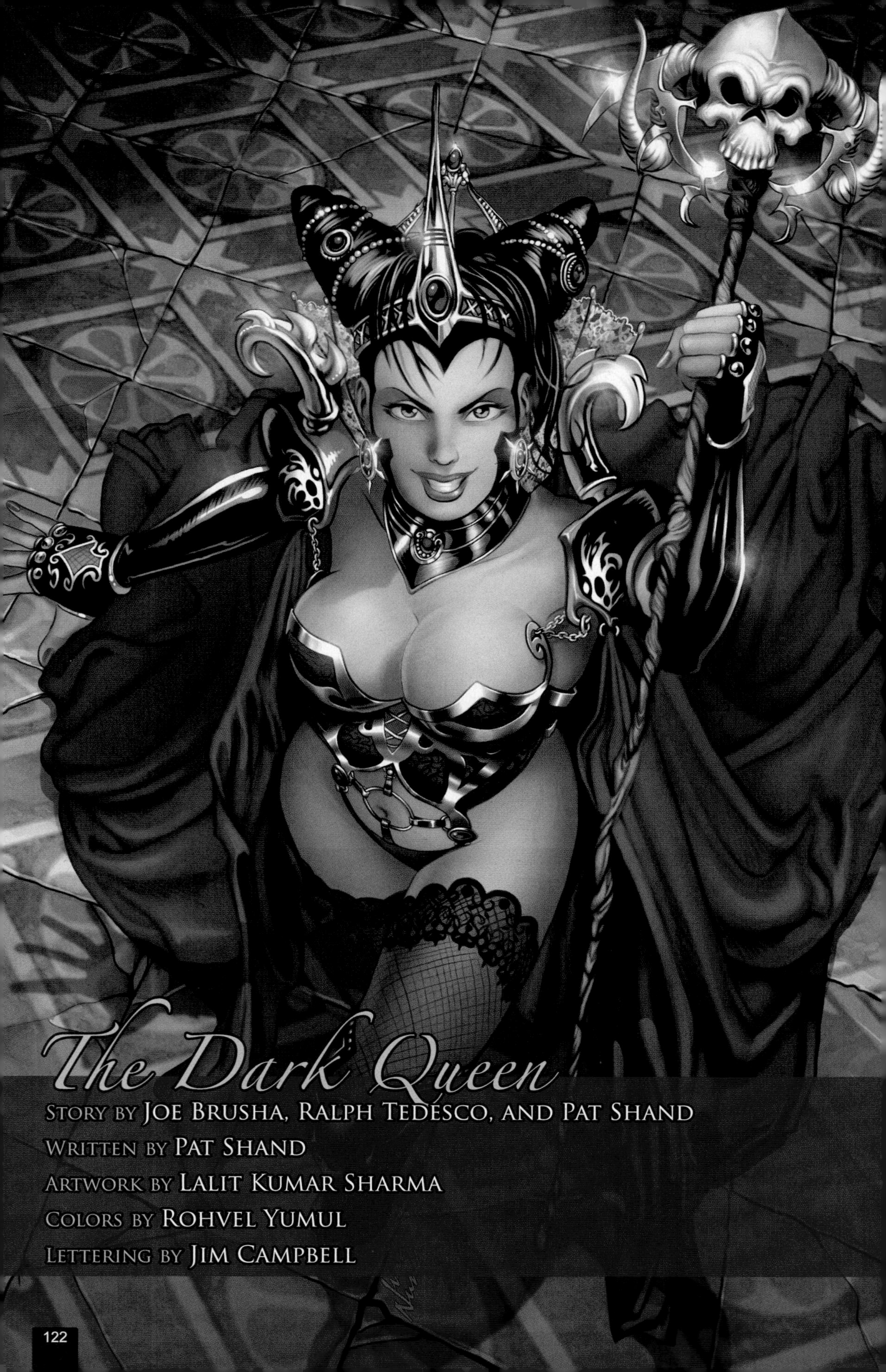

The Dark Queen

Story by Joe Brusha, Ralph Tedesco, and Pat Shand

Written by Pat Shand

Artwork by Lalit Kumar Sharma

Colors by Rohvel Yumul

Lettering by Jim Campbell

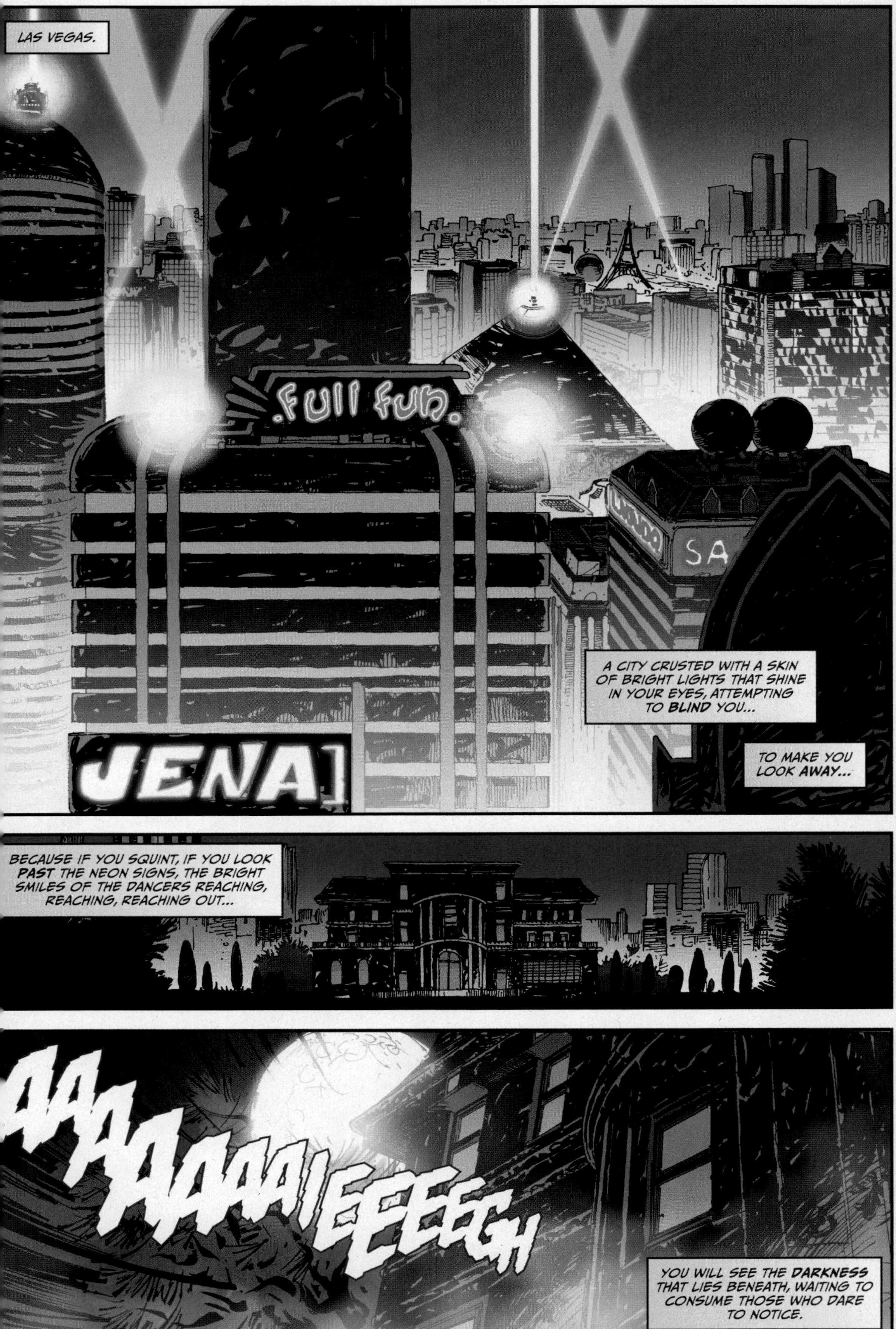
LAS VEGAS.
.FULL FUN.
JENA
SA
A CITY CRUSTED WITH A SKIN OF BRIGHT LIGHTS THAT SHINE IN YOUR EYES, ATTEMPTING TO BLIND YOU...
TO MAKE YOU LOOK AWAY...
BECAUSE IF YOU SQUINT, IF YOU LOOK PAST THE NEON SIGNS, THE BRIGHT SMILES OF THE DANCERS REACHING, REACHING, REACHING OUT...
AAAAAAAAAIEEEEGH
YOU WILL SEE THE DARKNESS THAT LIES BENEATH, WAITING TO CONSUME THOSE WHO DARE TO NOTICE.

IN THE HOME OF MALEC, THE DARK ONE, A MONSTER DWELLS.

SHE WAS ONCE HIS BRIDE. THE DARK QUEEN, A TYRANT EVEN MORE FEARED THAN HER LOVER. SHE GAVE HIM POWER. SHE GAVE HIM EVERYTHING.

THIS IS A MINOR SETBACK.

THEN SHE DIED.

YOU HAVE ALREADY GAINED CONTROL OF THIS FORM...

AND HE BROUGHT HER BACK WRONG.

WE WILL FIX THIS.

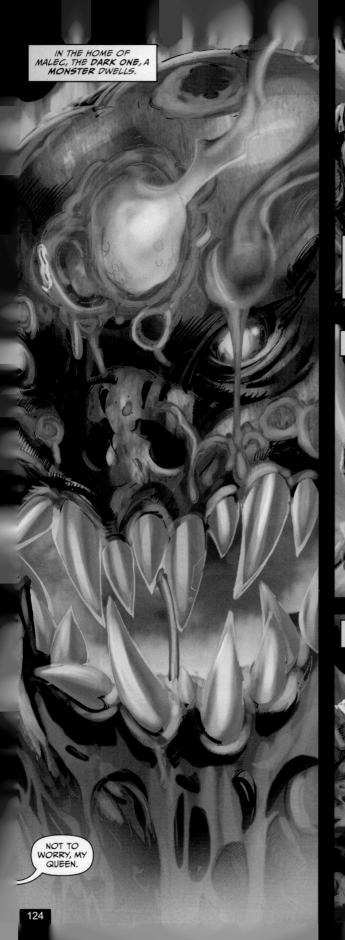

NOT TO WORRY, MY QUEEN.

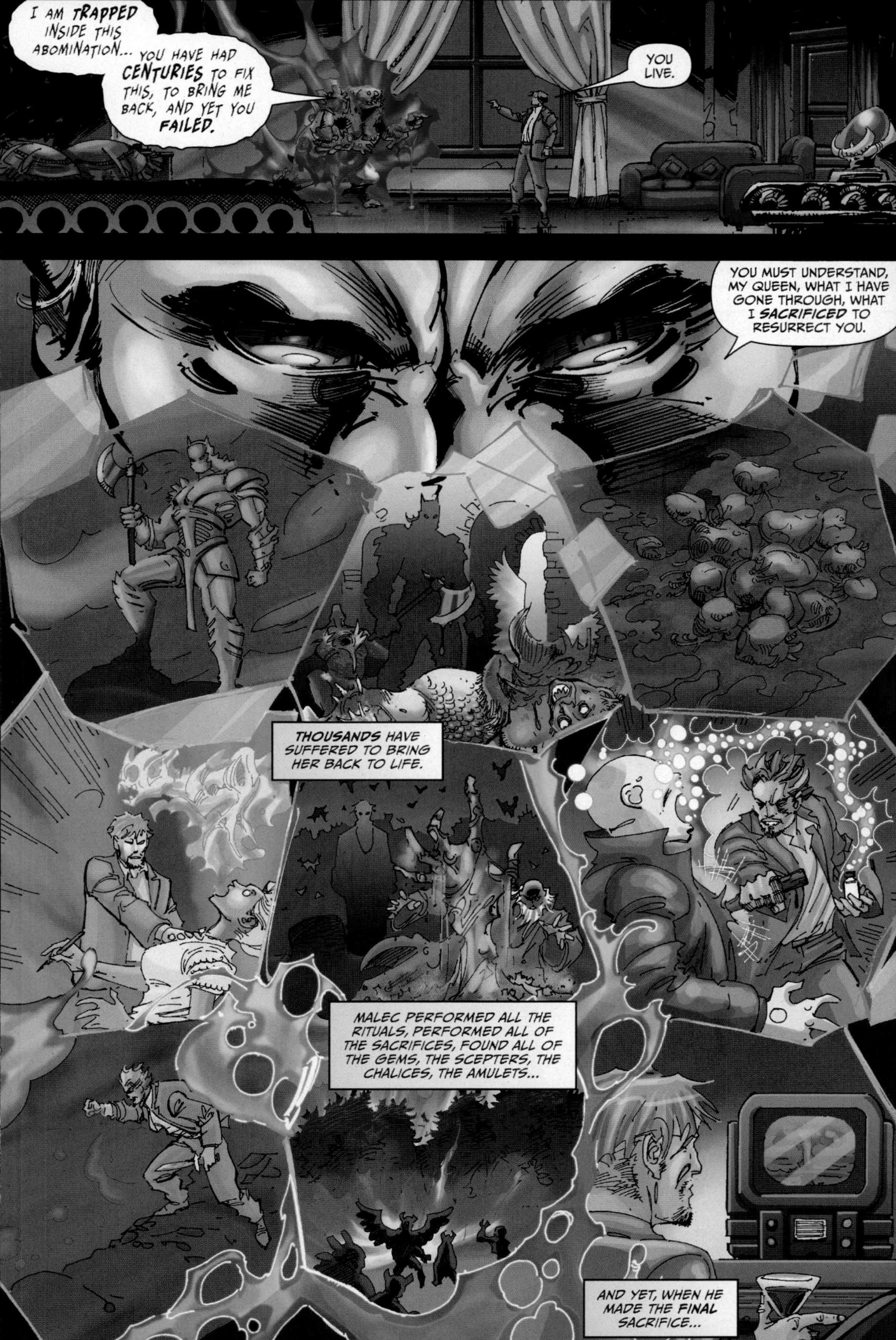

I AM TRAPPED INSIDE THIS ABOMINATION... YOU HAVE HAD CENTURIES TO FIX THIS, TO BRING ME BACK, AND YET YOU FAILED.
YOU LIVE.
YOU MUST UNDERSTAND, MY QUEEN, WHAT I HAVE GONE THROUGH, WHAT I SACRIFICED TO RESURRECT YOU.
THOUSANDS HAVE SUFFERED TO BRING HER BACK TO LIFE.
MALEC PERFORMED ALL THE RITUALS, PERFORMED ALL OF THE SACRIFICES, FOUND ALL OF THE GEMS, THE SCEPTERS, THE CHALICES, THE AMULETS...
AND YET, WHEN HE MADE THE FINAL SACRIFICE...

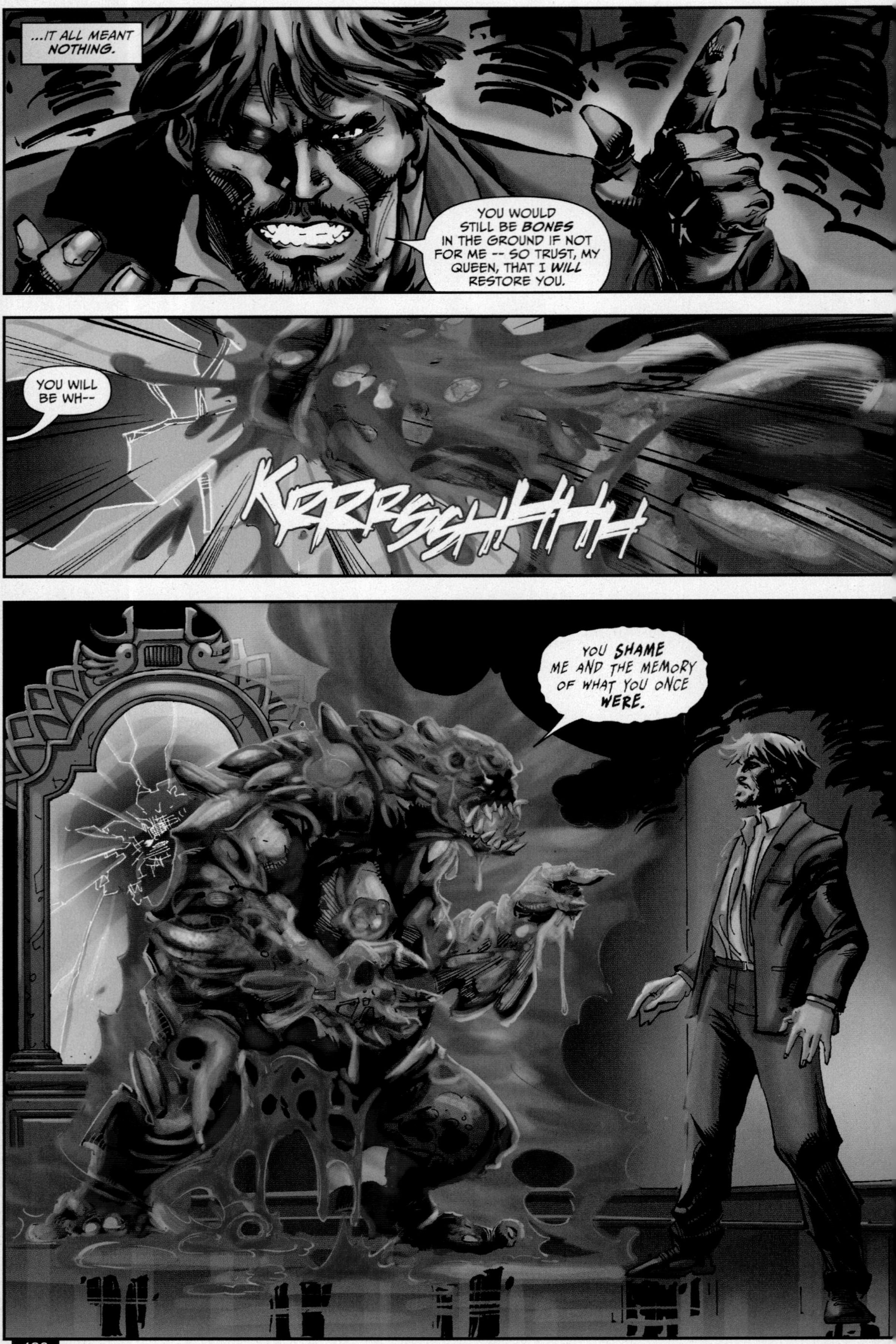
...IT ALL MEANT NOTHING.
YOU WOULD STILL BE BONES IN THE GROUND IF NOT FOR ME -- SO TRUST, MY QUEEN, THAT I WILL RESTORE YOU.
YOU WILL BE WH--
KRRRSCHHHHH
YOU SHAME ME AND THE MEMORY OF WHAT YOU ONCE WERE.

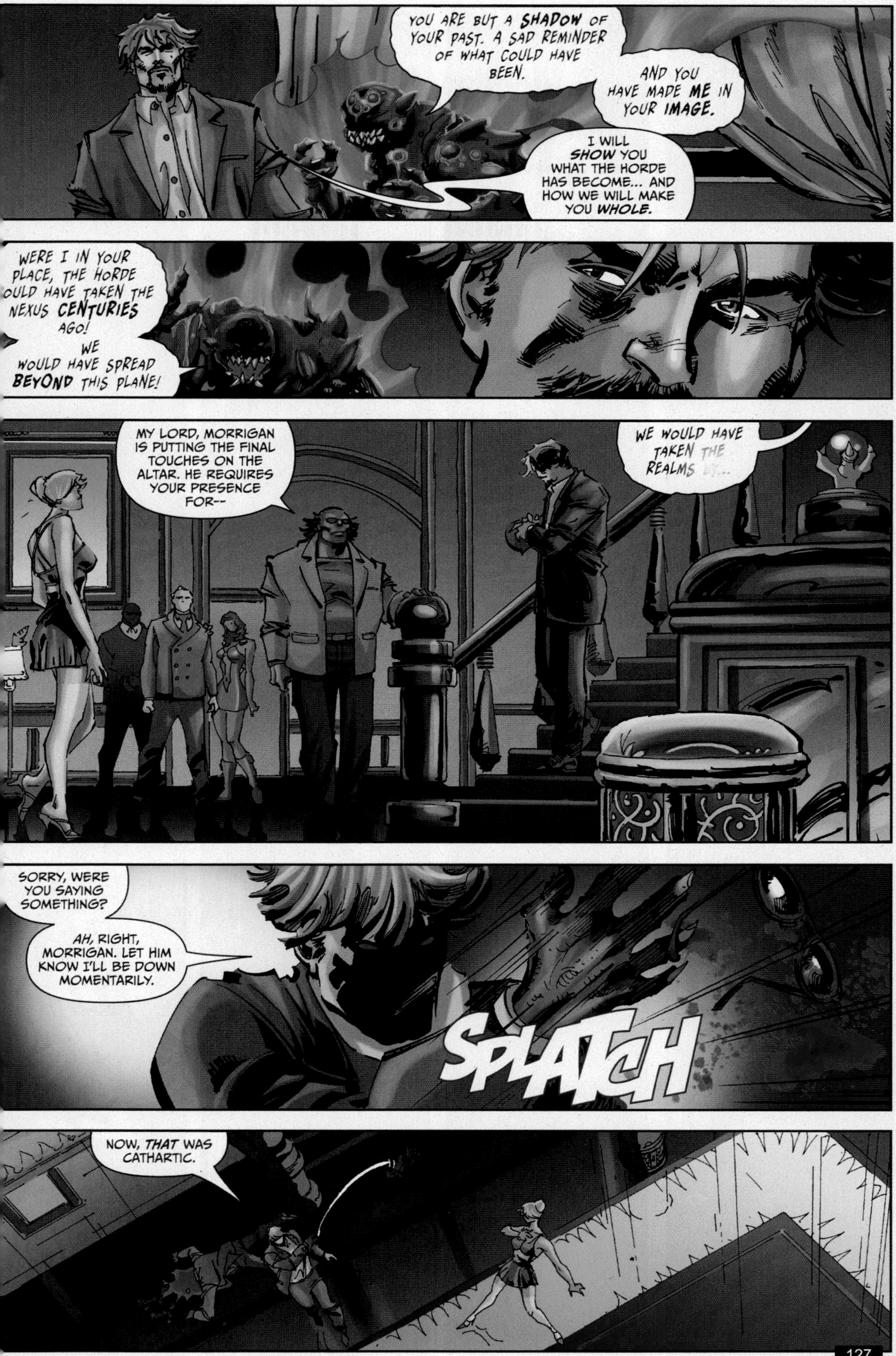
YOU ARE BUT A SHADOW OF YOUR PAST. A SAD REMINDER OF WHAT COULD HAVE BEEN.
AND YOU HAVE MADE ME IN YOUR IMAGE.
I WILL SHOW YOU WHAT THE HORDE HAS BECOME... AND HOW WE WILL MAKE YOU WHOLE.
WERE I IN YOUR PLACE, THE HORDE OULD HAVE TAKEN THE NEXUS CENTURIES AGO!
WE WOULD HAVE SPREAD BEYOND THIS PLANE!
MY LORD, MORRIGAN IS PUTTING THE FINAL TOUCHES ON THE ALTAR. HE REQUIRES YOUR PRESENCE FOR--
WE WOULD HAVE TAKEN THE REALMS BY...
SORRY, WERE YOU SAYING SOMETHING?
AH, RIGHT, MORRIGAN. LET HIM KNOW I'LL BE DOWN MOMENTARILY.
SPLATCH
NOW, THAT WAS CATHARTIC.

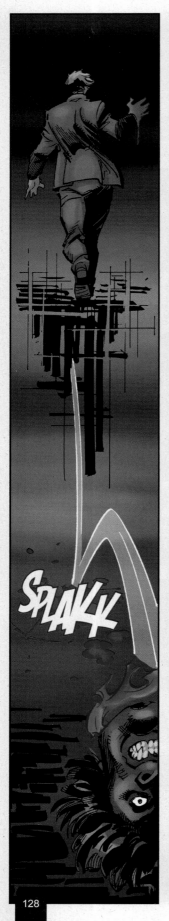

SPLAKK

TSSSSSS

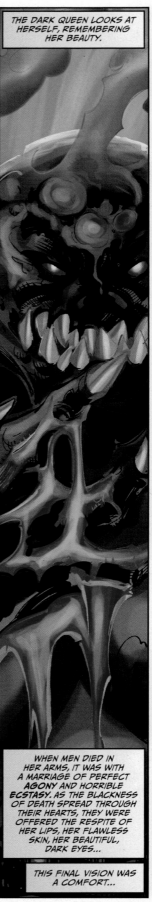

THE DARK QUEEN LOOKS AT HERSELF, REMEMBERING HER BEAUTY.

WHEN MEN DIED IN HER ARMS, IT WAS WITH A MARRIAGE OF PERFECT AGONY AND HORRIBLE ECSTASY. AS THE BLACKNESS OF DEATH SPREAD THROUGH THEIR HEARTS, THEY WERE OFFERED THE RESPITE OF HER LIPS, HER FLAWLESS SKIN, HER BEAUTIFUL, DARK EYES...

THIS FINAL VISION WAS A COMFORT...

NOW, THERE IS NO RESPITE...

AIIHHHEEEE

NOW, THERE IS ONLY THE MONSTER...

THE MONSTER THAT HAD BEEN DWELLING BEYOND THE SURFACE OF LIGHTS AND SMILES FOR LONGER THAN ANYONE NOTICED.

BEFORE SHE WAS CORRUPTED BY THE POWER OF THE DARK HORDE, LUCINDA LIVED A LIFE NOT UNLIKE THE OTHER PRINCESSES OF MYST.

ISOLATED BY OVER-PROTECTIVE PARENTS, SHE DWELLED IN HER CASTLE ALONE, ROAMING THE HALLS LIKE A GHOST, WAITING FOR A VALIANT KNIGHT TO COME RESCUE HER.

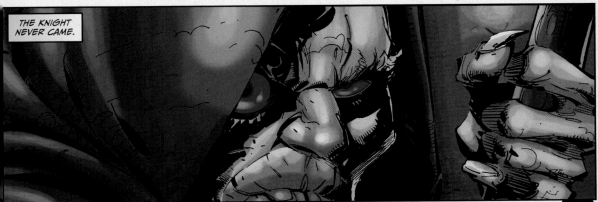

THE KNIGHT NEVER CAME.

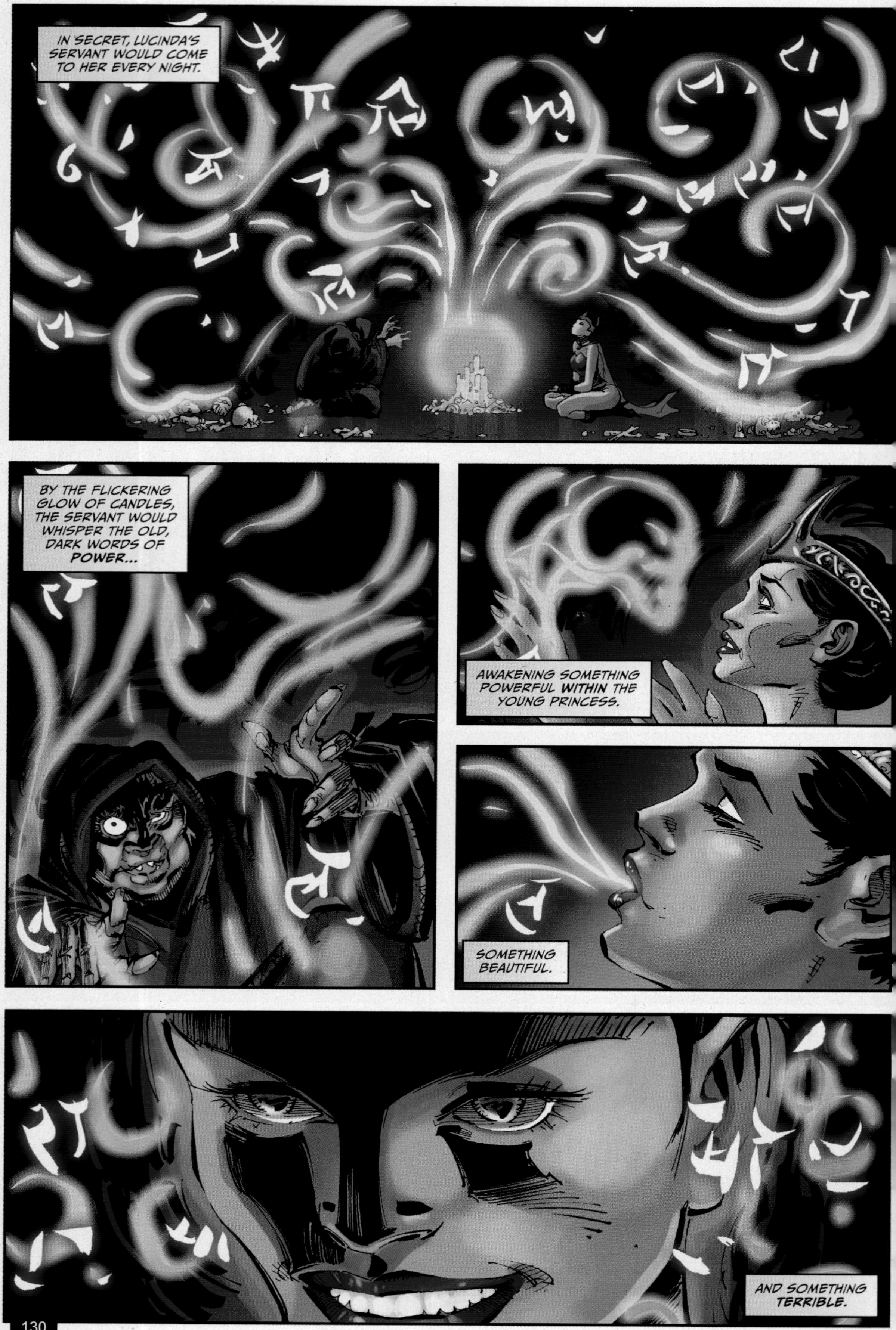
IN SECRET, LUCINDA'S SERVANT WOULD COME TO HER EVERY NIGHT.
BY THE FLICKERING GLOW OF CANDLES, THE SERVANT WOULD WHISPER THE OLD, DARK WORDS OF POWER...
AWAKENING SOMETHING POWERFUL WITHIN THE YOUNG PRINCESS.
SOMETHING BEAUTIFUL.
AND SOMETHING TERRIBLE.

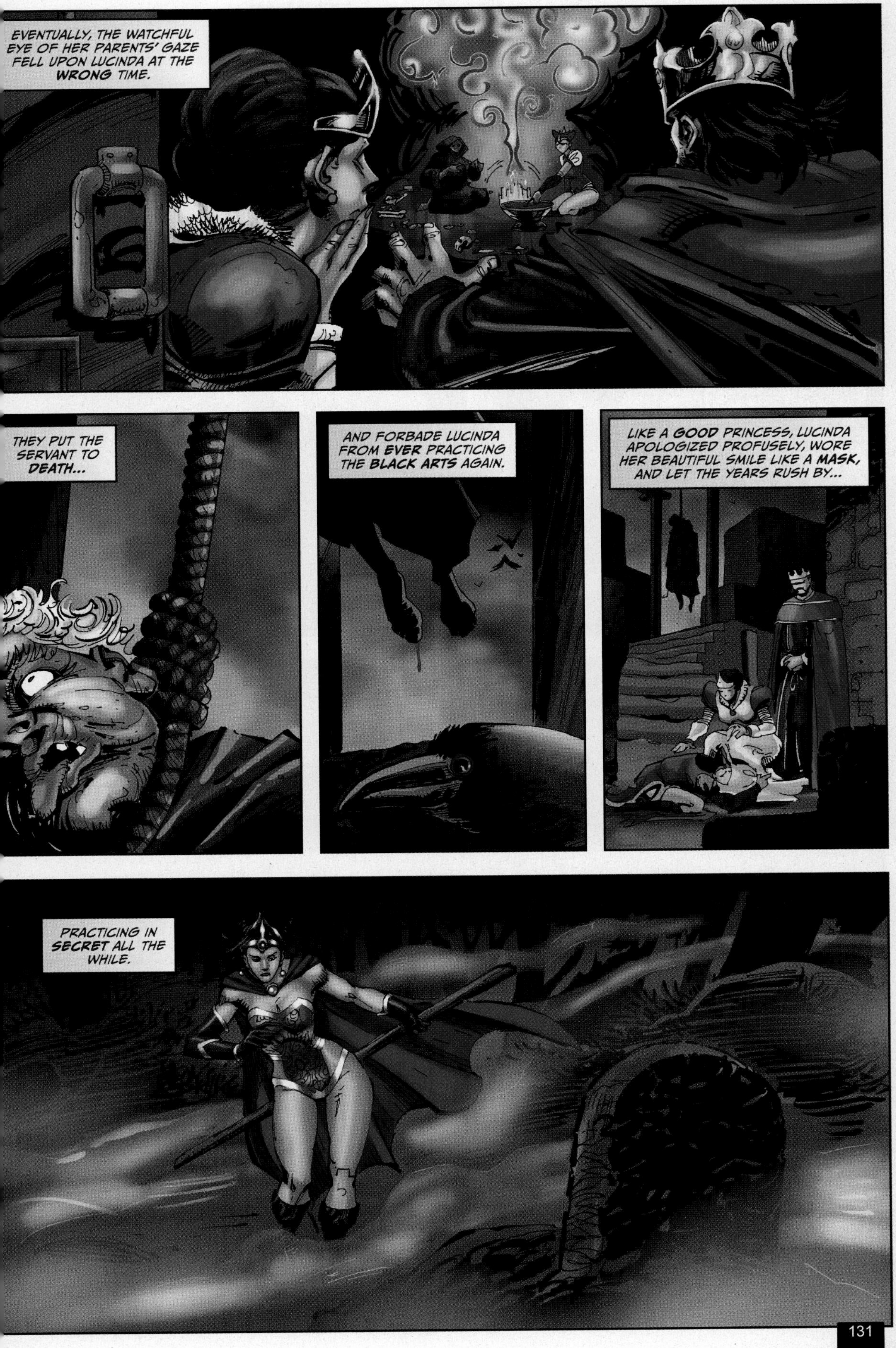
EVENTUALLY, THE WATCHFUL EYE OF HER PARENTS' GAZE FELL UPON LUCINDA AT THE WRONG TIME.
THEY PUT THE SERVANT TO DEATH...
AND FORBADE LUCINDA FROM EVER PRACTICING THE BLACK ARTS AGAIN.
LIKE A GOOD PRINCESS, LUCINDA APOLOGIZED PROFUSELY, WORE HER BEAUTIFUL SMILE LIKE A MASK, AND LET THE YEARS RUSH BY...
PRACTICING IN SECRET ALL THE WHILE.

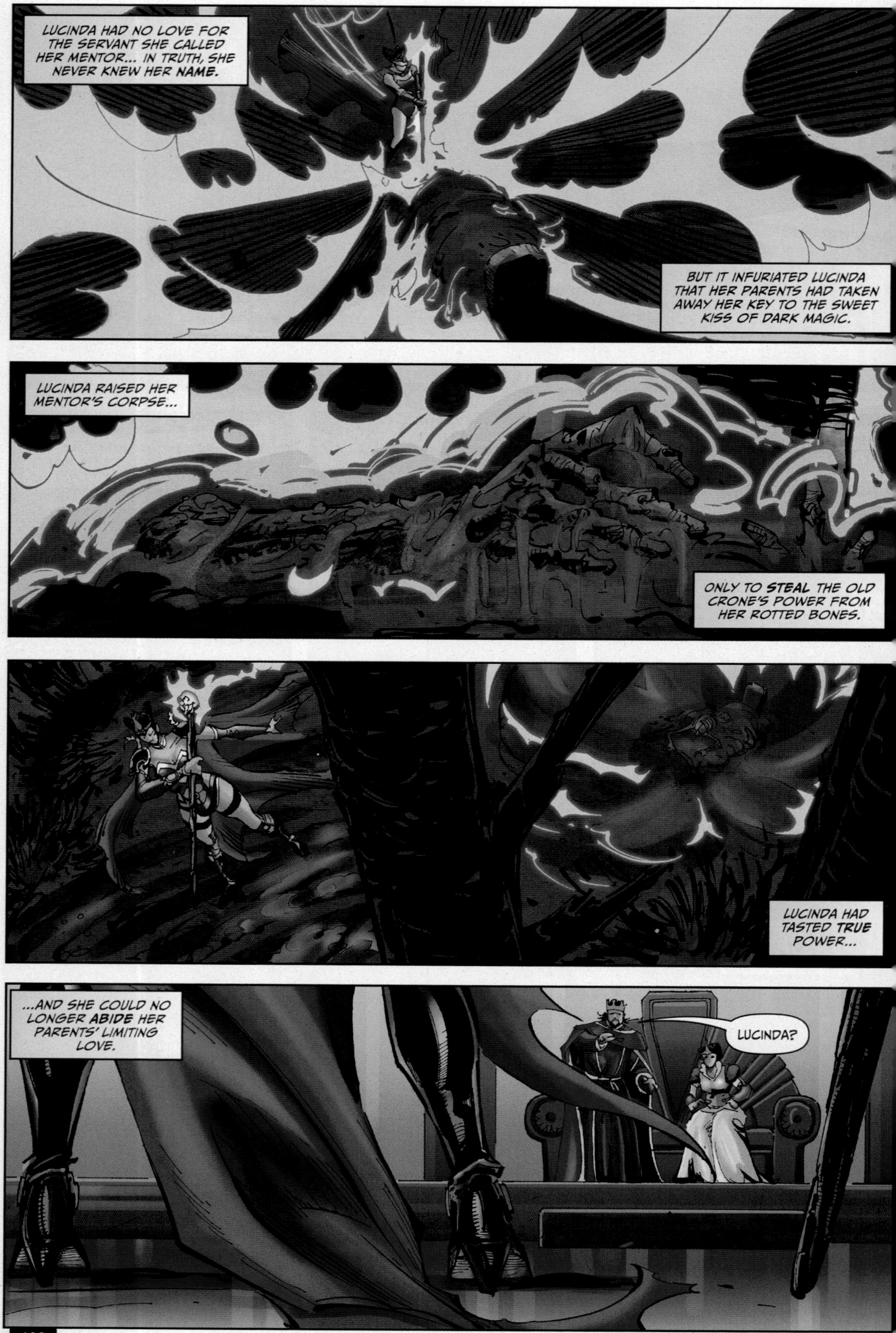
LUCINDA HAD NO LOVE FOR THE SERVANT SHE CALLED HER MENTOR... IN TRUTH, SHE NEVER KNEW HER NAME.
BUT IT INFURIATED LUCINDA THAT HER PARENTS HAD TAKEN AWAY HER KEY TO THE SWEET KISS OF DARK MAGIC.
LUCINDA RAISED HER MENTOR'S CORPSE...
ONLY TO STEAL THE OLD CRONE'S POWER FROM HER ROTTED BONES.
LUCINDA HAD TASTED TRUE POWER...
...AND SHE COULD NO LONGER ABIDE HER PARENTS' LIMITING LOVE.
LUCINDA?

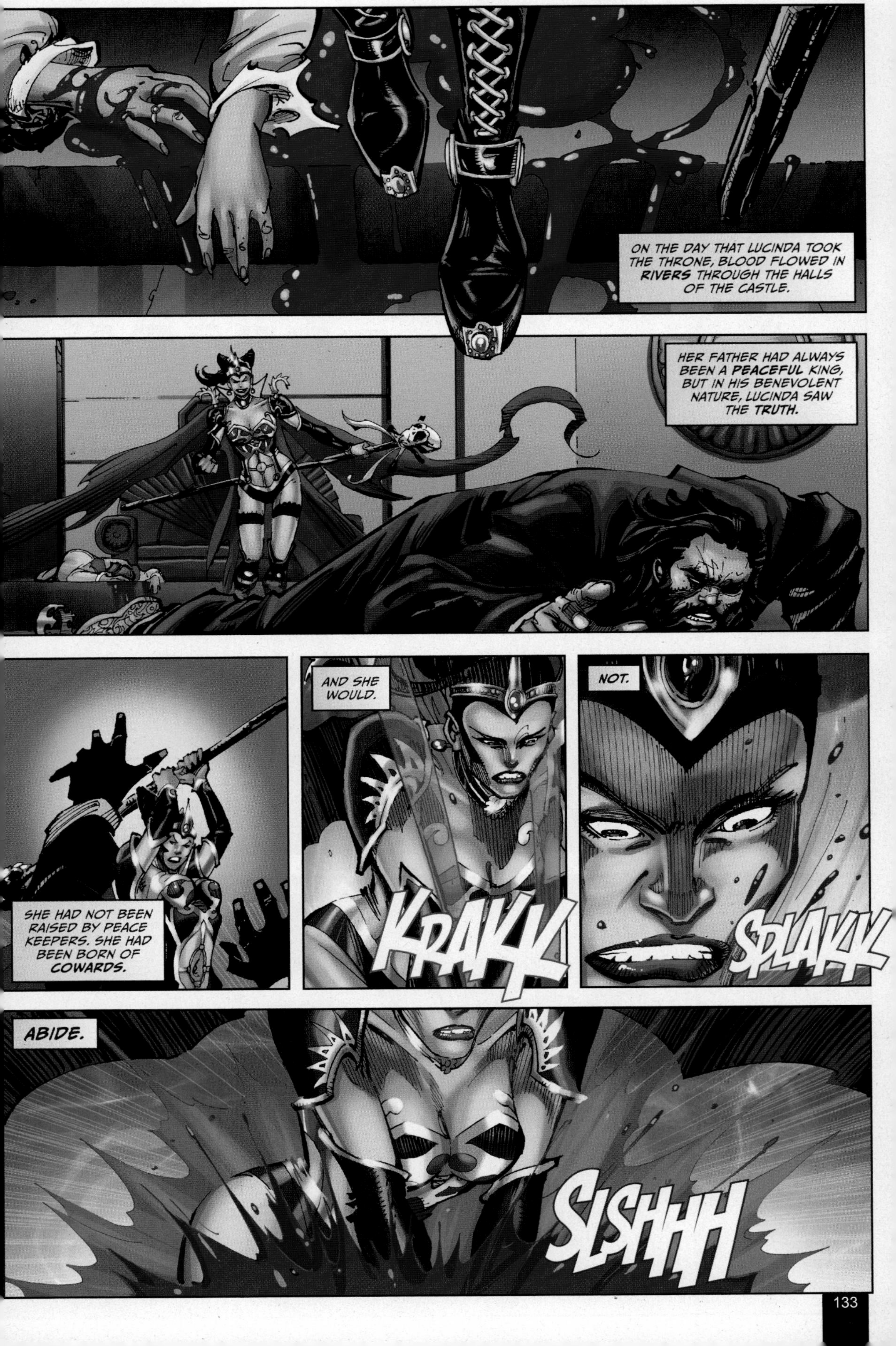
ON THE DAY THAT LUCINDA TOOK THE THRONE, BLOOD FLOWED IN RIVERS THROUGH THE HALLS OF THE CASTLE.
HER FATHER HAD ALWAYS BEEN A PEACEFUL KING, BUT IN HIS BENEVOLENT NATURE, LUCINDA SAW THE TRUTH.
SHE HAD NOT BEEN RAISED BY PEACE KEEPERS. SHE HAD BEEN BORN OF COWARDS.
AND SHE WOULD.
KRAKK
NOT.
SPLAKK
ABIDE.
SLSHHH

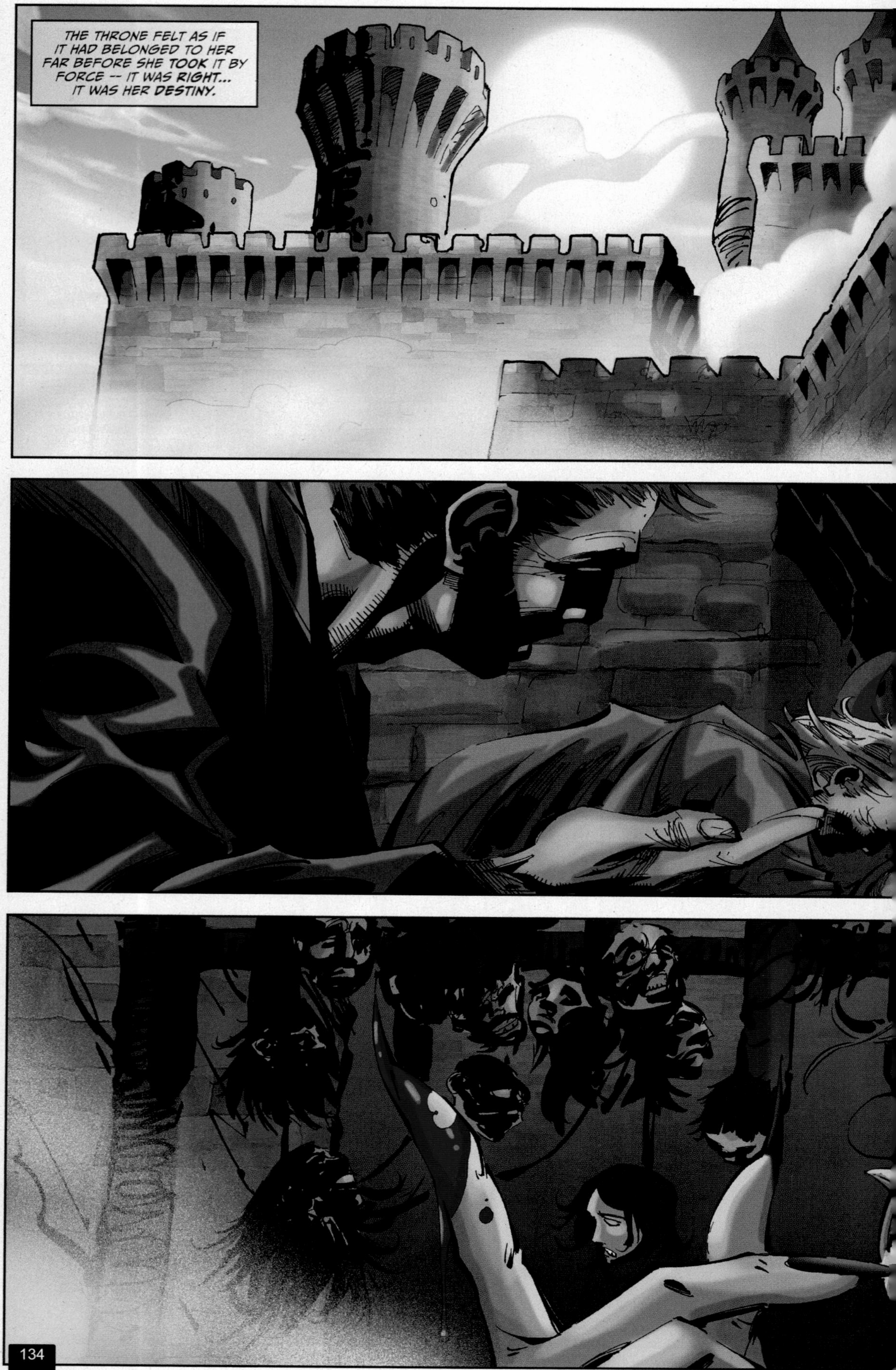
THE THRONE FELT AS IF IT HAD BELONGED TO HER FAR BEFORE SHE TOOK IT BY FORCE -- IT WAS RIGHT... IT WAS HER DESTINY.

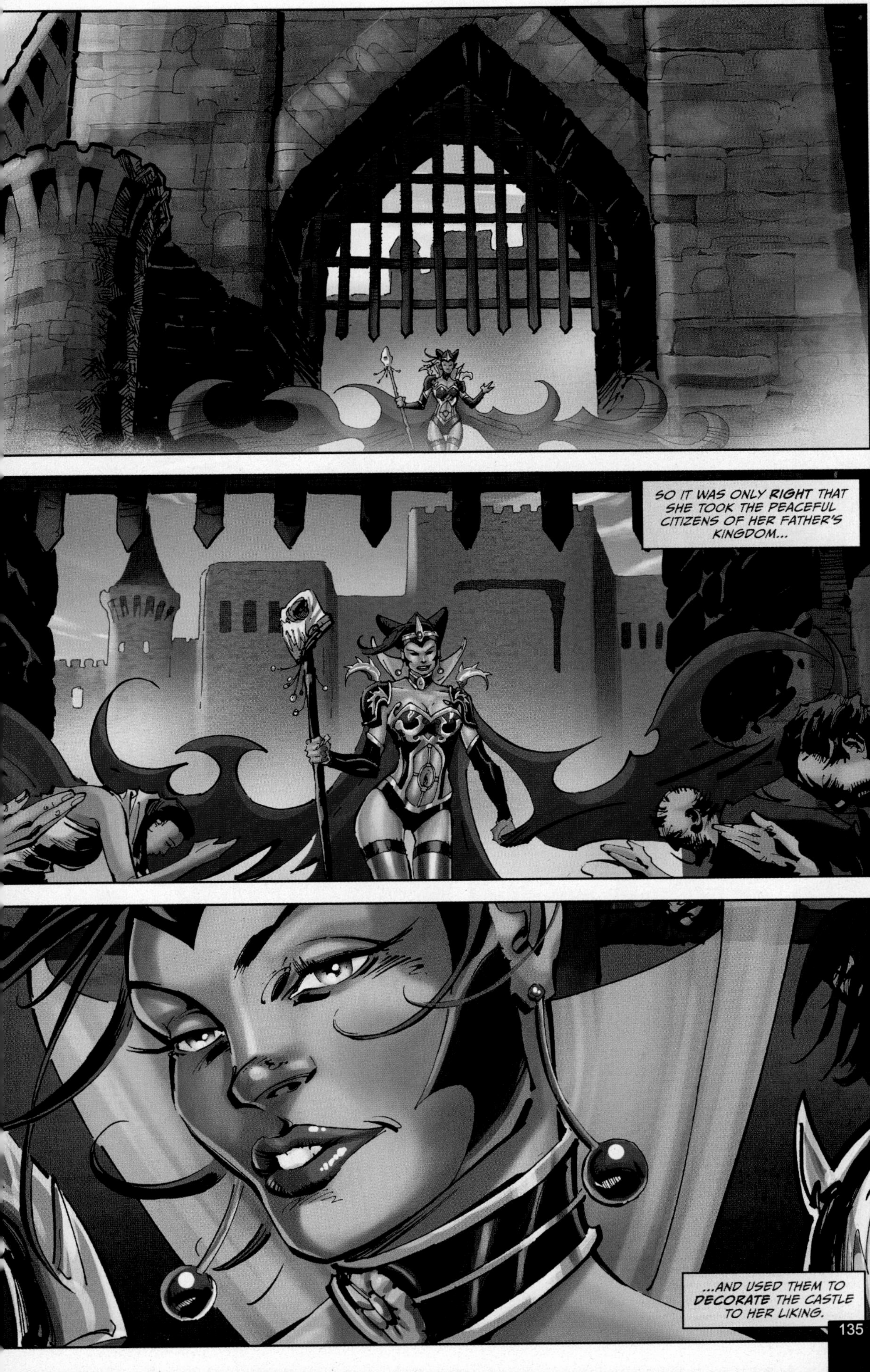
SO IT WAS ONLY RIGHT THAT SHE TOOK THE PEACEFUL CITIZENS OF HER FATHER'S KINGDOM...
...AND USED THEM TO DECORATE THE CASTLE TO HER LIKING.

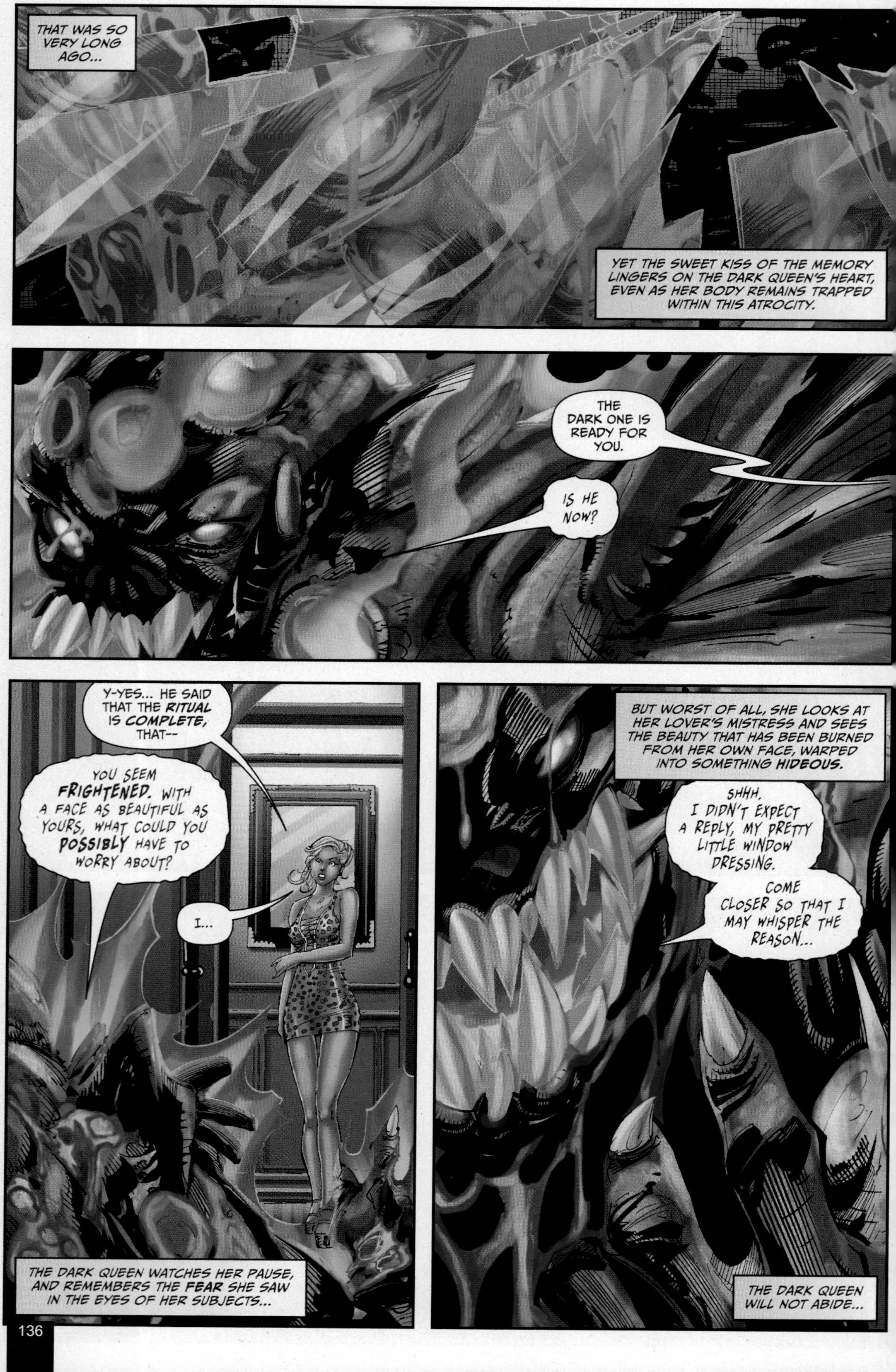
THAT WAS SO VERY LONG AGO...
YET THE SWEET KISS OF THE MEMORY LINGERS ON THE DARK QUEEN'S HEART, EVEN AS HER BODY REMAINS TRAPPED WITHIN THIS ATROCITY.
THE DARK ONE IS READY FOR YOU.
IS HE NOW?
Y-YES... HE SAID THAT THE RITUAL IS COMPLETE, THAT--
YOU SEEM FRIGHTENED. WITH A FACE AS BEAUTIFUL AS YOURS, WHAT COULD YOU POSSIBLY HAVE TO WORRY ABOUT?
I...
THE DARK QUEEN WATCHES HER PAUSE, AND REMEMBERS THE FEAR SHE SAW IN THE EYES OF HER SUBJECTS...
BUT WORST OF ALL, SHE LOOKS AT HER LOVER'S MISTRESS AND SEES THE BEAUTY THAT HAS BEEN BURNED FROM HER OWN FACE, WARPED INTO SOMETHING HIDEOUS.
SHHH. I DIDN'T EXPECT A REPLY, MY PRETTY LITTLE WINDOW DRESSING.
COME CLOSER SO THAT I MAY WHISPER THE REASON...
THE DARK QUEEN WILL NOT ABIDE...

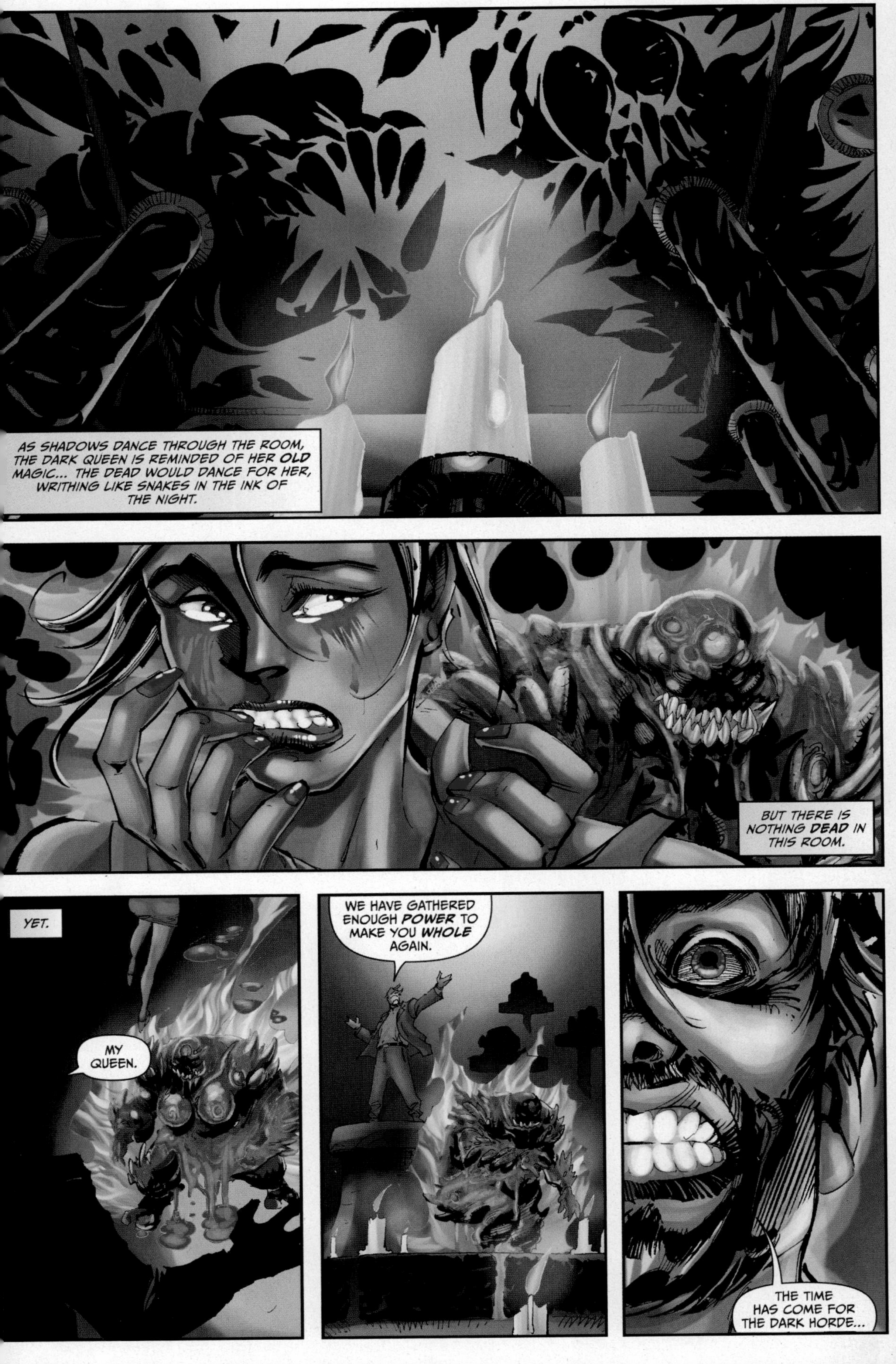
AS SHADOWS DANCE THROUGH THE ROOM, THE DARK QUEEN IS REMINDED OF HER OLD MAGIC... THE DEAD WOULD DANCE FOR HER, WRITHING LIKE SNAKES IN THE INK OF THE NIGHT.
BUT THERE IS NOTHING DEAD IN THIS ROOM.
YET.
MY QUEEN.
WE HAVE GATHERED ENOUGH POWER TO MAKE YOU WHOLE AGAIN.
THE TIME HAS COME FOR THE DARK HORDE...

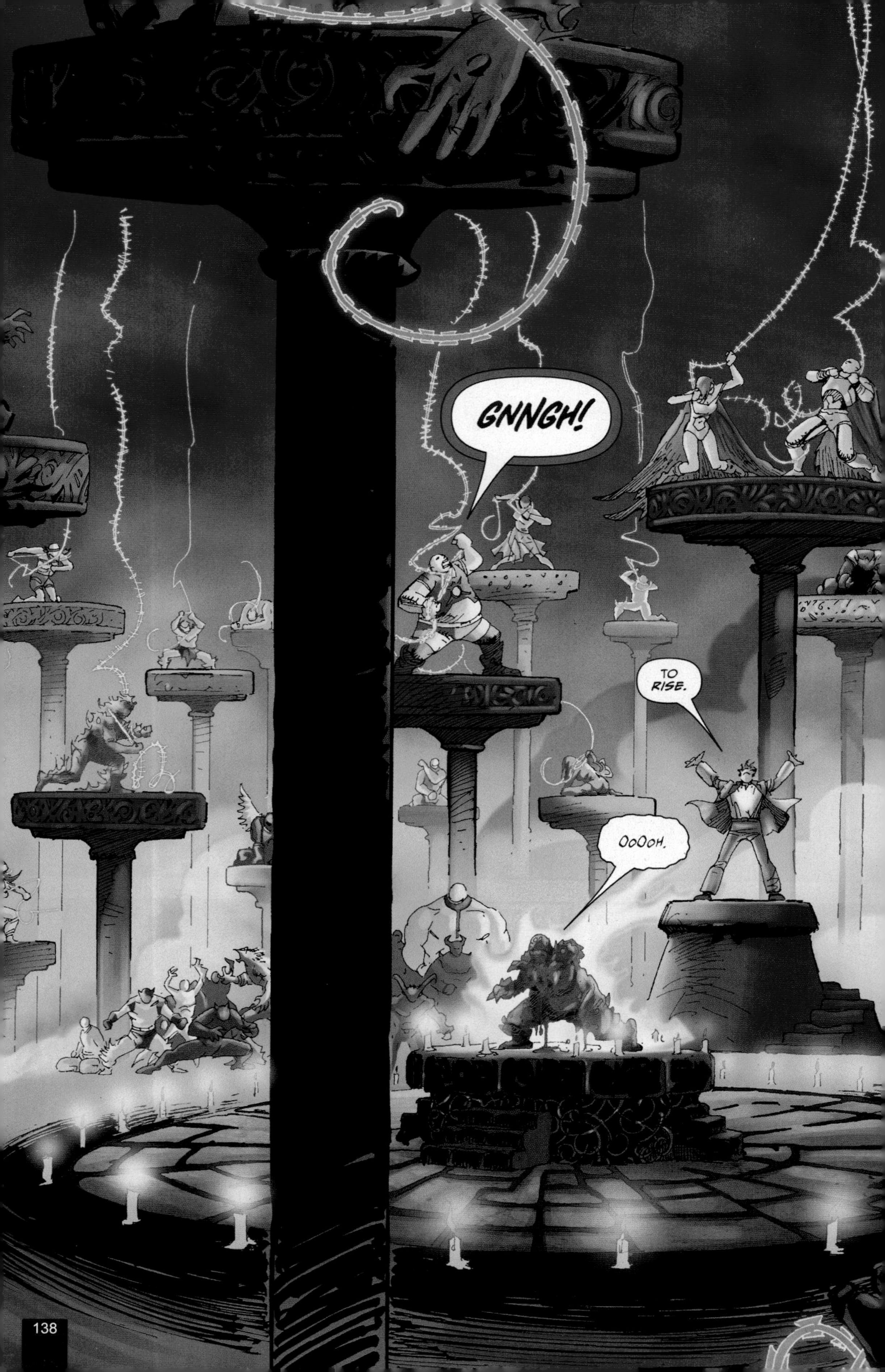
GNNGH!
TO RISE.
OOOOH.

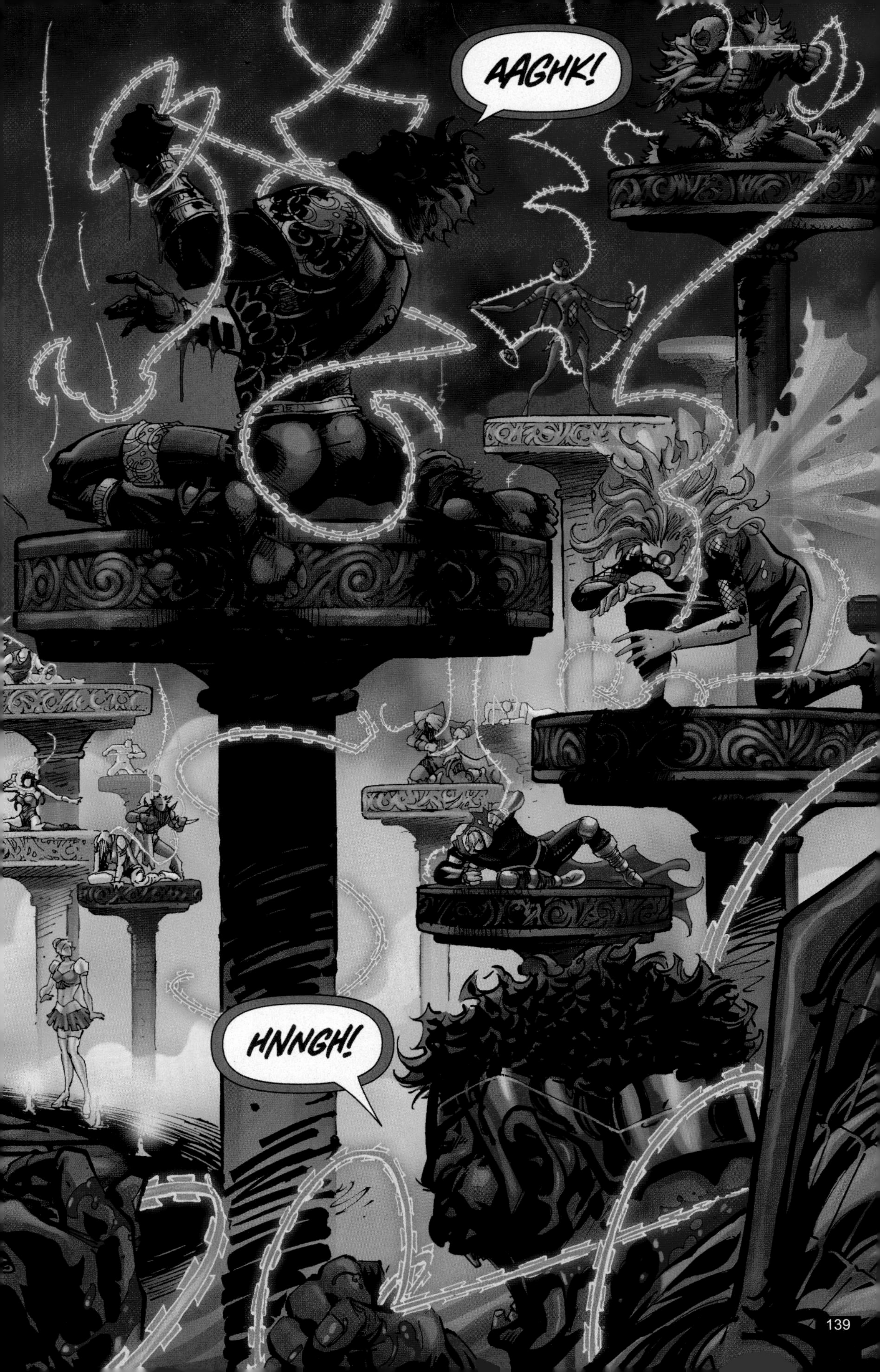
AAGHK!
HNNGH!

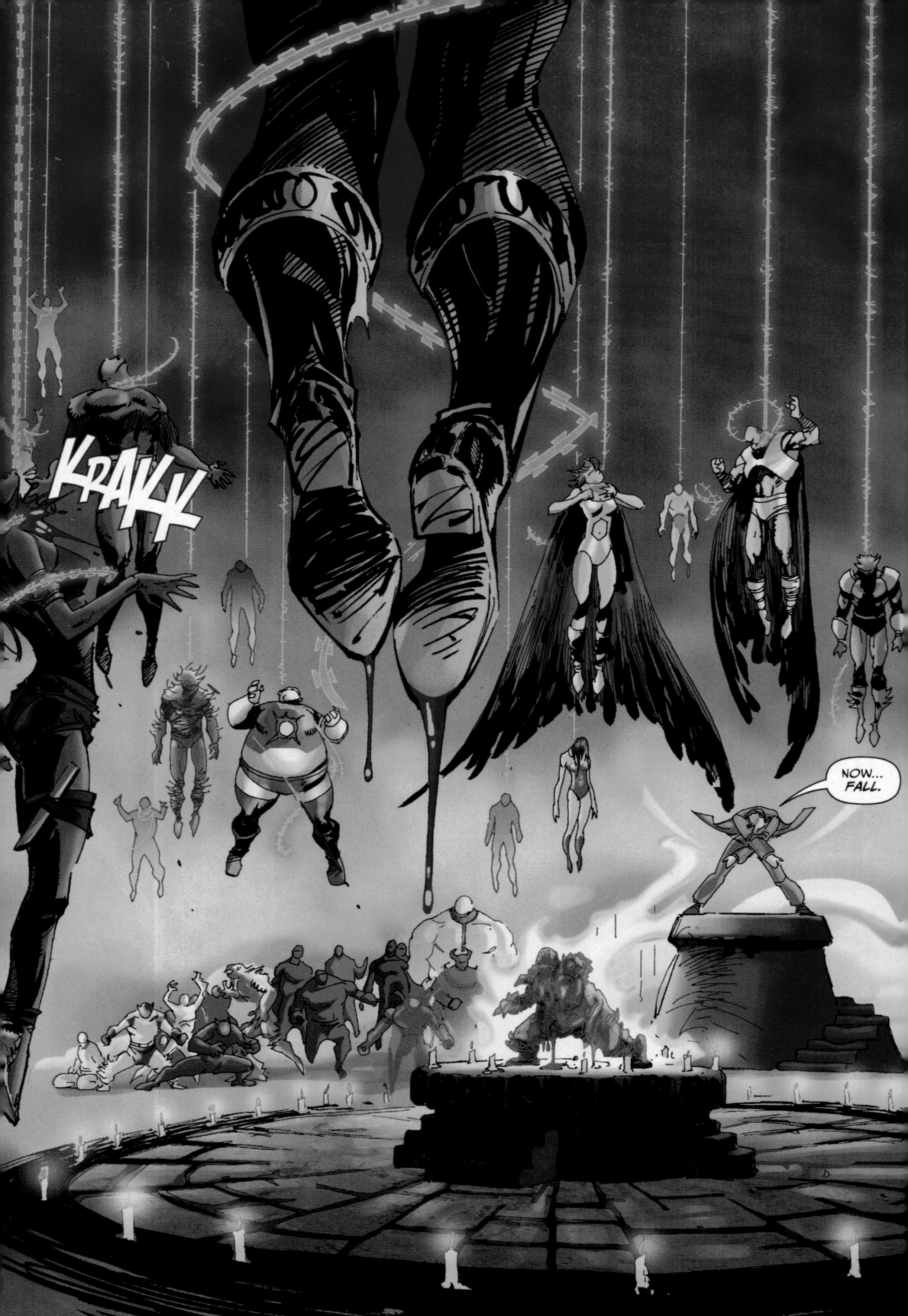
KRAKK
NOW... FALL.

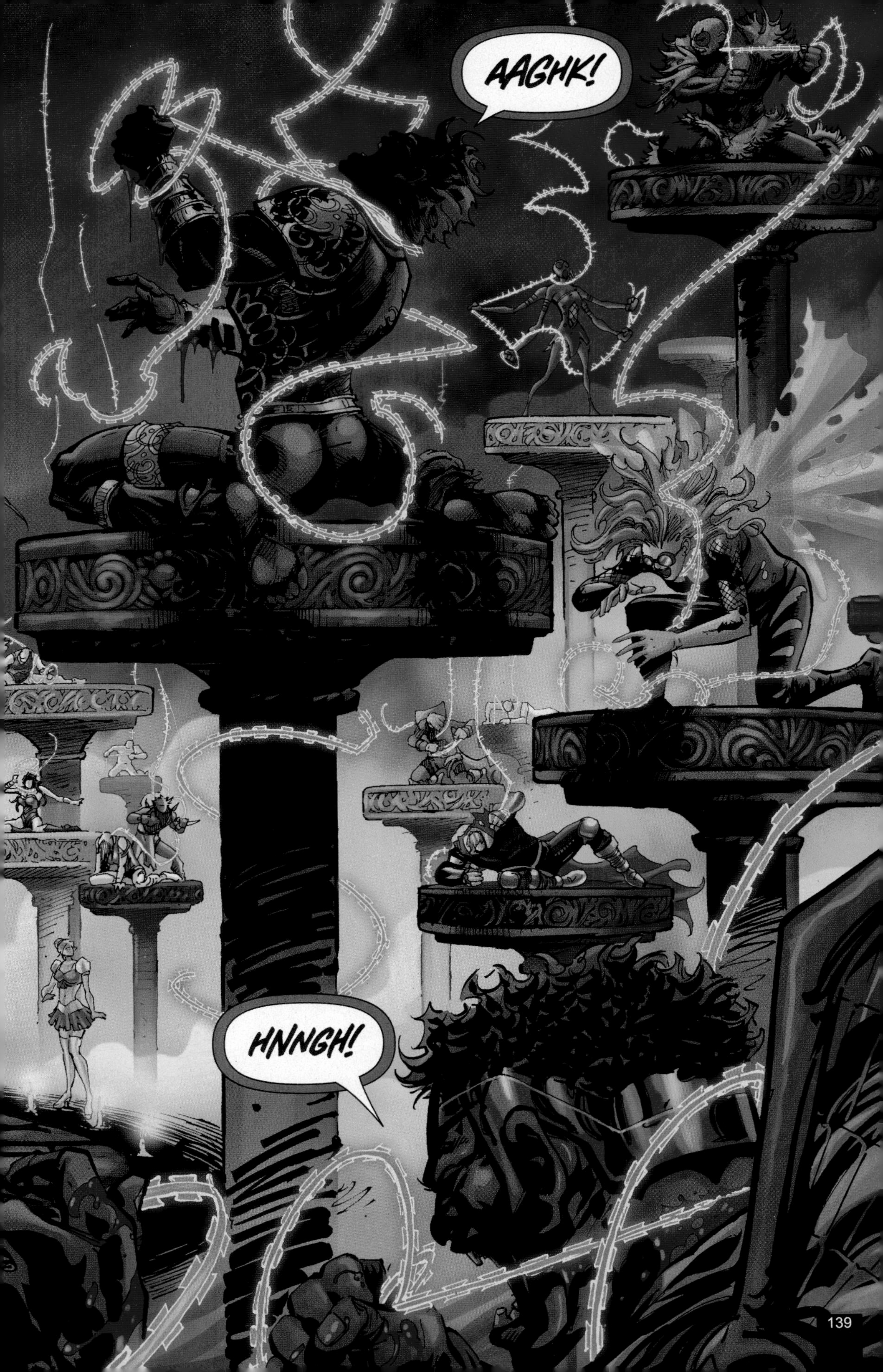
AAGHK!
HNNGH!

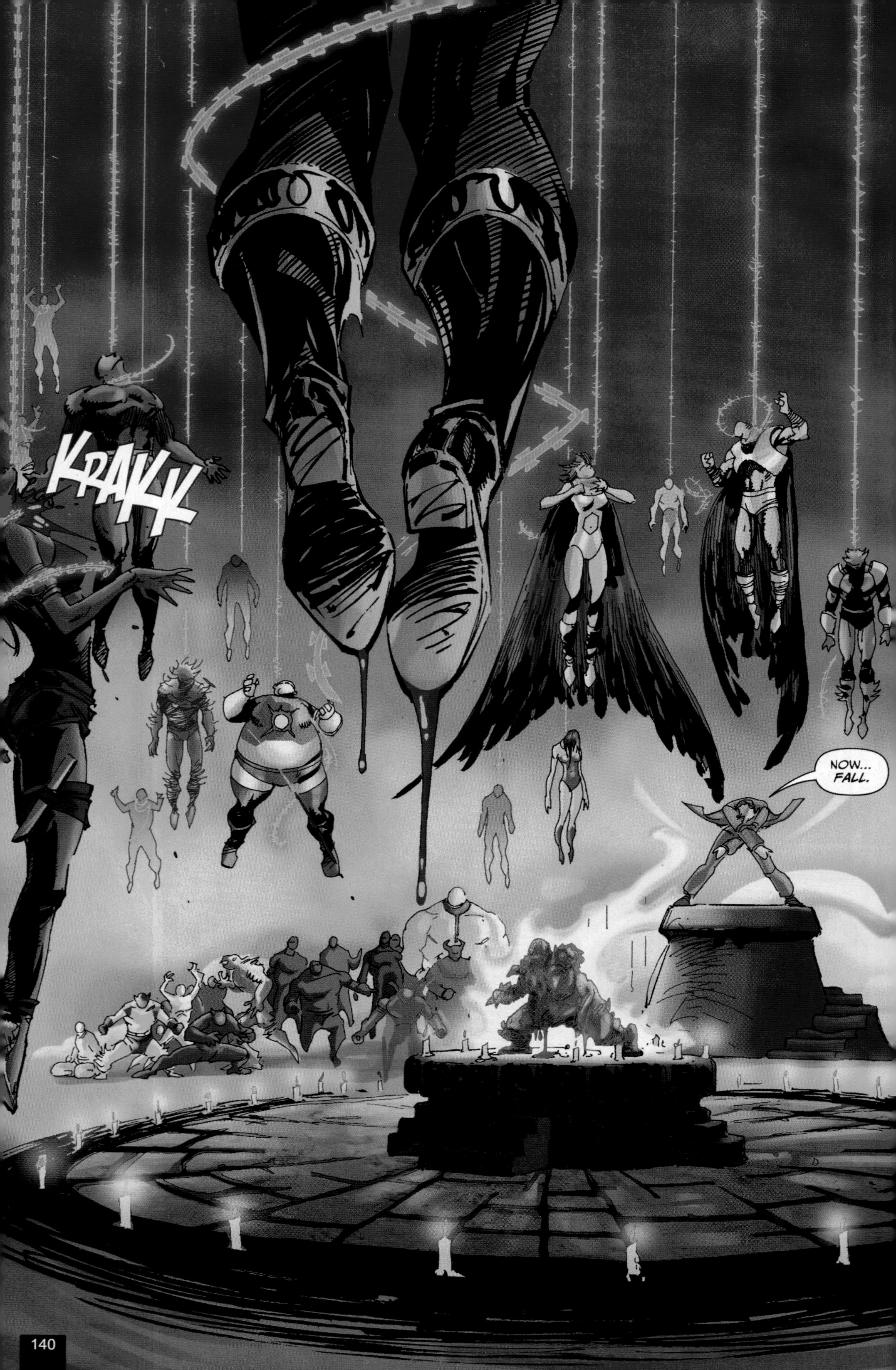
KRAKK
NOW... FALL.

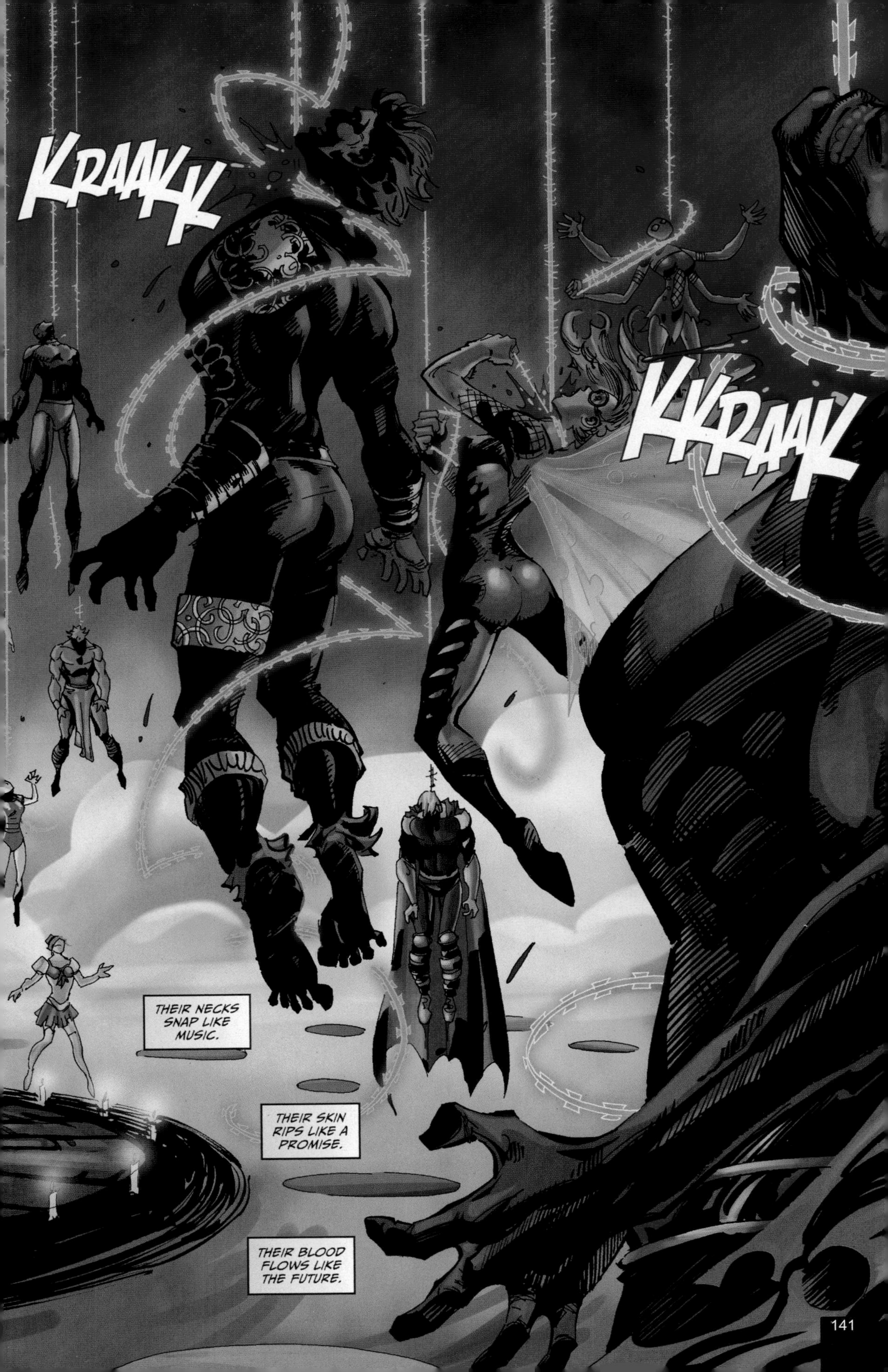
KRAAKK
KKRAAK
THEIR NECKS SNAP LIKE MUSIC.
THEIR SKIN RIPS LIKE A PROMISE.
THEIR BLOOD FLOWS LIKE THE FUTURE.

THE DARK QUEEN **KNOWS** THE RITUAL...

HER BLACK, ROTTING HEART **QUICKENS** IN HER MELTING CHEST...

SHE IS FALLING APART, DRIPPING, DROPPING, SHIFTING, BURNING...

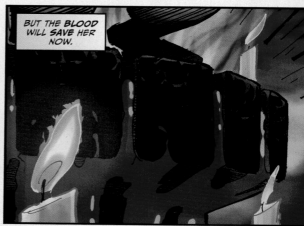

BUT THE BLOOD WILL **SAVE** HER NOW.

JUST LIKE IT SAVED HER THEN.

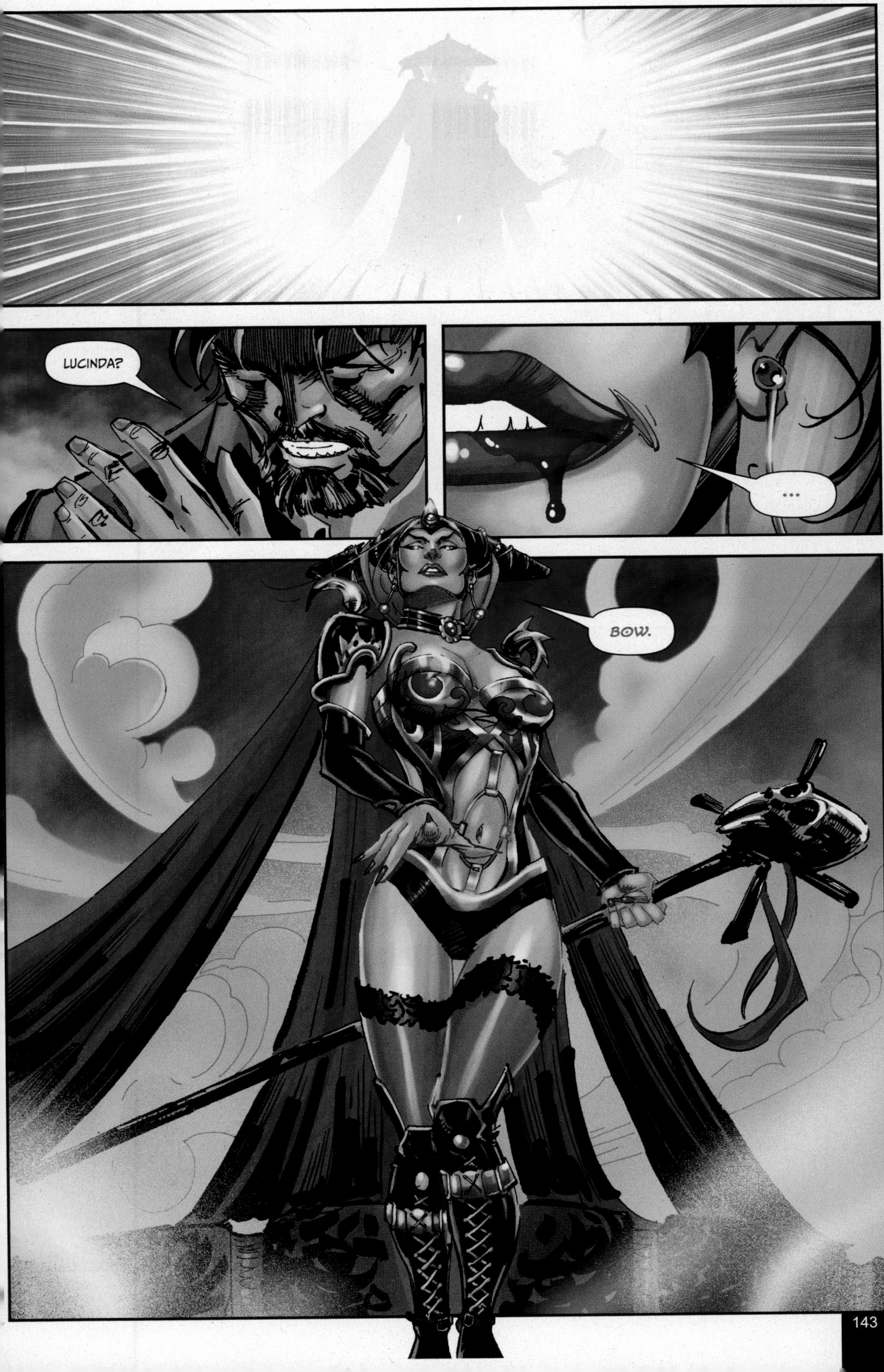
LUCINDA?
...
BOW.

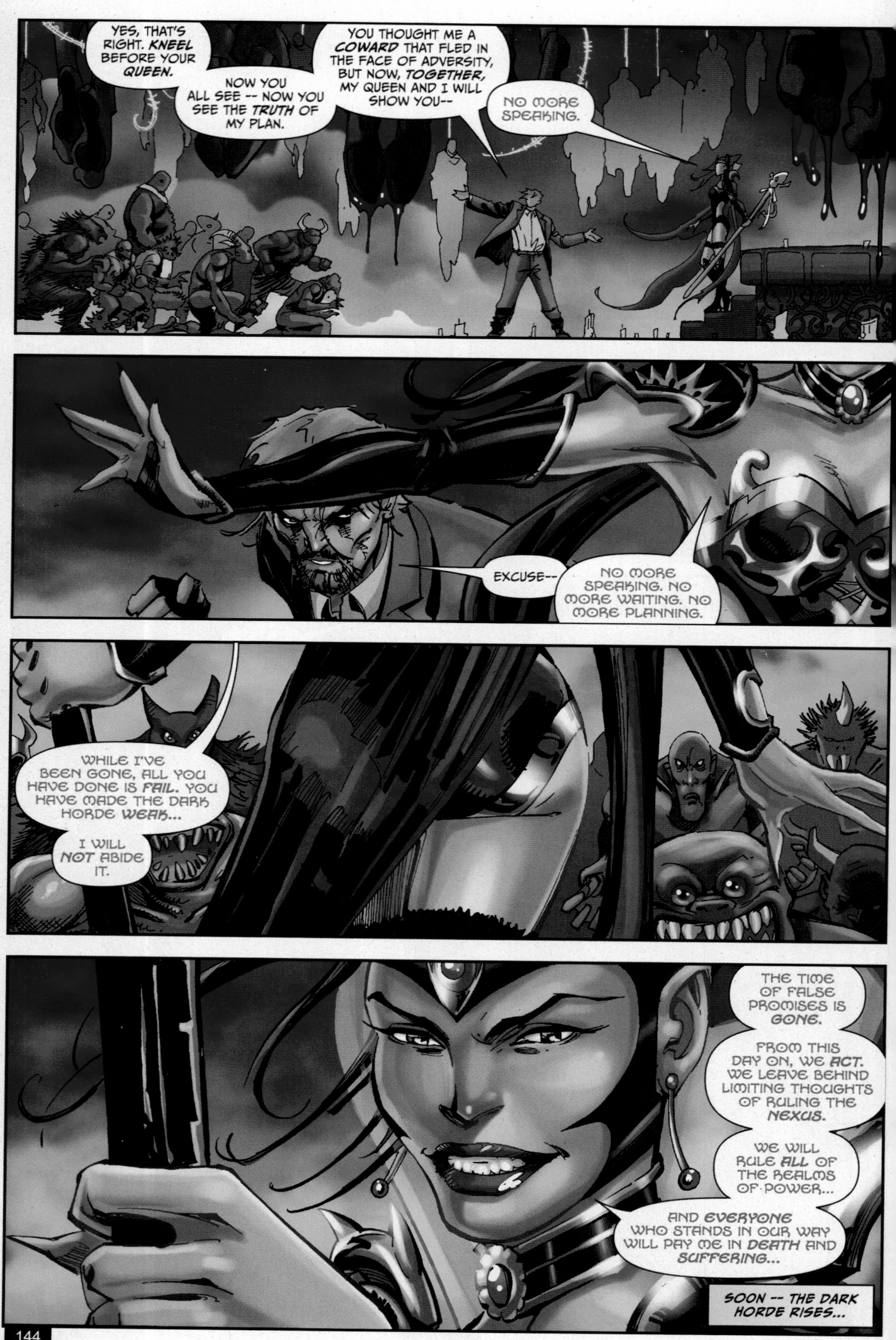
YES, THAT'S RIGHT. KNEEL BEFORE YOUR QUEEN.
NOW YOU ALL SEE -- NOW YOU SEE THE TRUTH OF MY PLAN.
YOU THOUGHT ME A COWARD THAT FLED IN THE FACE OF ADVERSITY, BUT NOW, TOGETHER, MY QUEEN AND I WILL SHOW YOU--
NO MORE SPEAKING.
EXCUSE--
NO MORE SPEAKING. NO MORE WAITING. NO MORE PLANNING.
WHILE I'VE BEEN GONE, ALL YOU HAVE DONE IS FAIL. YOU HAVE MADE THE DARK HORDE WEAK...
I WILL NOT ABIDE IT.
THE TIME OF FALSE PROMISES IS GONE.
FROM THIS DAY ON, WE ACT. WE LEAVE BEHIND LIMITING THOUGHTS OF RULING THE NEXUS.
WE WILL RULE ALL OF THE REALMS OF POWER...
AND EVERYONE WHO STANDS IN OUR WAY WILL PAY ME IN DEATH AND SUFFERING...
SOON -- THE DARK HORDE RISES...

Grimm Fairy Tales

Volume 14

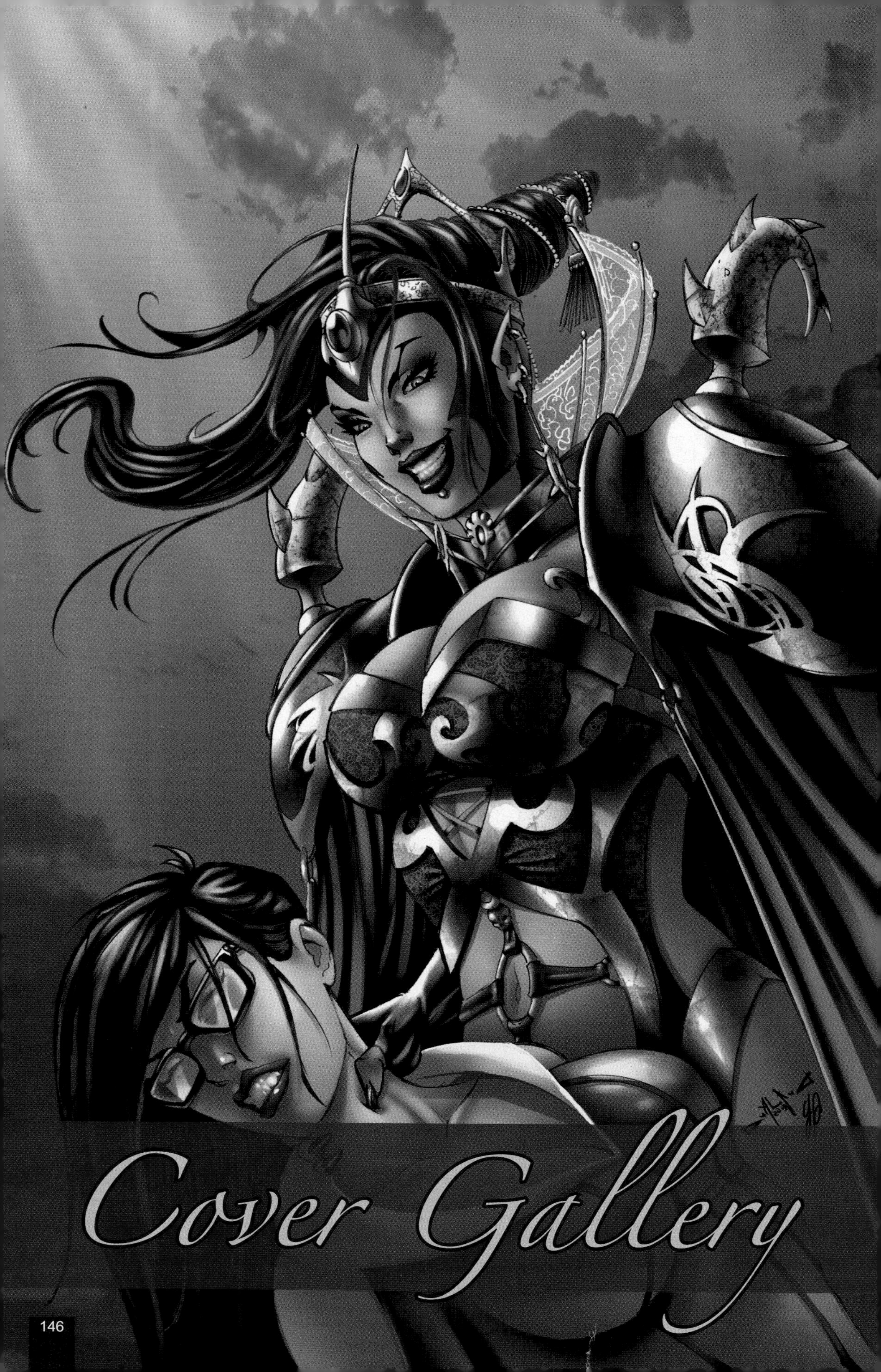

Cover Gallery

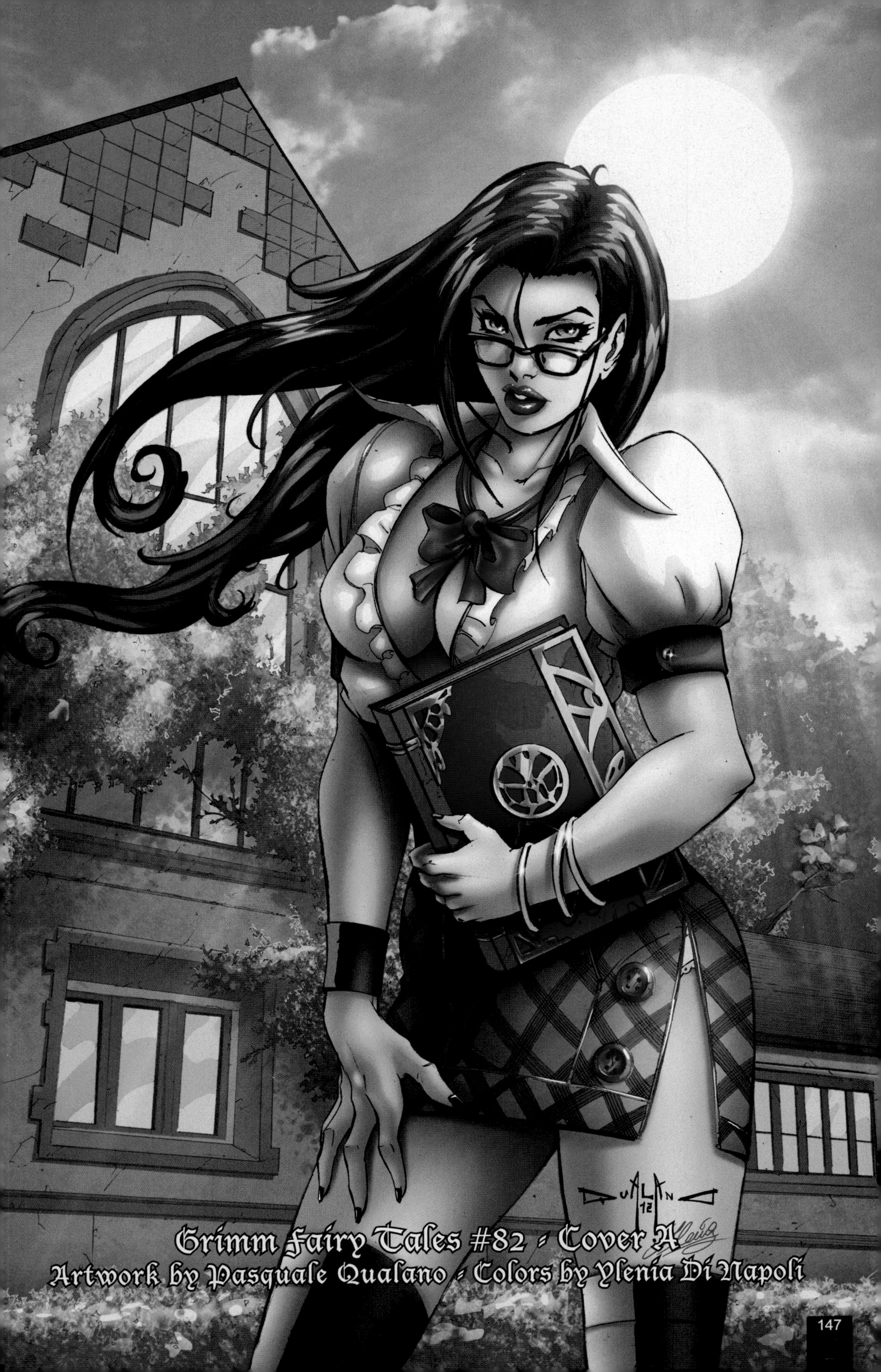
QUALANO 12

Grimm Fairy Tales #82 - Cover A
Artwork by Pasquale Qualano - Colors by Ylenia Di Napoli

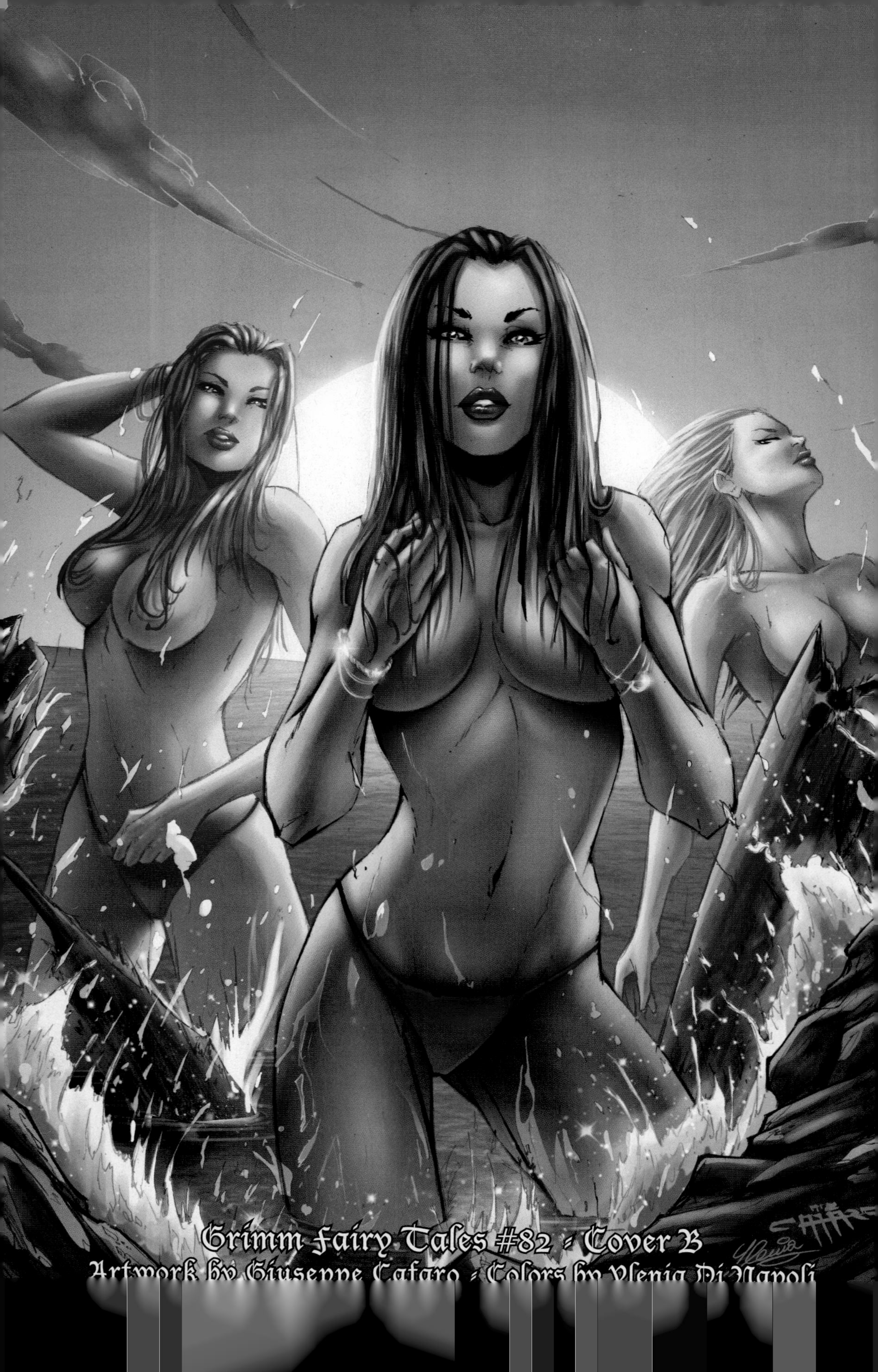

Grimm Fairy Tales #82 - Cover B
Artwork by Giuseppe Cafaro - Colors by Ylenia Di Napoli

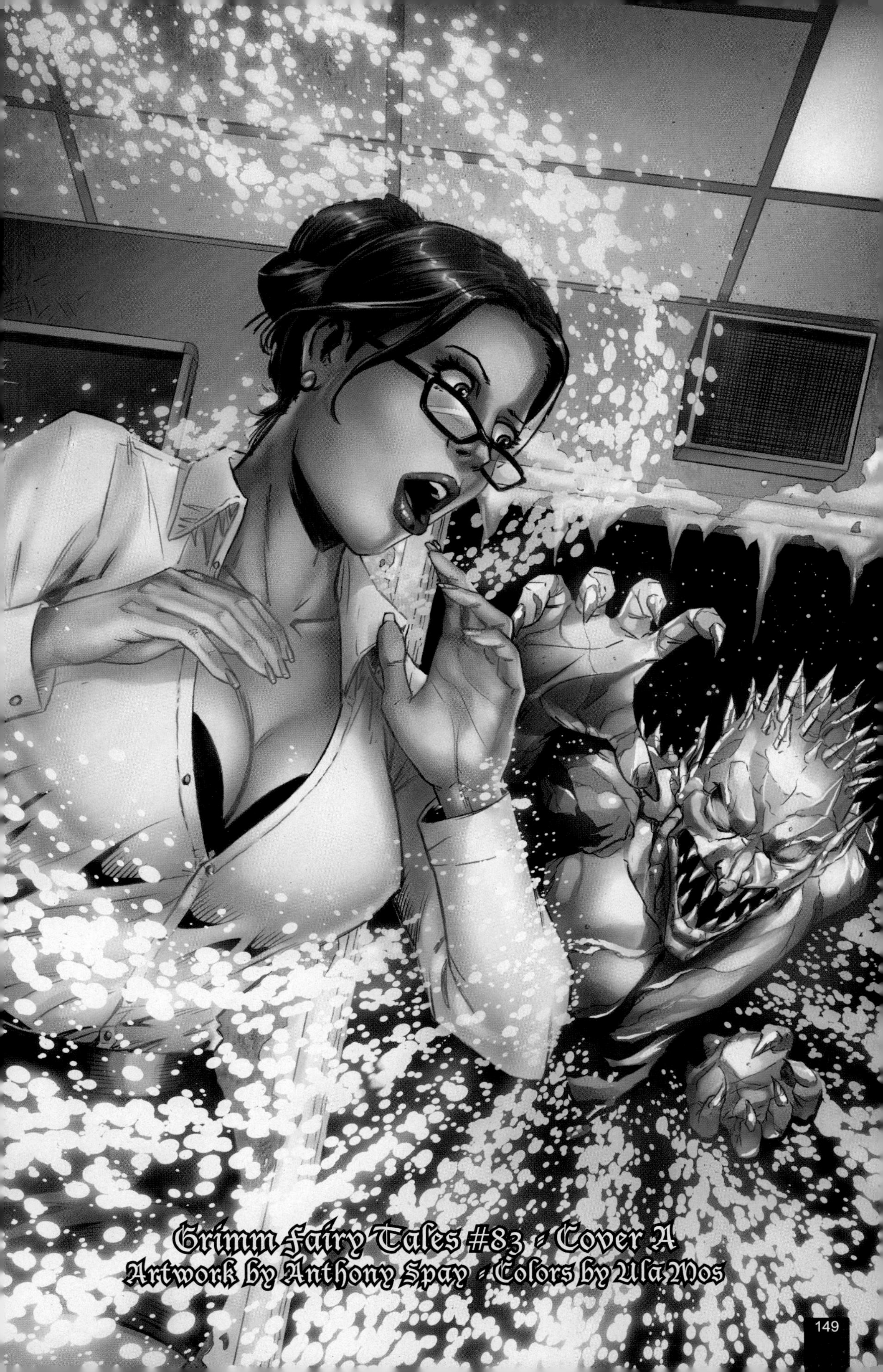

Grimm Fairy Tales #83 - Cover A
Artwork by Anthony Spay - Colors by Ula Mos

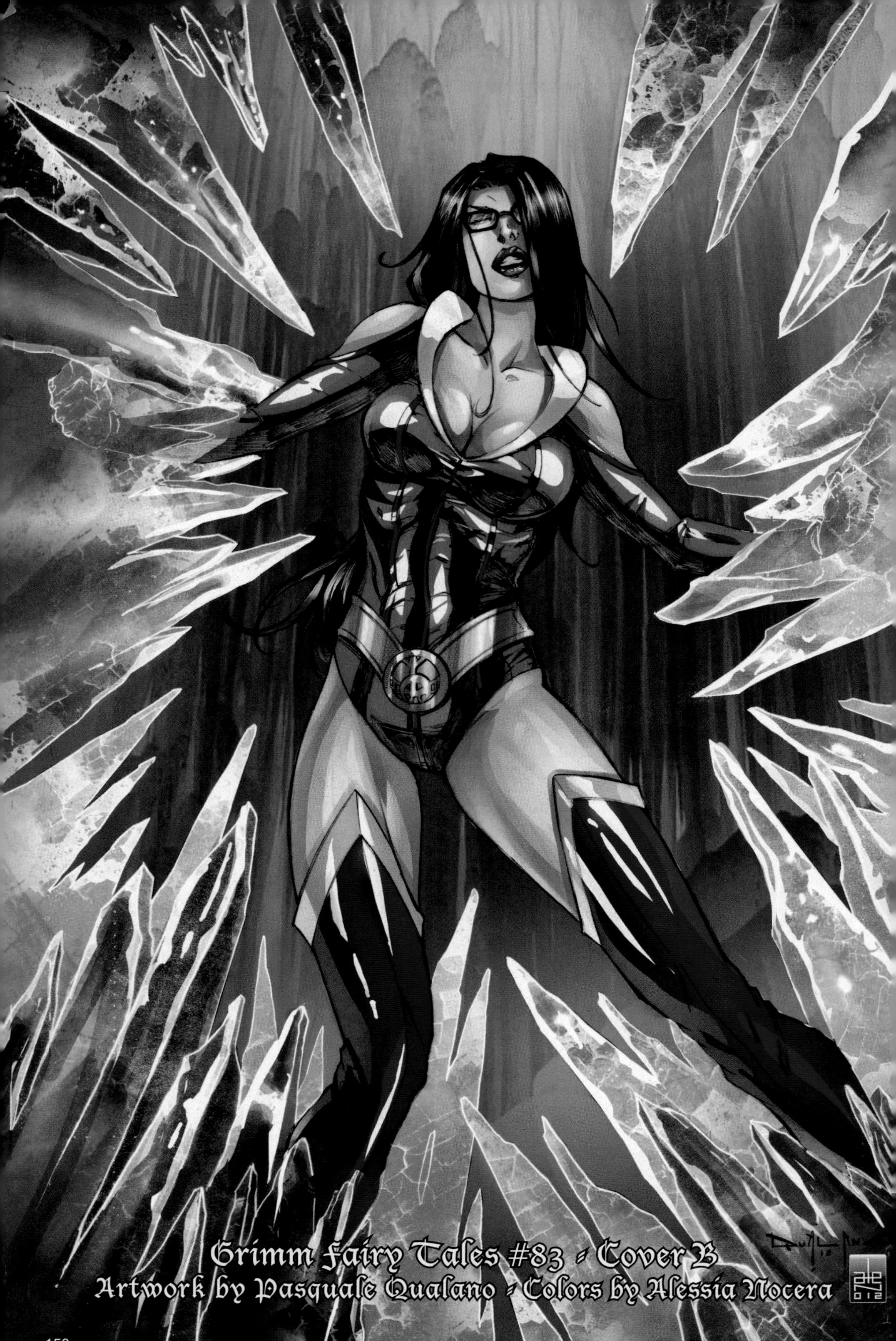

Grimm Fairy Tales #83 - Cover B
Artwork by Pasquale Qualano - Colors by Alessia Nocera

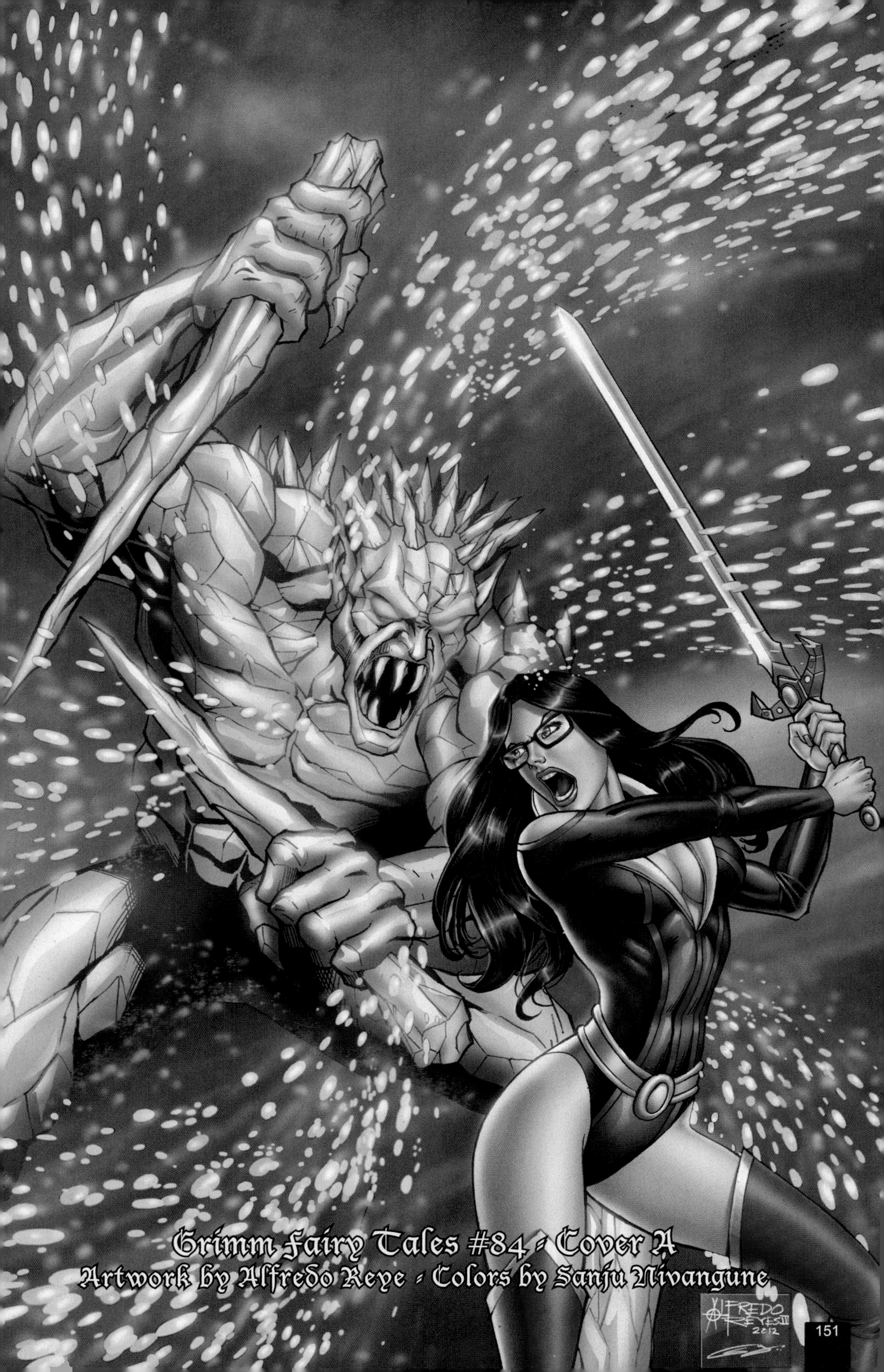
ALFREDO REYES III 2012

Grimm Fairy Tales #84 - Cover A
Artwork by Alfredo Reye - Colors by Sanju Nivangune

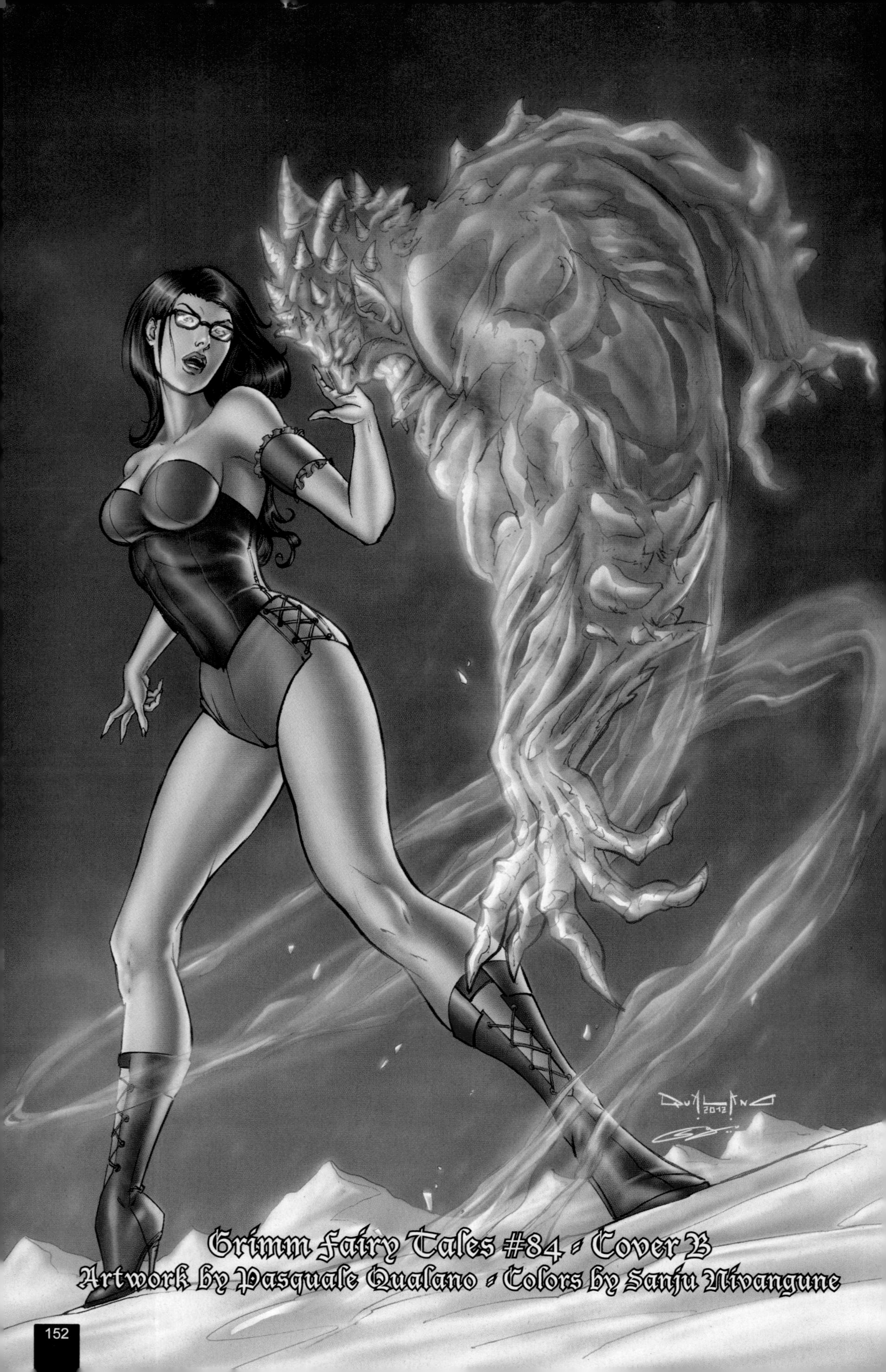

Grimm Fairy Tales #84 - Cover B
Artwork by Pasquale Qualano - Colors by Sanju Nivangune

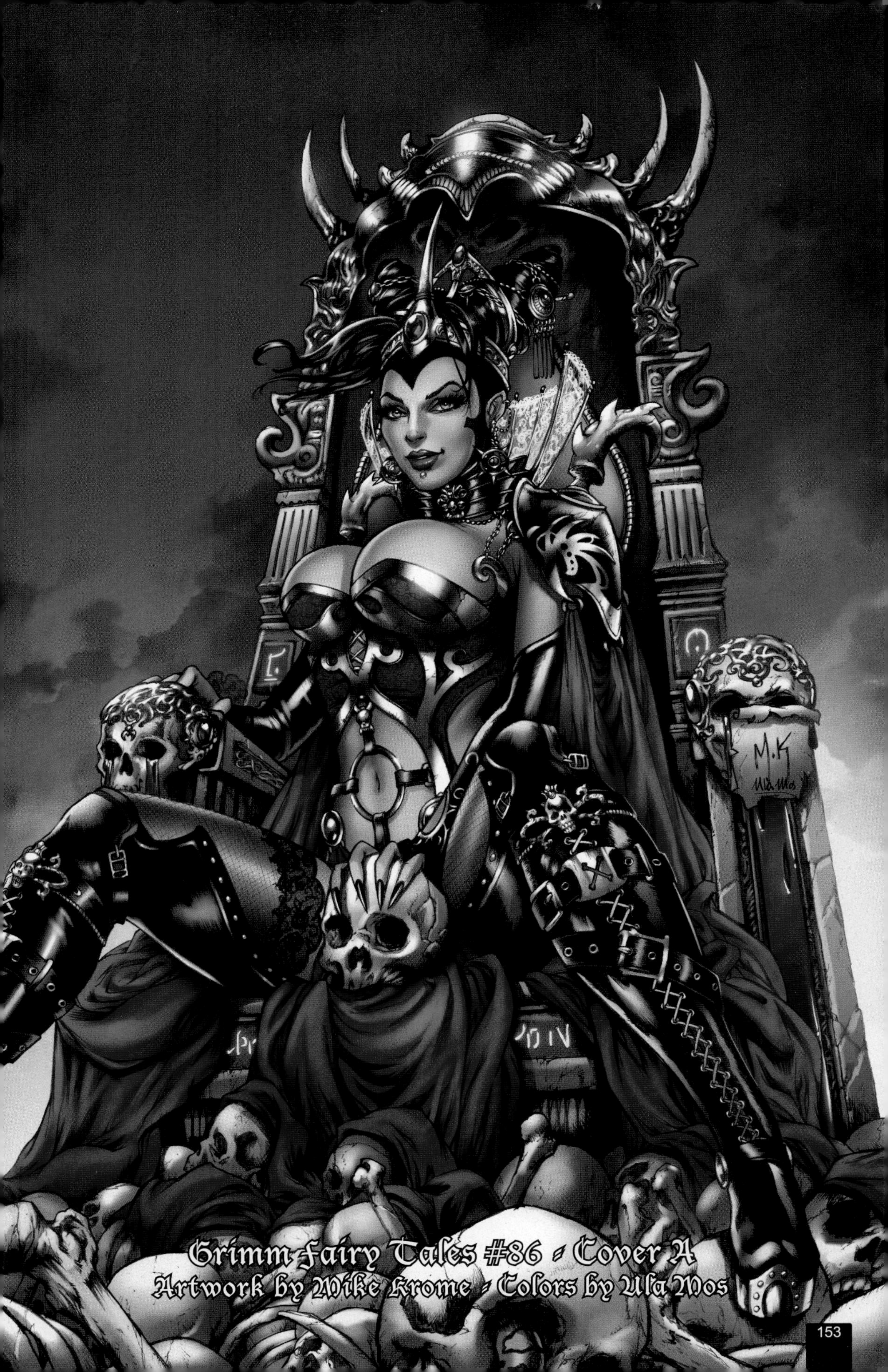

Grimm Fairy Tales #86 - Cover A
Artwork by Mike Krome - Colors by Ula Mos

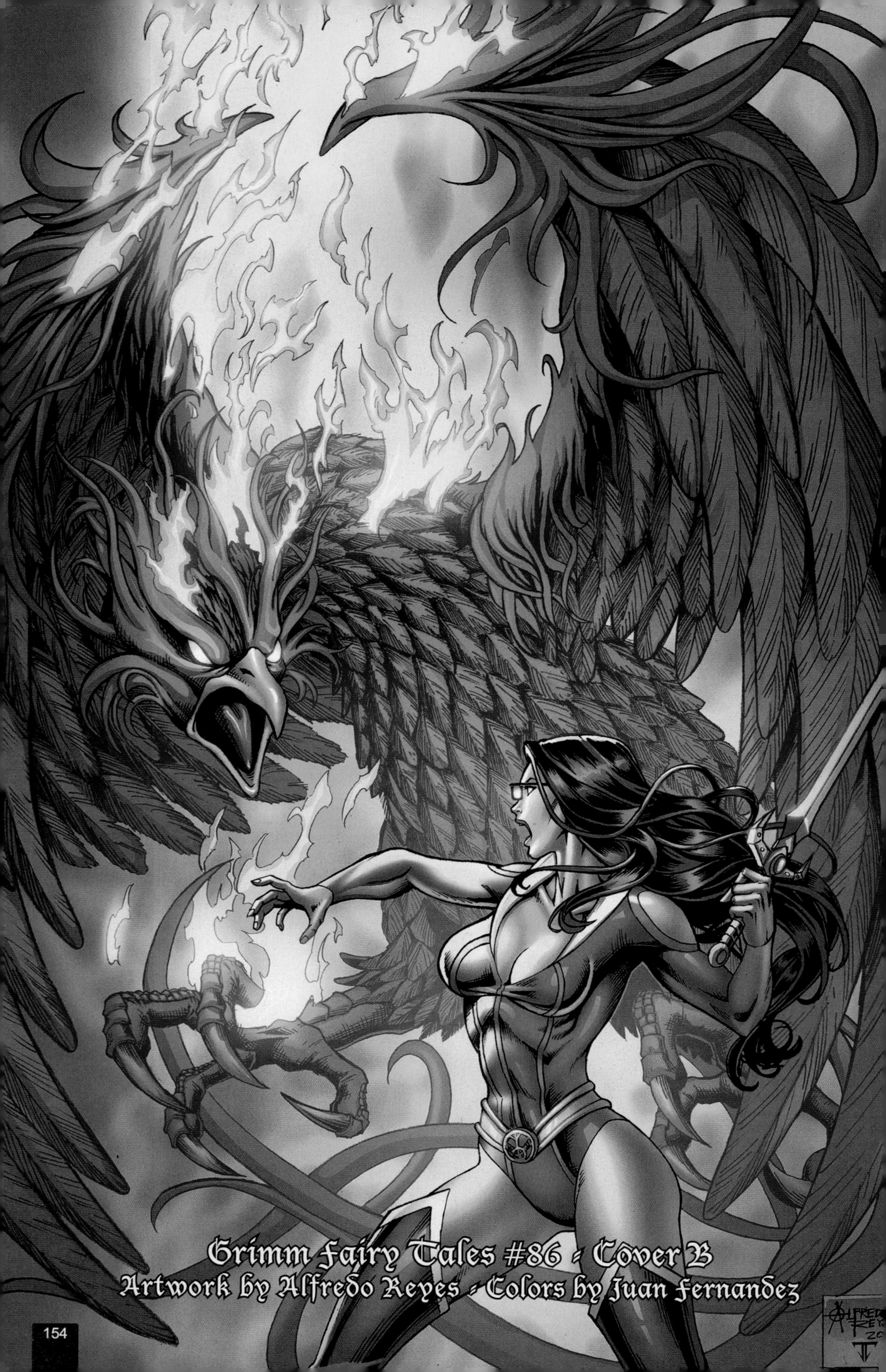

Grimm Fairy Tales #86 - Cover B
Artwork by Alfredo Reyes - Colors by Juan Fernandez

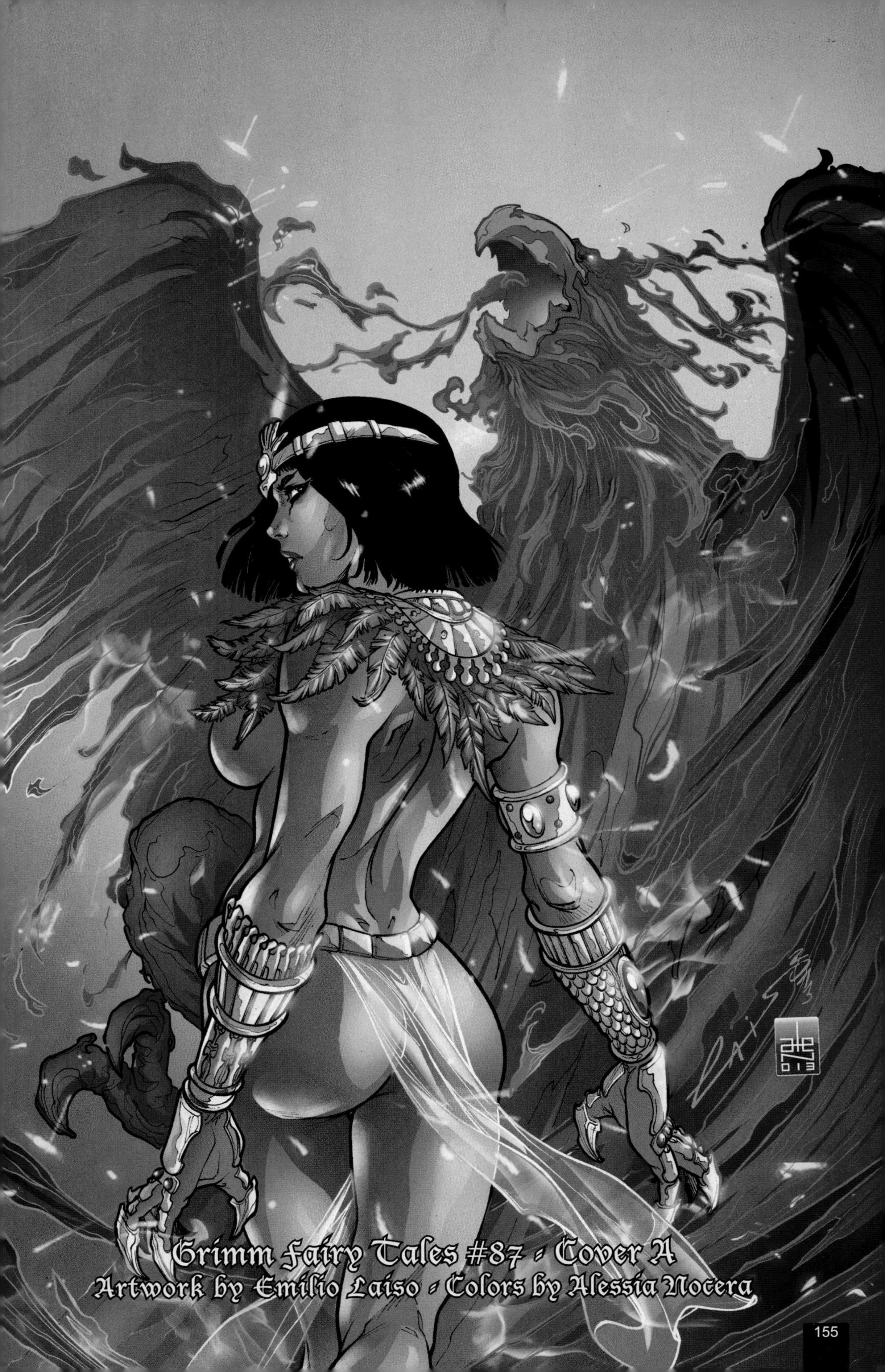

Grimm Fairy Tales #87 - Cover A
Artwork by Emilio Laiso - Colors by Alessia Nocera

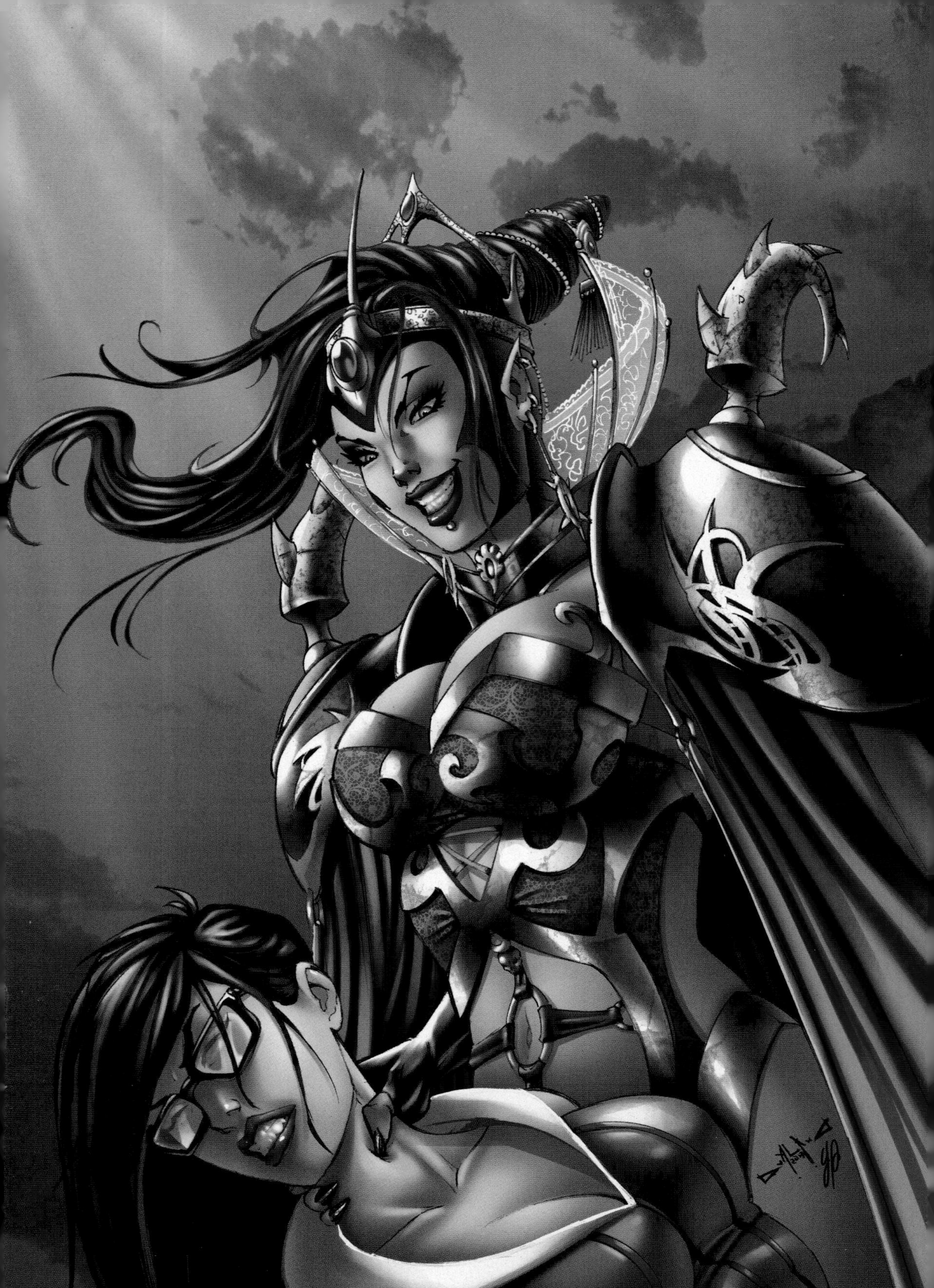

Grimm Fairy Tales #87 - Cover B
Artwork by Pasquale Qualano - Colors by Ylenia Di Napoli

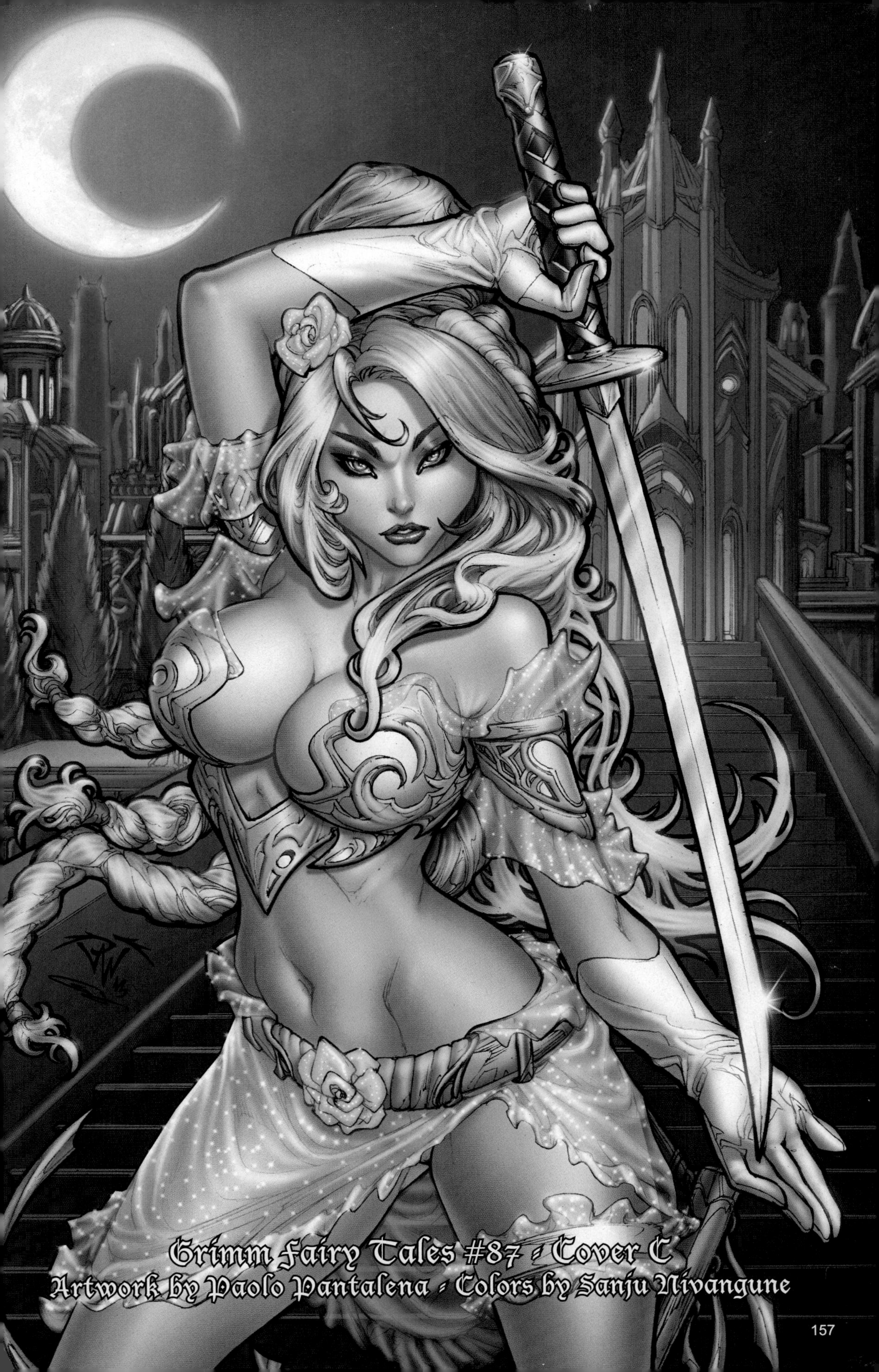

Grimm Fairy Tales #87 - Cover C
Artwork by Paolo Pantalena - Colors by Sanju Nivangune

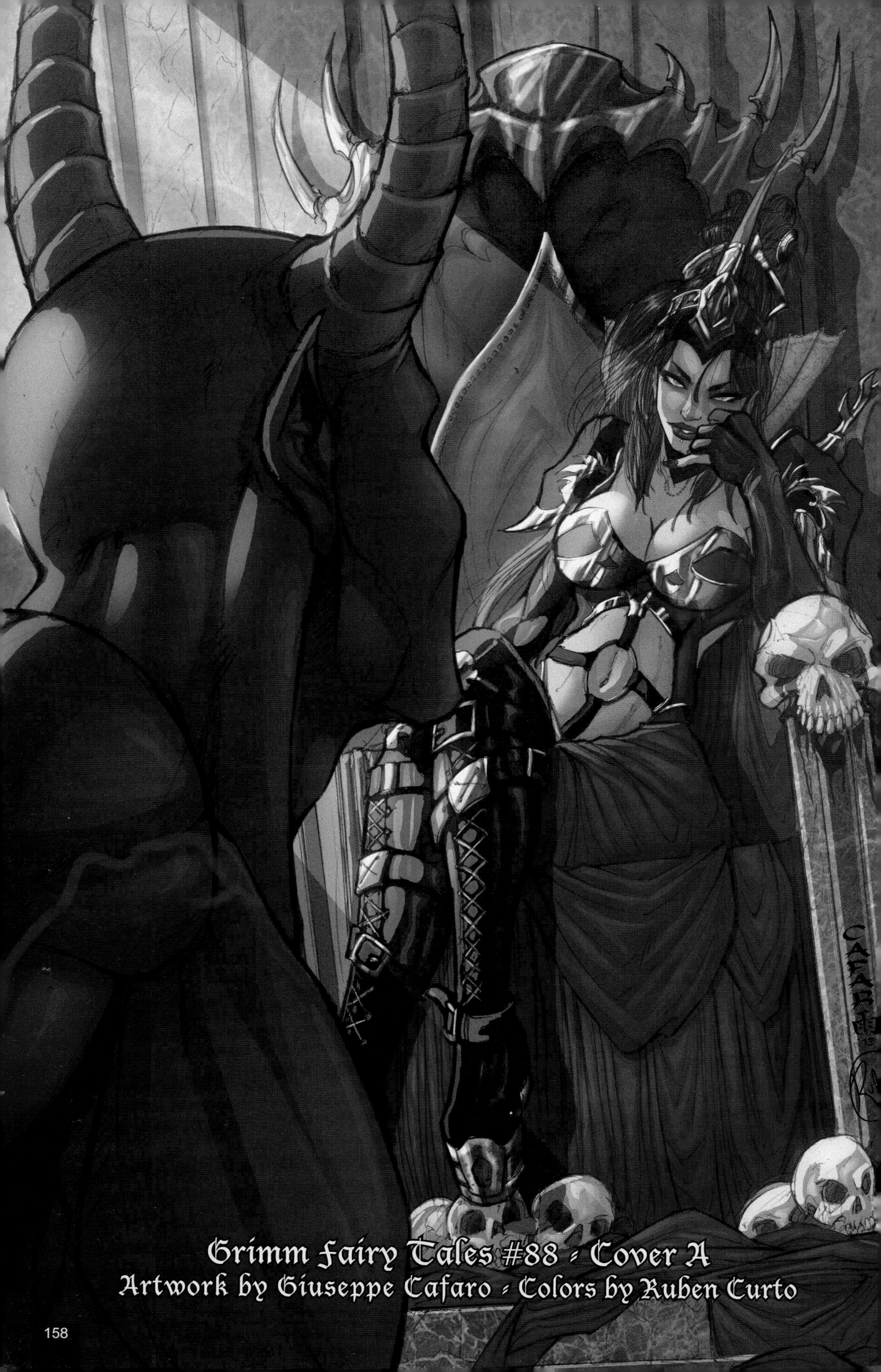

Grimm Fairy Tales #88 - Cover A
Artwork by Giuseppe Cafaro - Colors by Ruben Curto

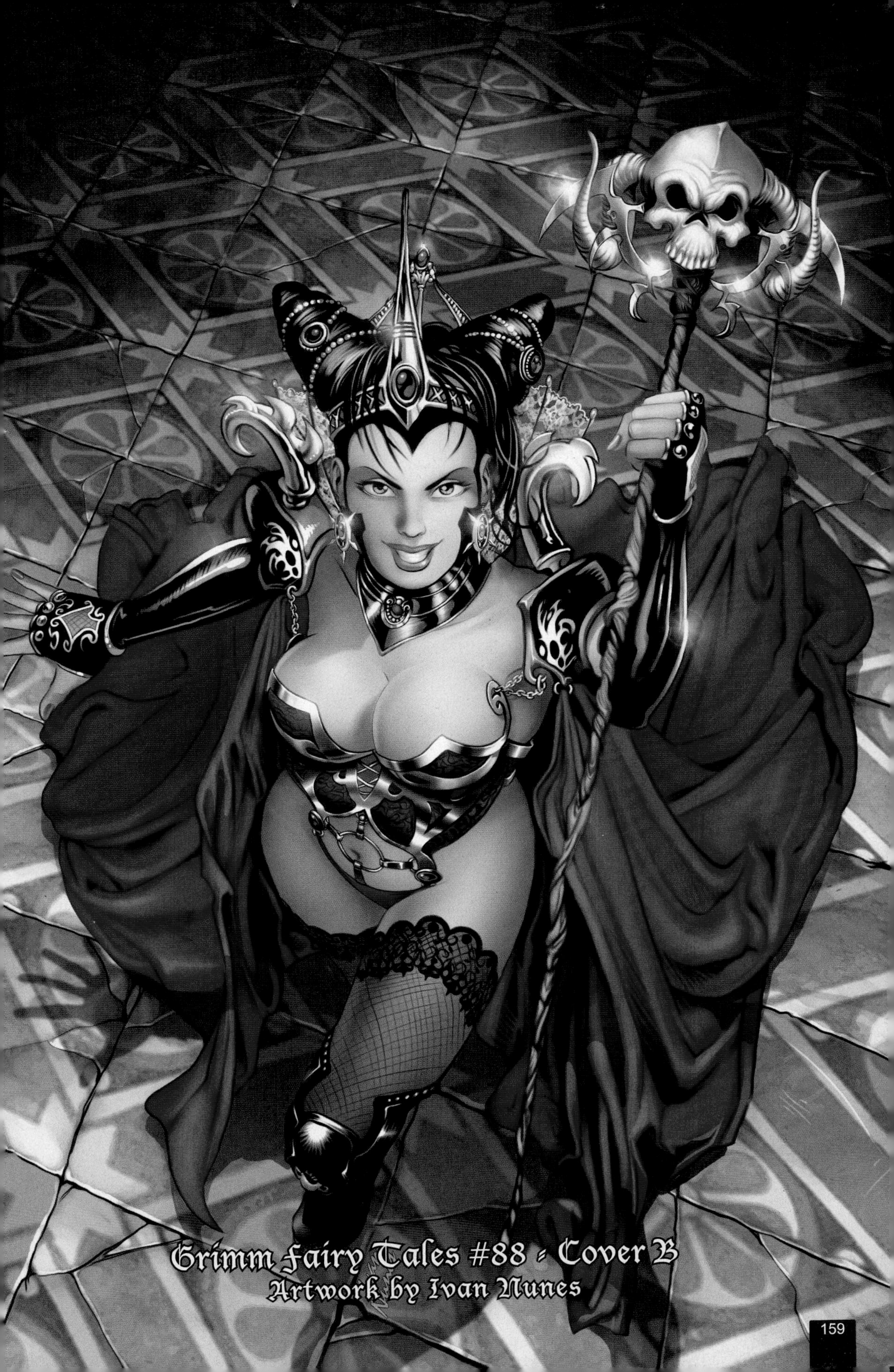

Grimm Fairy Tales #88 - Cover B
Artwork by Ivan Nunes

Grimm Fairy Tales

Volume 14